R Data Visualization Recipes

A cookbook with 65+ data visualization recipes for smarter decision-making

Vitor Bianchi Lanzetta

BIRMINGHAM - MUMBAI

R Data Visualization Recipes

First published: November 2017

Production reference: 1201117

Published by Packt Publishing Ltd.
Livery Place
35 Livery Street
Birmingham
B3 2PB, UK.
ISBN 978-1-78839-831-2

www.packtpub.com

Credits

Author
Vitor Bianchi Lanzetta

Reviewer
Radovan Kavicky

Commissioning Editor
Amey Varangaonkar

Acquisition Editor
Viraj Madhav

Content Development Editor
Tejas Limkar

Technical Editor
Danish Shaikh

Copy Editor
Tasneem Fatehi

Project Coordinator
Manthan Patel

Proofreader
Safis Editing

Indexer
Tejal Daruwale Soni

Graphics
Tania Dutta

Production Coordinator
Shantanu Zagade

About the Author

Vitor Bianchi Lanzetta is a young economist and data science enthusiast. As soon as his graduation began at University of São Paulo, one of Latin America's most renowned universities, he was introduced to R by his statistics professor. it was love at first sight.

Since then, he has never stopped using it. He joined the university team to compete in the CFA Global Challenge, where he and his team had a whole valuation model translated into R along with a Monte Carlo simulation and a bunch of visualizations done through the language.

While researching commodity prices prediction, Vitor used R from adjusting simple conditional mean-based models to artificial neural networks, along with all the visualizations.

First, I would like to thank my family for all the support. Mom, dad, sister, love you beyond measure! I thank Amanda Carolina Teixeira, Ricardo Farias, and their families for being so nice to me. I wish you the best of success, happiness and love.

I also would like to thank Professor Adriano Azevedo Filho for introducing me to the language and Packt for trusting me this project. Special thanks to Tejas Limkar for all the hard work.

About the Reviewer

Radovan Kavický is the principal data scientist and president at GapData Institute based in Bratislava, Slovakia, where he harnesses the power of data and wisdom of economics for public good.

He is a macroeconomist by education and consultant and analyst by professional background, with 8+ years of experience in consulting for clients from public and private sectors. He has strong mathematical and analytical skills and is able to deliver top-level research and analytical work.

From MATLAB, SAS & Stata switched to Python, R & Tableau.

Radovan is a member of the Slovak Economic Association (SEA) and evangelist of open data, open budget initiative and open government partnership. He is founder of PyData Bratislava, R <- Slovakia, and SK/CZ Tableau User Group (skczTUG).

He is a speaker at @TechSummit (Bratislava, 2017) and @PyData (Berlin, 2017), and member of the global Tableau #DataLeader network (2017).

You can follow him on Twitter at @radovankavicky, @GapDataInst, or @PyDataBA. His full profile and experience are available at https://www.linkedin.com/in/radovankavicky/ and https://github.com/radovankavicky.

GapData Institute: https://www.gapdata.org

<p>**Practical Data Science, Data Visualization in Python, R & Tableau; Open Data and Public Administration in Slovakia**

www.PacktPub.com

For support files and downloads related to your book, please visit www.PacktPub.com.

Did you know that Packt offers eBook versions of every book published, with PDF and ePub files available? You can upgrade to the eBook version at www.PacktPub.com and as a print book customer, you are entitled to a discount on the eBook copy. Get in touch with us at service@packtpub.com for more details.

At www.PacktPub.com, you can also read a collection of free technical articles, sign up for a range of free newsletters and receive exclusive discounts and offers on Packt books and eBooks.

https://www.packtpub.com/mapt

Get the most in-demand software skills with Mapt. Mapt gives you full access to all Packt books and video courses, as well as industry-leading tools to help you plan your personal development and advance your career.

Why subscribe?

- Fully searchable across every book published by Packt
- Copy and paste, print, and bookmark content
- On demand and accessible via a web browser

Customer Feedback

Thanks for purchasing this Packt book. At Packt, quality is at the heart of our editorial process. To help us improve, please leave us an honest review on this book's Amazon page at https://www.amazon.com/dp/1788398319.

If you'd like to join our team of regular reviewers, you can e-mail us at customerreviews@packtpub.com. We award our regular reviewers with free eBooks and videos in exchange for their valuable feedback. Help us be relentless in improving our products!

Table of Contents

Preface   1

Chapter 1: Installation and Introduction   7

    Introduction   7

    Installing and loading graphics packages   8

        How to do it...   8

        How it works...   9

        There's more   12

        See also...   12

    Using ggplot2, plotly, and ggvis   13

        Getting ready   13

        How to do it...   14

        How it works...   16

        There's more   20

        See also   20

    Making plots using primitives   21

        How to do it...   21

        How it works...   25

        There's more...   29

Chapter 2: Plotting Two Continuous Variables   31

    Introduction   32

    Plotting a basic scatterplot   32

        How to do it...   33

        How it works...   34

        There's more...   35

    Hacking ggvis add_axis() function to operate as a title function   36

        Getting ready   36

        How to do it...   36

        How it works...   37

    Plotting a scatterplot with shapes and colors   38

        How to do it...   38

        How it works...   40

    Plotting a shape reference palette for ggplot2   41

        How to do it...   42

        How it works...   42

There's more...   43
Dealing with over-plotting, reducing points   43
How to do it...   43
How it works...   45
There's more...   45
Dealing with over-plotting, jittering points   46
How to do it...   46
How it works...   48
Dealing with over-plotting, alpha blending   49
How to do it...   49
How it works...   51
There's more...   51
Rug the margins using geom_rug()   52
How to do it...   52
How it works...   54
Adding marginal histograms using ggExtra   55
Getting ready   55
How to do it...   55
How it works...   57
Drawing marginal histogram using gridExtra   57
Getting ready   57
How to do it...   58
How it works...   60
Crafting marginal plots with plotly   60
How to do it...   61
How it works...   61
Adding regression lines   62
How to do it...   62
How it works...   64
Adding quantile regression lines   65
Getting ready   65
How to do it...   66
How it works...   67
Drawing publish-quality scatterplots   68
Getting ready   69
How to do it...   71
How it works...   73
See also   73
Chapter 3: Plotting a Discrete Predictor and a Continuous Response   75

Introduction 75
Installing car package and getting familiar to data 76
How to do it... 76
How does it works... 77
There is more 77
See also 78
Drawing simple box plots 78
Getting ready 78
How to do it... 78
How it works... 80
Adding notches and jitters to box plots 81
Getting ready 81
How to do it... 82
How it works... 83
Drawing bivariate dot plots using ggplot2 84
Getting ready 84
How to do it... 84
How does it work... 87
There is more 87
Using more suitable colors for geom_dotplot 87
Getting ready 88
How to do it... 88
How it works... 90
Combining box with dot plots 91
Getting ready 91
How it works... 91
How it works... 93
See also 94
Using point geometry to work as dots using ggvis, plotly and ggplot2 94
Getting ready... 95
How it works... 95
How it works... 97
There is more 98
Crafting simple violin plots 98
How to do it... 99
How it works... 101
Using stat_summary to customize violin plots 101
Getting ready 101
How it works... 102

How it works...	104
There is more...	105
Manually sorting and coloring violins	**105**
Getting ready	106
How to do it...	106
How it works...	108
Using joy package to replace violins	**109**
Getting ready	109
How to do it...	109
How it works...	110
See also	111
Creating publication quality violin plots	**111**
Getting Ready	112
How to do it...	112
How it works...	115
See also	115
Chapter 4: Plotting One Variable	**117**
Introduction	**117**
Creating a simple histogram using geom_histogram()	**118**
Getting ready	119
How to do it...	119
How does it work...	121
Creating an histogram with custom colors and bins width	**122**
Getting ready	123
How to do it...	124
How it works...	126
Crafting and coloring area plots using geom_area() and more	**127**
Getting ready	127
How to do it...	127
How it works...	129
Drawing density plots using geom_density()	**130**
How to do it...	130
How it works...	132
See also	133
Drawing univariate colored dot plots with geom_dotplot()	**133**
Getting ready	134
How to do it...	134
How it works...	135
See also	138

Crafting univariate bar charts   138
    Getting ready   138
    How to do it...   138
    How it works...   140
Using rtweet and ggplot2 to plot twitter words frequencies   142
    Getting ready...   142
    How to do it...   143
    How it works...   145
    See also   146
Drawing publish quality density plot   147
    How to do it...   147
    How it works...   149

Chapter 5: Making Other Bivariate Plots   151

Introduction   151
Creating simple stacked bar graphs   152
    Getting ready   152
    How to do it...   152
    How it works...   155
Crafting proportional stacked bar   156
    Getting ready   156
    How to do it...   157
    How it works...   158
    See also   160
Plotting side-by-side bar graph   161
    Getting ready   161
    How to do it...   161
    How it works...   164
    See also   164
Plotting a bar graphic with aggregated data using geom_col()   165
    Getting ready   165
    How to do it...   165
    How it works...   167
Adding variability estimates to plots with geom_errrorbar()   167
    Getting ready   168
    How to do it...   168
    How it works...   169
    There's more...   170
    See also   170
Making line plots   170

Getting ready | 171
How to do it... | 171
How it works... | 173
Making static and interactive hexagon plots | 174
Getting ready | 174
How to do it... | 174
How it works... | 175
There is more... | 176
Adjusting your hexagon plot | 176
Getting ready | 176
How to do it... | 177
How it works... | 178
See also | 179
Developing a publish quality proportional stacked bar graph | 179
Getting ready | 179
How to do it... | 180
How it works... | 181
Chapter 6: Creating Maps | 183
Introduction | 183
Making simple maps - 1854 London Streets | 184
Getting ready | 184
How to do it... | 184
How it works... | 186
Creating an interactive cholera map using plotly | 187
Getting ready | 188
How to do it... | 188
How it works... | 189
Crafting choropleth maps using ggplot2 | 190
Getting ready | 191
How to do it... | 191
How it works... | 192
Zooming in on the map | 194
Getting ready | 194
How to do it... | 194
How it works... | 196
See also | 196
Creating different maps based on different map projection types | 197
Getting ready | 197
How to do it... | 197

How it works... 200
See also 200
Handling shapefiles to map Afghanistan health facilities 201
Getting ready 201
How to do it... 201
How it works... 204
See also 205
Crafting an interactive globe using plotly 205
Getting ready 206
How to do it... 206
How it works... 208
Creating high quality maps 209
Getting ready 209
How to do it... 210
How it works... 211
See also 212

Chapter 7: Faceting 213
Introduction 213
Creating a faceted bar graph 214
How to do it... 214
How it works... 216
Crafting faceted histograms 218
Getting ready 218
How to do it... 218
How it works... 219
Creating a facet box plot 220
How to do it... 220
How it works... 222
Crafting a faceted line plot 222
Getting ready 223
How to do it... 223
How it works... 225
There is more 225
Making faceted scatterplots 226
Getting ready 226
How to do it... 226
How it works... 228
Creating faceted maps 228
Getting ready 229

How to do it...	229
How it works...	231
See also	233
Drawing facets using plotly	**233**
How to do it...	233
How it works...	235
See also	236
Plotting a high quality faceted bar graph	**236**
How to do it...	237
How it works...	239

Chapter 8: Designing Three-Dimensional Plots	**241**
Introduction	**241**
Drawing a simple contour plot using ggplot2	**242**
How to do it...	242
How it works...	244
Picking a custom number of contour lines	**246**
How to do it...	247
How it works...	248
Using the directlabels package to label the contours	**249**
Getting ready	249
How to do it...	250
How it works...	251
See also	251
Crafting a simple tile plot with ggplot2	**251**
How to do it...	251
How it works...	253
Creating simple raster plots with ggplot2	**255**
How to do it...	255
How it works...	257
There is more	259
Designing a three-dimensional plot with plotly	**259**
Getting ready	259
How to do it...	259
How it works...	261
Crafting a publication quality contour plot	**261**
How to do it...	262
How it works...	263

Chapter 9: Using Theming Packages	**265**

Introduction 265
Drawing a bubble plot 266
    Getting ready 266
    How to do it... 266
    How it works... 268
Popular themes with ggthemes 269
    Getting Ready 269
    How to do it... 269
    How it works... 273
    There's more... 273
    See also 274
Applying sci themes with ggsci 274
    Getting Ready 274
    How to do it... 274
    How it works... 277
    See also 277
Importing new fonts with the extrafont package 277
    Getting Ready 278
    How to do it... 278
    How it works... 279
    There's more... 280
Using ggtech to mimic tech companies themes 280
    Getting Ready 281
    How to do it... 281
    How it works... 282
    There's more... 283
    See also 283
Wrapping a custom theme function 284
    Getting ready 284
    How to do it... 284
    How it works... 286
    See also 286
Applying awesome themes and checking misspells with hrbrthemes 287
    Getting Ready 287
    How to do it... 287
    How it works... 290
    There's more... 291
    See also 291
Chapter 10: Designing More Specialized Plots 293

Introduction	293
Drawing wonderful facets zoom with the ggforce package	294
Getting Ready	294
How to do it...	294
How it works...	296
See also	296
Drawing sina plots with ggforce	297
Getting Ready	297
How to do it...	297
How it works...	299
Using ggrepel to plot non-overlaying texts	299
Getting Ready	300
How to do it...	300
How it works...	301
There's more...	302
See also	302
Visualizing relational data structures with ggraph	302
Getting Ready	303
How to do it...	303
How it works...	306
See also	307
Draw alternative lollipop and density plots with ggalt	307
Getting Ready	308
How to do it...	308
How it works...	311
See also	312
Chapter 11: Making Interactive Plots	313
Introduction	313
Using ggiraph to create interactive plots	314
Getting ready	314
How to do it...	314
How it works...	316
See also	317
Using gganimate to craft animated ggplots	317
Getting ready	317
How to do it...	318
How it works...	319
See also	320
Crafting animated plots with tweenr	320

Getting ready 321
How to do it... 321
How it works... 324
See also 325

Chapter 12: Building Shiny Dashboards 327
Introduction 327
Installing and loading a shiny package 327
How to do it... 328
How it works... 330
Creating basic shiny interactive plots 330
Getting ready 331
How to do it... 331
How it works... 332
See also 333
Developing intermediate shiny interactive plots 334
Getting ready 334
How to do it... 334
How it works... 336
There's more... 336
Building a shiny dashboard 336
Getting ready 337
How to do it... 337
How it works... 339
See also 340

Index 341

Preface

Visualizations are amazing to investigate. You can explore data, reach insights, and transmit them directly to your audience. When several paragraphs may be needed to prove a point, good figures do it better in just a glance; they literally do. Fortunately, as computers keep evolving, crafting first-class graphs is not that difficult anymore.

R has proven itself an amazing tool for both data analysis and visualization. It all began by as an open source, well-designed, and multi-propose programming language that did not require much programming background to use. So, as R rose in popularity, a vivid and helpful community has also arisen.

The community itself has done much to keep improving the language. They have designed and shared tons of packages, which brings us to here and now. This book is full of examples on how to easily brew pretty graphics using very popular packages. It aims for teaching the nuts and bolts related to many different visuals, along with very useful tricks to adapt and enhance your figures.

Examples range from static scatterplots built using `ggplot2` to interactive globes formed by `plotly`. Learn how to plot the most tweeted words by some user, draw true 3D interactive surfaces, and build `shiny` dashboards. Also you will learn how to apply a theme that will support your analysis.

What this book covers

Chapter 1, *Installation and Introduction*, teaches how to install the three most popular R visualization packages: `ggplot2`, `ggvis`, and `plotly`. This chapter introduces the ways a package can be installed: either from a CRAN repository or a GitHub one. You also get to know how to call functions from those packages while going through some examples demonstrating the basic framework of those packages.

Chapter 2, *Plotting Two Continuous Variables*, dives into scatterplots, the most popular way to plot two continuous variables. We learn how to change shapes, colors and sizes. The main problem imbued to scatterplots is called over plotting; this chapter explores related solutions. Also we see how to draw marginal plots and produce high-quality scatterplots.

Chapter 3, *Plotting a Discrete Predictor and a Continuous Response,* covers distributions over categories, a great way to explore your data. It can be handled using R to draw one box plots, bivariate dot plots, and violin plots. Learn how to draw and combine each of them. Meet nice additional features while learning the art of crafting to publish quality violin plots.

Chapter 4, *Plotting One Variable,* covers histograms, density plots, area plots, univariate dot plots, and univariate bar graphs. Learn how to brew these visuals under different R packages. Meet the useful modifications achieved by little code tweaks.

Chapter 5, *Making Other Bivariate Plots.* Trust this chapter to build bars of all kinds, line graphs, hexagon plots, and deploy variability estimates (error bars). Bars can be displayed as stacked, proportional, and/or side by side. Despite the wide variability of bars available, there are also some useful tricks to learn.

Chapter 6, *Creating Maps,* Demonstrating spatial correlation is mustily done through maps. Learn how points, lines, and polygons can be used to craft maps through R packages. Meet the John Snow cholera map, Tolkien's Middle Earth map, and an interactive globe of banking crisis. Also learn how to read shapefiles from temporary directories and how projection types can be coerced.

Chapter 7, *Faceting,* covers an important device that allows comprehension on more complex data relations. Recipes within this chapter teach how different kinds of visuals can easily reach out for faceting using `ggplot2`. Additionally, this chapter teaches how those can be coerced into interactive visuals by relying on the `plotly` package.

Chapter 8, *Designing Three-Dimensional Plots.* Although `ggplot2` is not capable of drawing true 3D surfaces, it can draw their 2D representations. This chapter demonstrates the craft of contour, tile, and raster plots using `ggplot2`. It also demonstrates how to draw true and interactive 3D surfaces using `plotly`.

Chapter 9, *Using Theming Packages,* teaches how several themming packages can be used to coerce several themes to a ggplot. These range from themes inspired by The Simpsons and Star Trek to respectful academic journal themes. Also learn how to wrap a theme of your own into a function.

Chapter 10, *Designing More Specialized Plots.* Meet the complementary `ggplot2` packages: ggforce, ggrepel, ggraph, and ggalt. These can be used to simple tasks like zooming in to more complex tasks like avoiding labels and texts inside the graph to overlay each other.

Chapter 11, *Making Interactive Plots*, explains how the ggiraph, gganimate, and tweenr packages can be used to create ggplot2 based animations and design interactive features. Animations are an useful way to denote how data variables have evolved with wonderful applications to all kinds of visuals.

Chapter 12, *Building Shiny Dashboards*. shiny allows the user to make interactive web applications direct from R. The package shinydashboard makes easier to create dash boards using shiny. This recipe demonstrates how to construct those while customizing styles, side bars, and more.

What you need for this book

First things first, download the latest version of R (https://cran.r-project.org/). Additionally, recipes were written using a IDE named RStudio (free version). I do prefer to write R codes under RStudio IDE; if you do not have the software yet, you can get it from https://www.rstudio.com/products/rstudio/download/.

Who this book is for

If you are looking to create custom data visualization solutions using the R programming language and are stuck somewhere in the process, this book will come to your rescue. Prior exposure to packages such as ggplot2 will be useful but not necessary. Some programming knowledge of R is required for this book.

Conventions

In this book, you will find a number of text styles that distinguish between different kinds of information. Here are some examples of these styles and an explanation of their meaning. Code words in text, database table names, folder names, filenames, file extensions, pathnames, dummy URLs, user input, and Twitter handles are shown as follows: "This chapter covers basic aspects of three of them: ggplot2, plotly, and ggvis."

A block of code is set as follows:

```
> install.packages(c('devtools','plotly','ggvis'))
> devtools::install_github('hadley/ggplot2')
```

New terms and **important words** are shown in bold. Words that you see on the screen, for example, in menus or dialog boxes, appear in the text like this: "Open your RStudio, go to **Tools | Install Packages...**"

 Warnings or important notes appear like this.

 Tips and tricks appear like this.

Reader feedback

Feedback from our readers is always welcome. Let us know what you think about this book-what you liked or disliked. Reader feedback is important for us as it helps us develop titles that you will really get the most out of. To send us general feedback, simply email feedback@packtpub.com, and mention the book's title in the subject of your message. If there is a topic that you have expertise in and you are interested in either writing or contributing to a book, see our author guide at www.packtpub.com/authors.

Customer support

Now that you are the proud owner of a Packt book, we have a number of things to help you to get the most from your purchase.

Downloading the example code

You can download the example code files for this book from your account at http://www.packtpub.com. If you purchased this book elsewhere, you can visit http://www.packtpub.com/support and register to have the files emailed directly to you. You can download the code files by following these steps:

1. Log in or register to our website using your email address and password.
2. Hover the mouse pointer on the **SUPPORT** tab at the top.
3. Click on **Code Downloads & Errata**.

4. Enter the name of the book in the **Search** box.
5. Select the book for which you're looking to download the code files.
6. Choose from the drop-down menu where you purchased this book from.
7. Click on **Code Download**.

Once the file is downloaded, please make sure that you unzip or extract the folder using the latest version of:

- WinRAR / 7-Zip for Windows
- Zipeg / iZip / UnRarX for Mac
- 7-Zip / PeaZip for Linux

The code bundle for the book is also hosted on GitHub at `https://github.com/PacktPublishing/R-Data-Visualization-Recipes`. We also have other code bundles from our rich catalog of books and videos available at `https://github.com/PacktPublishing/`. Check them out!

Errata

Although we have taken every care to ensure the accuracy of our content, mistakes do happen. If you find a mistake in one of our books-maybe a mistake in the text or the code-we would be grateful if you could report this to us. By doing so, you can save other readers from frustration and help us improve subsequent versions of this book. If you find any errata, please report them by visiting `http://www.packtpub.com/submit-errata`, selecting your book, clicking on the **Errata Submission Form** link, and entering the details of your errata. Once your errata are verified, your submission will be accepted and the errata will be uploaded to our website or added to any list of existing errata under the Errata section of that title. To view the previously submitted errata, go to `https://www.packtpub.com/books/content/support` and enter the name of the book in the search field. The required information will appear under the **Errata** section.

Piracy

Piracy of copyrighted material on the internet is an ongoing problem across all media. At Packt, we take the protection of our copyright and licenses very seriously. If you come across any illegal copies of our works in any form on the internet, please provide us with the location address or website name immediately so that we can pursue a remedy. Please contact us at copyright@packtpub.com with a link to the suspected pirated material. We appreciate your help in protecting our authors and our ability to bring you valuable content.

Questions

If you have a problem with any aspect of this book, you can contact us at questions@packtpub.com, and we will do our best to address the problem.

1
Installation and Introduction

Following recipes are covered in this chapter:

- Installing and loading graphics packages
- Using ggplot2, plotly, and ggvis
- Making plots using primitives

Introduction

R is a free open language and environment for statistical computing and graphics. It particularly gained wide popularity among scientists from different fields, journalists, and private companies. There are various reasons for that, openness and gratuity may be couple of them. Also, R requires minimal programming background and has a vibrant online community.

From community, a bunch of useful graphical packages had come. This chapter covers basic aspects of three of them: ggplot2, plotly, and ggvis. The first one (ggplot2) has been there for a long time, is very mature, and is very useful to build non-interactive graphics.

Both plotly and ggvis are much younger packages, which can build interactive plots. Both are shiny compatible and can well address the matter of web applications. Beginning with installation and loading, this chapter goes all the way through explaining the basic framework of all those three packages, while demonstrating how to use ggplot2 primitives.

Installing and loading graphics packages

Before starting, there are some habits you may want to cultivate in order to keep improving your R skills. First of all, whenever you program there may be some challenges to face. Usually those are tackled either by out-thinking the problem or by doing some research. You might want to remember what the problem was about and the solution, be that for times you face it again later or even for studying hours, keep a record of problems and solutions.

 Speaking for me, making a library-like folder and gathering some commented examples on problems and resolutions was, and still is, of great help. Naming files properly and taking good use of comments (# are used to assign comments with R) makes the revision much easier.

R Markdown documents are pretty useful if want to keep a track of your own development and optionally publish for others to see. Publishing the learning process is a good way to self-promote. Also, keep in mind that R is a programming language and often those can correctly pull a problem out in more than one way, be open-minded to seek different solutions.

First things first, in order to make good use of a package, you need to install the package and know how to call a package's function.

 If your R Session is running for a long time, there is a good chance that a bunch of packages are already loaded. Before installing or updating a package it's a good practice to restart R so that the installation won't mess with related loaded packages.

How to do it...

Run the following code to install the graphics packages properly:

```
> install.packages(c('devtools','plotly','ggvis'))
> devtools::install_github('hadley/ggplot2')
```

How it works...

Most of the book covers three graphic packages—ggplot2, plotly, and ggvis. In order to install a new package, you can type the function install.packages() into the console. That function works for packages available at CRAN-like repositories and local files. In order to install packages from local files, you need to name more than just the first argument. Entering ?install.packages into RStudio console shall lead you to the function documentation at the **Help** tab.

Instants after running the recipe, all the packages (devtools included) covered in this chapter might already be properly installed. Check the **Packages** tab in your RStudio application (speed up the search by typing into the search engine); if everything went fine, these four may be shown under **User Library**. Following image shows how it might look like:

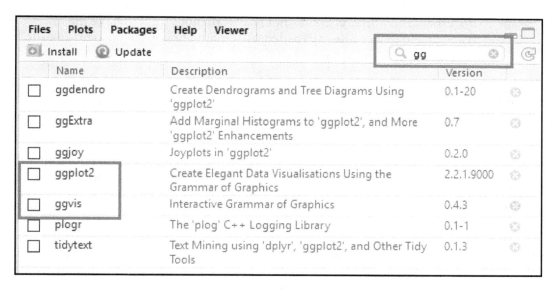

Figure 1.1 - RStudio package window (bottom right corner).

If it fails, you may want to check the spelling and the internet connection. This function also gives some outputs that stand for warnings, progress reports, and results. Look for a message similar to package '<Package Name>' successfully unpacked and MD5 sums checked to make sure that all went fine. Checking the output is a good practice in order to know if the plan worked. It also give good clues about troubleshooting.

You may want to call a non-existing package (be creative here) and a package already installed and see what happens. Sometimes incompatibilities avoid proper download and installation. For example, missing Java or the proper architecture of Java may prevent you from installing the rJava package.

Realize that a package's name must be in the string format in order to work (remember to use ' '). It's also important to check the spelling. The function (calling and arguments) is case sensitive; if you miss even one letter or case, you will not find the desired package. Also note that the arguments where drew into a c() function. That is a vector (try ?c in the console).

? sign is actually a function that comes along base package called **utils**. Typing ?<function name> will always lead you to documentation whenever there is one to display. All functions coming from CRAN packages, base R and maybe the majority of GitHub ones have related documentation files, yet, if it's not base R do not forget to have the respective package already loaded. Alternatively you can also make calls like this: ?<package name>::<function name>.

As first argument of the install.packages() function, a vector of strings was given. That said, multiple packages can be downloaded and installed simultaneously. The same function might not install only the packages asked, but all the packages each of them rely on.

Once the packages are installed, you have a bunch of new functions at your disposal. In order to get to know these functions, you can seek the packages' documentation online. Usually, the documentations can be found at repositories (CRAN, GitHub, and so on).

Now with a bunch of new functions at hand, the next step is to call a function from a specific package. There are several ways of doing that. One possible way to do it is typing <package name>::<package function>, latest code block done that when called install_github(), a function from coming from devtools package, so it was called this way: devtools::install_github().

There are pros and cons about calling a function this way. As for pros, you mostly avoid any name conflict that could possible happen between packages. Other than that, you also avoid loading the whole package when you only need to call a single function. Thus, calling a function this way may be useful in two occasions:

- Name conflict is expected
- Only few functions from that package may be requested and only a few times

Otherwise, if a package is required many times, typing `<package name>::` before every function is anti-productive. It's possible to load and attach the whole package at once. Via RStudio interface, right below the window that shows environment objects, there is a window with a **package** tab. Below the **package** tab it's possible to check the box in order to load a package and uncheck to detach them.

Try to detach `ggplot2` by unchecking the box; keep an eye on that box. You can load packages using functions. The `require()` and `library()` functions can be assigned to this task. Both don't need `' '` in order to function well like `install.packages()` does, but if you call the package name as a string it stills works. Note that both functions can only load one package a time.

Although `require()` and `library()` work in a very similar way, they do not work exactly the same. If `require()` fails it throws a warning, `library()` on the other hand will trow an error. There is more, `require()` returns a logical value that stands for TRUE when the load succeeds and FALSE when it fails; `library()` returns no value.

For common loading procedures that is not a difference that should made into account, but if you want to create a function or loop that depends on loading a package and checking if it succeed, you may find easier to make it using `require()`. Using the logical operator `&` (and), it's possible to load all three packages at once and store the result in a single variable. Calling this variable will state TRUE if there is success for all and FALSE if a single one fails. This is done as follows:

```
> lcheck <- require(ggplot2) & require(plotly) & require(ggvis)
> lcheck
```

`lcheck` won't tell you which and how many packages failed. Try assigning `c( require(ggplot2), require(plotly), reqruire(ggvis))` instead. Each element returning a FALSE is the package that is giving you trouble; this means better chances at troubleshooting.

For now you might be able to install R packages - from CRAN, Git repositories or local files - load and call a functions from an specific package. Now that you are familiar with R package's installation and loading procedures, the next section gives an introduction to the `ggplot2` package framework.

There's more

Installation is also possible via **RStudio features**, which may seen more user friendly for newcomers. Open your RStudio, go to **Tools > Install Packages...**, type the packages' names (separate them with space or comma), and hit install. It fills the `install.package()` function and shows it in your console.

This is most indicated when you are not absolutely sure about the package name, but have a good clue. There is automatic suggestion thing that shall help you out to figure exactly what the package name is. You can also install packages from local files by using this feature. Look for an option called **Install from** and switch it to **Package Archive File** instead of **Repository**.

RStudios also gives you a **Check For Packages Updates...** option right below **Install Packages...** Hit it once in a while to make sure your packages are properly updated. Along with the packages to be updated it also shows what is new about them.

See also...

- `ggplot2` tidyverse reference manual: http://ggplot2.tidyverse.org/reference/
- `ggvis` CRAN-R documentaion: https://cran.r-project.org/web/packages/ggvis/ggvis.pdf
- `plotly` figure reference: https://plot.ly/r/reference/

Using ggplot2, plotly, and ggvis

ggplot2, ggvis, and plotly have proven to be very useful graphical packages in the R universe. Each of them gained a respectful sum of popularity among R users, being recalled for the several graphical tasks each of them can handle in very elegant manners.

The purpose of this section is to give a brief introduction on the general framework of ggplot2 via some basic examples, and relate how to tackle similar quests using ggvis and plotly. Along the way, some pros and cons from each package will be highlighted.

 Whenever you need to choose between some packages (and base R), it's important to balance the tasks each one were designed to handle, the amount of work it will require for you to achieve your goal (learning time included), and the time you actually have. It's also good to consider scale gains in future uses. For example, mastering ggplot2 may not seem a smart choice for a single time task but might pay-off if you're expecting lots of graphical challenges in the future.

Keep in mind that all the three packages are eligible for a large convoy of tasks. There are some jobs that a specific package is more suitable for and even some tasks that can be considered almost impracticable for others. This point will become clearer as the book goes on.

Getting ready

The only requirement this section holds is to have the ggplot2, ggvis, and plotly packages properly installed. Go back to *Installing and loading graphics packages* recipe if that is not the case. Once the installation is checked, it's time to know ggplot2 framework.

How to do it...

First things first, in order to plot using `ggplot2`, data must come from a data frame object. Data can come from more than one data frame but it's mandatory to have it arranged into objects from the data frame class.

1. We took the `cars` data set to fit this first graphic. It's good to actually get to know the data before plotting, so let's do it using the `?`, `class()`, and `head()` functions:

   ```
   > ?cars
   > class(cars)
   > head(cars)
   ```

2. Plots coming from `ggplot2` can be stored by objects. They would fit two classes at same time, `gg` and `ggplot`:

   ```
   > library(ggplot2)
   > plot1 <- ggplot(cars, aes(x = speed, y = dist))
   ```

    Objects created by the `ggplot()` function get to be from classes `gg` and `ggplot` at the same time. That said, you can to refer to a plot crafted by `ggplot2` as a `ggplot`.

3. The three packages work more or less in a layered way. To add what we call layers to a `ggplot`, we can use the `+` operator:

   ```
   > plot1 + geom_point()
   ```

    The + operator is in reality a function.

Result is shown by the following figure:

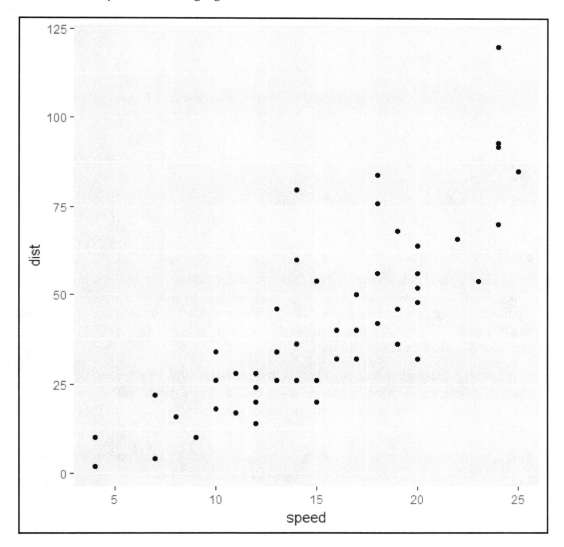

Figure 1.2 - Simple ggplot2 scatterplot.

4. Once you learn this framework, getting to know how `ggvis` works becomes much easier, and vice-versa. A similar graphic can be crafted with the following code:

```
> library(ggvis)
> ggvis(data = cars, x = ~speed, y = ~dist) %>% layer_points()
```

5. `plotly` would feel a little bit different, but it's not difficult at all to grasp how it works:

```
> library(plotly)
> plot_ly(data = cars, x = ~speed, y = ~dist, type = 'scatter',
mode = 'markers')
```

Let's give these nuts and bolts some explanations.

How it works...

In order to have a brief data introduction, step 1 starts by calling `?cars`. This is a very useful way to get to meet variables and background related to almost every data set coming from a package. Once `ggplot2` requires data coming from data frames, `class()` function is checking if is that the case, answer is affirmative. At the end of this step `head()` function is checking upon the first six observations.

Moving on to step 2, after loading `ggplot2`, it demonstrates how to store the basic coordinate mapping and aesthetics into an object called `plot1` (try it on the `class()` function). In order to set the basics, it uses a function (`ggplot()`) that initializes every single `ggplot`.

 Storing a plot coming from `ggplot2`, `ggvis`, or `plotly` package into an object is optional, though very useful way to proceed.

To properly set `ggplot()`, start by declaring data set using `data` argument. After that, some basic aesthetics and coordinates are assigned. Different figures can ask and work along with different aesthetics, for the majority of cases those are named inside the `aes()` function.

As the books goes on you're going to get used to the ways how aesthetics can be declared-in or outside the `aes()` function. For now, let's acknowledged that inside `aes()` it's possible to call data frame variables by name and they may be displayed in legends.

Checking `?aes()` shows "`...`" as argument, popularly known as three-dots but technically named **ellipsis**. It allows the user to pass an arbitrary number and variety of arguments. So as `ggplot2` does lazy-evaluation (only evaluates arguments as they are requested, you could make up arguments and pass them into the `aes()` function with zero or only little trouble to the function. Perceive the following:

```
> plot1 <- ggplot(cars, aes(x = speed,y = dist, gorillaTroubleShooter = T,
sight = 'Legolas'))
```

It would work as good as the earlier version. Just don't forget to name the arguments and you got yourself a good way to create some Easter eggs at your code (also a good way to confuse unaware developers). Both `aes()` and `ggplot()` play core roles in building graphics within this package.

Until step 2, only coordinate mapping was set at object named `plot1`, calling for it alone displays an empty graphic. Step 3 uses `%+%` to add a layer, the layer called (`geom_point()`) took care of fixing a geometry to the graphic. Besides the plus sign, `ggplots` are usually constructed by two families of functions (layers): `geom_*`and `stat_*`. While the first family comes with a fixed geometry and a default statistical transformation, the second one comes with fixed statistical transformations and a default geometry (this is grammar of graphics for real), defaults can be tweaked.

 `plot1 + stat_identity(geom = 'point')` works just the same as step 3. Argument `geom` is set for `'point'` as default for `stat_identity()`, it's fine to skip it. The reason I declared it was to reinforce that if you call for a statistical transformation you can pick the geometry and it goes the other way round (if you call for a geometry you can change the statistical transformation).

Behind the scene, `geom_point()` called the `layer()` function, which set a couple of arguments that culminated in the creation of a scatterplot. One may want to modify the axis labels and add a regression line. It can be done by simply adding more layers to the plot using the plus sign. One can stack as many layers desired, as shown next:

```
> plot1 + geom_point() +
> labs(x = "Speed (mpg)", y = "Distance (ft)") +
> geom_smooth(method = "lm", se = F) +
> scale_y_continuous(breaks = seq(0, 125, 25))
```

Result is exhibited by figure 1.3:

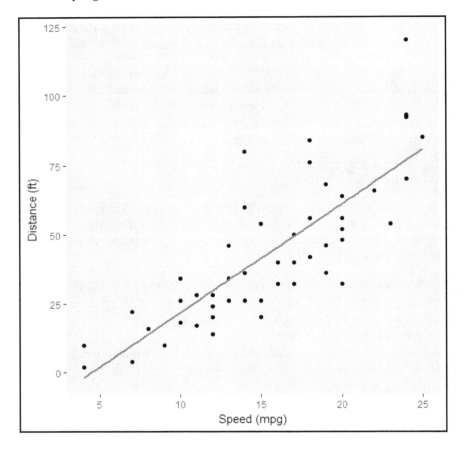

Figure 1.3 - Adding up several layers to a ggplot.

Combining `ggplot2`'s sum operator (that is actually a function) and functions allows the user to make plots in a layered, iterative way. It splits complex graphics construction into several simple steps. It's also very intuitive and does not get any harder as you practice.

Yet, there are limitations. The difficulty to make interactive graphics by itselft may be one. These tasks, in the majority of the cases, are very well handled by both `ggvis` and `plotly` as stand alone packages. This leads us to steps 4 and 5.

Calling `plotly::ggplotly()` after bringing a `ggplot` up will coerce it into an interactive plot. It may fail sometimes. Do not forget to have `plotly` installed.

Step 4 loads `ggvis` package using `library()` and then gives birth to an interactive plot. It holds many similarities with `ggplot2`. Function `ggvis()` handles basic coordinating mapping while pipe operator (`%>%`) is used to add up a layer called by the `layer_points()` function. Remember, pipe operator and not plus sign.

`ggvis` understands different arguments declared using = (ever scaled) and := (never scaled). Also, ~ must come before the variable names.

Function names may change and also does the operator used to add up layers from `ggplot2` to `ggvis`, but essentially the underlying logic keeps still. Layers coming from `ggvis` has several correspondences with `ggplot2`'s ones; refer to the *See also* section to track some. In comparison with `ggplot2`, `ggvis` is much younger and some utilities may be yet to come, also data don't need to come from a data frame object.

Step 5 draws an interactive `plotly` graph. A single function (`plot_ly()`) takes care of coordinate mapping and geometry. It can be designed a little more layered using the `add_traces()` function, but there is no real need for that when the plot is too simple. Instead of having many functions demanding statistical transformations and geometries those are declared by arguments inside the main function.

These three packages, `ggplot2`, `ggvis`, and `plotly`, are well coded and powerful graphic packages. Right before picking one of them to handle a task do ever consider some points like:

- What the package is able to do
- Time needed to master the skill set required
- Time required to handle the task
- Amount of time available
- Time to be saved later by the thing that you learned

Base R is also a feasible possibility. Whenever you face new challenges, it is a good thing to think through these points.

There's more

To have data coming solely from data frames is a strong restriction, but it does obligate the user to be explicit about the data and also draw a very clear line on what is ggplot2's concern (data visualization) and what is not (model visualization). In order to avoid headaches that come from downloading spreadsheets, setting up working directories, and loading data from files, we're taking an alternative way: getting data from packages instead.

 data.frame() may be the most convenient function to coerce vectors into data frames in R.

By doing this, we ensure that the readers only need to reach the R's console to reproduce recipes; we want nothing to do with web browsers (we're too cool for school, school meaning web browsers). We shall follow this approach to the end of the book. This recipe look over datasets base packages to do so. ggplot2 has some data frames of its own.

 Enter library(help = 'datasets') to general information on the other data sets.

It's also important to outline that the *gg* in the ggplot2 and ggvis refer to the Grammar of Graphics. That's a very important and inspiring theory that in had influenced ggplot2, ggvis, and plotly. The layered/iterative way that these packages handle plots might come from the Grammar of Graphics and makes graphics building much easier and reasonable. Learning this theory may give you heads into the process of learning these packages while learning these packages may give you heads when it comes to learn the Grammar of Graphics.

See also

- ggplot2 Cheatsheet made by Rstudio can be found at https://www.rstudio. com/wp-content/uploads/2015/03/ggplot2-cheatsheet.pdf

- Learn layers from ggplot2's author and a real R-universe star at http://rpubs. com/hadley/ggplot2-layers

- Did you know that gg's + is actually a shortcut for a function? A clue on that and some exercises are hidden at http://rpubs.com/hadley/97970

- Learn more about ggvis layers and how they can be translated into ggplot2 ones at http://ggvis.rstudio.com/layers.html

- Learn more about ggvis scaled and unscaled arguments at http://ggvis.rstudio.com/properties-scales.html

Making plots using primitives

Previously, a brief introduction on the frameworks of ggplot2, ggvis and plotly package was conducted. Next we are getting started with ggplot2 graphical primitives, using them in a series of recipes with related examples made with ggvis and plotly.

There are a total of eight graphical primitives at ggplot2, one of them already covered in this chapter (geom_point()). It's important to know the primitives well-what they do and when to use them. As fundamental building blocks, they play an essential role in the drawing process. A series of tasks can be handled relying on primitives when there is no dedicated function to handle some task; sometimes even if there is, primitives can handle it much better.

A good example are the dot plots. They have this dedicated geom_dotplot() function, but sometimes it is much easier to draw dot plots using geom_point(). Now, let's see how ggplot2 can brew figures using primitives and create related ones using ggvis and plotly.

How to do it...

1. After loading the package, primitives geom_point() and geom_path() can be stacked in order to plot lines with markers:

```
> library(ggplot2)
> plot1 <- ggplot( cars, aes(x = speed, y = dist))
> plot1 + geom_point() + geom_path()
```

The resulting output is shown by following figure:

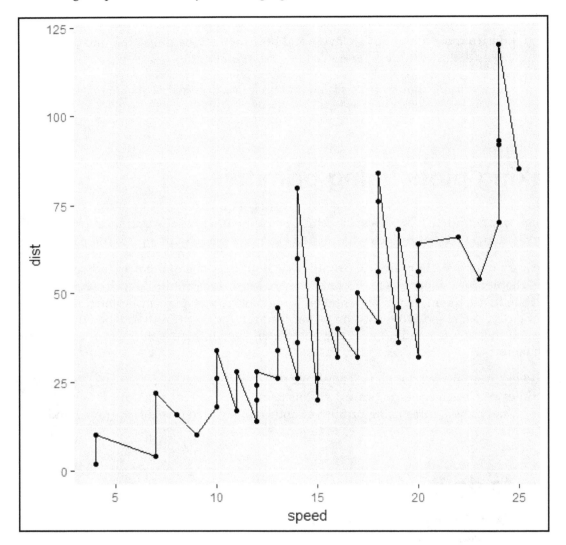

Figure 1.4 - Lines with markers plot made by ggplot2's primitives.

2. Same mission can be nailed by the `ggvis` package, relying on the following code:

```
> library(ggvis)
> ggvis(cars, x = ~speed, y = ~dist) %>% layer_points() %>%
layer_paths()
```

Following figure 1.5 displays a representation of the resulting graphic (only default theme will look different):

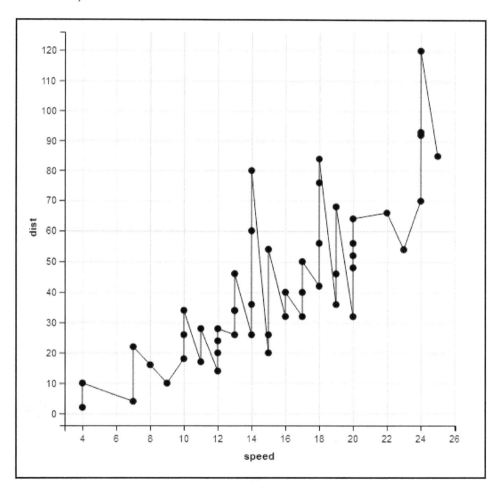

Figure 1.5 - Similar lines and markers plot done by ggvis.

3. Without using the translation function (`ggplotly()`) from `plotly` package, it's also possible to code a similar graphic from scratch relying only on `plotly`:

```
> library(plotly)
> plot_ly(cars, x = ~speed, y = ~dist, type = 'scatter', mode =
'lines+markers')
```

Following figure 1.6 exhibits a snapshot of the graphic brewed by the latest code:

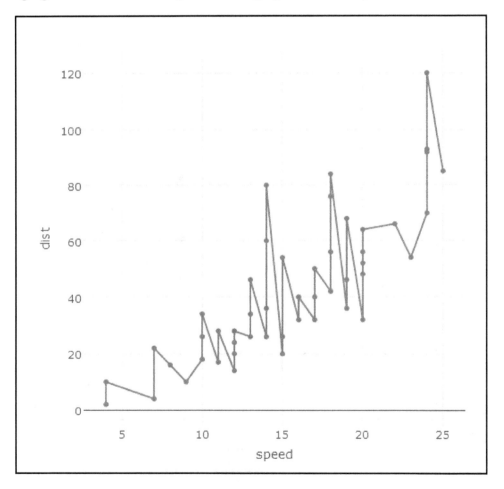

Figure 1.6 - Similar lines and markers plot done by plotly.

Let's understand how these are unfolding.

How it works...

Complete list of `ggplot2`'s primitives is given by
`geom_*`: `blank()`, `path()`, `ribbon()`, `polygon()`, `segment()`, `rect()`, `text()`, and `point()`. Every primitive starts with `geom_*` but not every `geom_*` is a primitive. In fact, the better odds stands for quite the opposite.

More or less, `geom_blank()` seems to be the simplest of the primitives. Calling it right after setting `ggplot()` will display a blank plot with axis already adjusted. It's mostly used to check axes limits given by data itself. Maybe you can find it useful for another task; suit yourself.

Other primitives may work in a similar way. That is the case for `geom_path()`, `geom_ribbon()`, and `geom_polygon()` functions. The first one draws lines between coordinates, second one looks like the first but thicker, requiring additional `aes()` arguments (`ymin` and `ymax`). Last function draws filled polygons.

By setting only the starting and ending points, `geom_segment()` adds a segment line. `geom_rect()` adds a rectangle to the plot, requiring four corners to do so (`xmin`, `xmax`, `ymin`, and `ymax`). `geom_text()` add texts to the given coordinates. Some graphics displays only texts for each observations instead of points, also a good way to display additional information.

The remaining primitive is `geom_point()`. It's the only primitive direct called so far, it plot points at given coordinates. Two important points must be highlighted here. One, getting to know the primitives might give you an idea about which function you will require the most and which one the least, but that is not all that `ggplot2` is capable of doing. Primitives are nothing but the building blocks used by other functions.

For the second point, as the previous recipe stated earlier, you can stack as many layers as you feel like. That is not less true for primitives functions, but it's good to know how they interact with one another. For example, calling geom_blank() after geom_point() may not override the points with a blank space.

After loading ggplot2 and setting base aes(), step 1 is creating a simple plot with lines and markers. While geom_point() displays the markers, geom_path() draws the lines between them. Note that the last function draws lines following the order given by data set rows, so we can call this function order-sensitive.

For many situations, reordering data will improve viz. This may be the case for dot, box, violin, bar plots, and others. If you want paths to be ordered within the x variable, geom_line() does that by itself, though it is not a primitive.

To this particular plot, the lines attach no meaning; they actually mislead. Lines are better designated to indicate some sort of order within the data, like chronological order. The only reason they were used was to demonstrate how primitives could be stacked to originate different viz from the one done before.

Step 2 is drawing a plot similar to the one crafted by step 1 but using ggvis instead. libray() loads the package while the ggvis() function is used to map the basic aesthetics. Following function (layer_points()) sets up the points to work as our markers and layer_paths() draws the lines between them.

Earlier section argued that ggvis is very similar to ggplot2 in the ways of coding graphics. This section actually demonstrated that. First, the function gets the data set and the variables are inputted as arguments. Pipe operators (%>%) are used instead of plus sign to stack up the layers, and layer_* works in a very similar way as geom_* does.

By step 3, a similar plotly graphic is crafted. Same function responsible for setting basic aesthetic mapping (plot_ly()) is also dealing geometries. Arguments type and mode set the geometries, both inputted with strings. These two arguments are meant to work together.

Setting `type = 'scatter'` enables the lines and markers modes. Each type has a whole particular convoy of modes attached to it; consult the reference manual to catch them all. The way we wanted to is to use markers and lines at same time so we built a string containing those two elements separated by the plus sign (`'lines+markers'`), and assigned it to `mode` argument.

 `mode = 'lines+markers'` works as good as `mode = 'markers+lines'`. Modes can be stacked and order does not matter.

Figures 1.4 to 1.6 five resembles much a time series, but they aren't and it may give the wrong intuition. There are observations for two variables and neither one is time. Notice how for some speeds values there are up to 4 different distances to stop. Note that the cars data frame is ordered first by speed and then by distance, paths obey the row order showed by data while for point geometry order doesn't really matter.

Adding path geometry was misleading, `geom_point()` would be enough. Goal here was to demonstrate primitives interaction and not to give a meaningful figure. Next, let's build fictional data and draw a graphic that tells the story the right way. Picture a small classroom with only 7 students. The teacher builds a data frame with studying hours and grades for each student.

Data can be created like this:

```
> allnames <- c('Phill','Ross','Kate','Patrice','Peter','James','Monica')
> classr <- data.frame(names = allnames)
> classr$hours <- c(4, 16, 8, 11, 6, 14, 8)
> classr$grades <- c(4, 9.5, 6, 4, 6, 9, 7.5)
```

`geom_text()` primitive could be used to summon a meaningful graphic:

```
> library(ggplot2)
> plot2 <- ggplot( classr, aes(x = hours, y = grades))
> plot2 + geom_text( aes( labels = names))
```

The result would be like shown in the following figure 1.7:

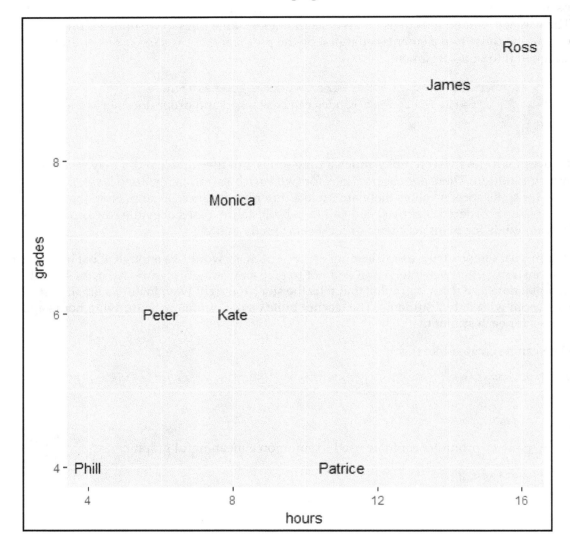

Figure 1.7 - Plotting grades and hours as texts using ggplot2's primitive.

Related `ggvis` and `plotly` codes are shown next:

```
> library(ggvis)
> ggvis(classr, x = ~hours, y = ~grades, text := ~names) %>% layer_text()
> library(plotly)
> plot_ly(classr, x = ~hours, y = ~grades, type = 'scatter', mode = 'text',
text = ~names)
```

This last brief example illustrates how to brew graphics using only primitives in a more meaningful way. It's very important to think about it. The better graphic is the one that tells the right story objectively and not the one with many layers.

There's more...

Did you know that both `ggvis` and `plotly` can guess which geometry you are looking for? Based on the basic aesthetics defined, they make a guess and adopt certain geometry. They look at how many variables of what kind (discrete or continuous) were inputted, and for some combinations they are able to make a guess.For the nearest example they would have guessed points geometry.

Figures breed by both packages will be displayed by the **Viewer** tab if you're using RStudio (They are interactive! Try hoovering the mouse over a `plotly` figure). Figures can be exported as web pages. Other than that, they can be exported as PNG, JPEG, and BMP, therefore losing the interactive property.

This recipe aimed to demonstrate how to construct plots using `ggplot2` primitives, and build similar graphs using other packages. A question you should always ask yourself is if the geometry adopted goes along with the data used. In other words, if the graphic tells the story that you are willing to.

The recipes's goal was to introduce you to the graphical primitives of `ggplot2` and draw simple graphics by using only primitives. Additional goal was to draw related graphics using the `ggvis` and `plotly` packages.

The next chapters dive deeper; each one shall tackle some families of graphics, highlighting nuts and bolts in the way to building high quality plots. As the book advances, so does the complexity involved. At some point, we are going to be plotting interactive globes, 3D surfaces and developing web applications. I find it pretty sicking cool, hope you enjoy it.

Chapter 2, *Plotting Two Continuous Variables*, takes care of scatterplots. It's a very popular kind of plot, and very useful too, but there is a big problem: over-plotting. Following chapter will not only teach how to craft scatterplots, but also teach how to deal with such problem and how to improve scatters by deploying marginal plots. Let it rip!

2
Plotting Two Continuous Variables

In this chapter, we will cover the following recipes:

- Plotting a basic scatterplot
- Hacking ggvis add_axis() function to operate as a title function
- Plotting a scatterplot with shapes and colors
- Plotting a shape reference palette for ggplot2
- Dealing with over-plotting, reducing points
- Dealing with over-plotting, jittering points
- Dealing with over-plotting, alpha blending
- Rug the margins using geom_rug()
- Adding marginal histograms using ggExtra
- Drawing marginal histogram using gridExtra
- Crafting marginal plots with plotly
- Adding regression lines
- Adding quantile regression lines
- Drawing publish-quality scatterplots

Introduction

Investigating the relationship between two variables may be much easier than investigating it for several variables simultaneously. There is one good reason for that: we can visualize bivariate relationships way better. Problems with numerous amount of variables are often split into several problems with only two variables.

There are several visualizations that supports the two variables context. The most popular of them may be the scatterplots. People are familiar with them, on the other hand there is a problem that haunts many scatterplots: over-plottingting. This chapter begins with recipes to draw very simple scatterplots, going all the way to explore solutions available when it comes to deal with over-plottingting, and demonstrate how enhance scattersplots by setting up marginal graphics.

Plotting a basic scatterplot

Scatterplots play a major role in the representation of two continuous variables. Making simple scatterplots is a very easy task to handle using `ggplot2`, `ggvis`, or `plotly`. This recipe uses a data frame called `iris` to draw plots, it comes with base R (`datasets` package).

 Before using data coming from a package, you may want to try entering `?<package name>::<data frame name>` into your console. For this recipe, that would go as: `?datasets::iris`. This is may lead you towards data documentation, this way you get to know each variable coming from the data frame.

From the various features presented by this data set, this recipe uses `Petal.Width` and `Petal.Length`. They respectively account for iris' petal widths and lengths measured in centimeters. Besides drawing the plots, this recipe also teaches how to add a title to them. So, move on to the coding!

How to do it...

1. Initialize a `ggplot` and then give it the point geometry:

```
> library(ggplot2)
> sca1 <- ggplot(data = iris, aes(x = Petal.Length, y =
Petal.Width))
> sca1 + geom_point() +
    ggtitle('Simple ggplot2 scatterplot')
```

Last lines gives the following illustration (figure 2.1):

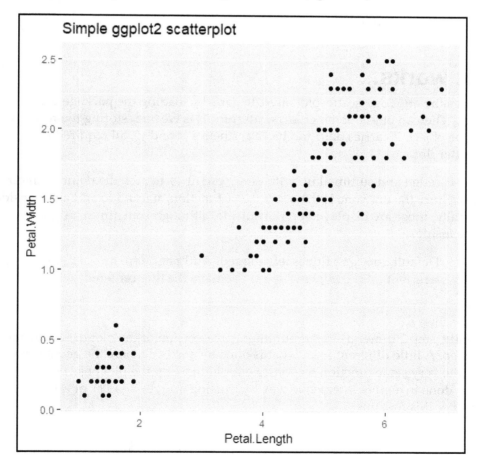

Figure 2.1 - Simple ggplot2 scatterplot.

2. `plotly` can reach very similar results:

```
> library(plotly)
> sca2 <- plot_ly(data = iris, x = ~Petal.Length, y = ~Petal.Width,
                   type = 'scatter', mode = 'markers')
> sca2 %>% layout(title = 'Simple plotly scatterplot')
```

3. Using `ggvis`, call `layer_points()` to add a geometry:

```
> library(ggvis)
> sca3 <- iris %>% ggvis(x = ~Petal.Length, y = ~Petal.Width)
> sca3 %>% layer_points()
```

Ahead lay the explanations.

How it works...

Step 1 brings the `ggplot2` scatterplot alive. It starts by loading the package using `library()`. Then an object name `sca1` (scatterplot 1) is created, storing the recently created `ggplot` type object. It carries data and basic aesthetics (x and y), all required in order to make a scatterplot.

Next, `sca1` is called and summed up with `geom_point()` to pick the point geometry. Until now no novelties, the only one is the `ggtitle()` function, stacked to add a title inside the plot. Normally, those are displayed on the outside, although sometimes it's good to have them at the inside.

> Default `ggplot2` title is left aligned. Add `theme(plot.title = element_text(hjust = .5))` to have the title centered.

Subsequently, step 2 draws a similar but interactive version of the plot drawn by the previous step. A little different from what is done by `ggplot2`, here the geometry was picked by the very same function responsible for initializing the plot object (`plot_ly()`). This can be done in a more interactive way by trusting `add_traces()` or `add_markers()` functions after this first one.

Entire plot was designed by `plot_ly()` alone, and then stored into the `sca2` object. By choosing `type = 'scatter'`, the marker mode was enabled, giving away a scatterplot. The yet unused `layout()` function joined the code with the aid of pipe operator (`%>%`). The `title` argument carried the string to be displayed as title.

Step 3 introduces a new way to create a `ggvis` type object. Rather than directly inputting data as first argument, pipe operator (`%>%`) declared data argument. Arguments x and y were called in the sequence and their names could be omitted once they were called in the right order.

 Pipe operator (`%>%`) hands previous object or function results to work as the first argument to the next function. It's not a base R operator, but it's very famous and is carried by many packages, such as `ggvis`, `plotly` and `dplyr`. Strictly, it's not an operator but a function used to chain a series of functions.

Out of curiosity, when the geometry is missing, `ggvis` takes care of guessing one. Try entering `sca3` into your console to see the guessing taking place.

There's more...

Did you note that the `ggplot2` plot title is left aligned while `plotly`'s is centered? Those are set by default and can be changed. For instance, one can centrally align the `ggplot`'s title by summing the following code line:

```
> theme(plot.title = element_text( hjust = .5))
```

Also, note that the `ggvis` plot was the only one without a title. That happened because package version 0.4.3 did not had an easy way to add titles, although it's possible to sort of hack (in a good sense) the `add_axis()` function coerce a title. Next recipe teaches how to do it.

Hacking ggvis add_axis() function to operate as a title function

Version 0.4.3 of ggvis does not have a function to add titles to plots, but still there is a known way to hack the add_axis() function to work as a title function. If a user expects to explore this device many times, it's advised to wrap it into a function. Besides making the code more readable, it's a quicker way to address the problem.

Getting ready

This recipe does not only teach how to craft the hack function but also to experiment it on the previous plot, so make sure to have sca3 from the earlier recipe loaded into your environment. Alternatively, you can use another ggvis object of your own.

How to do it...

1. Wrap the add_axis() function with several arguments declared to work as a title function:

```
> library(ggvis)
> ggvis_title <- function(vis, plot_title, title_size = 18, shift =
0, ...){
    add_axis(vis, 'x', ticks = 0, orient = 'top',
            properties = axis_props( axis = list(strokeWidth = 0),
                                     labels = list(strokeWidth =
0),
                                     grid = list(strokeWidth = 0),
                                     title = list(fontSize =
title_size, dy = -shift, ...)),
            title = plot_title)
  }
```

2. Try it on the previous plot:

```
> sca3 %>% ggvis_title('simple ggvis scatterplot')
```

The result looks like the following image:

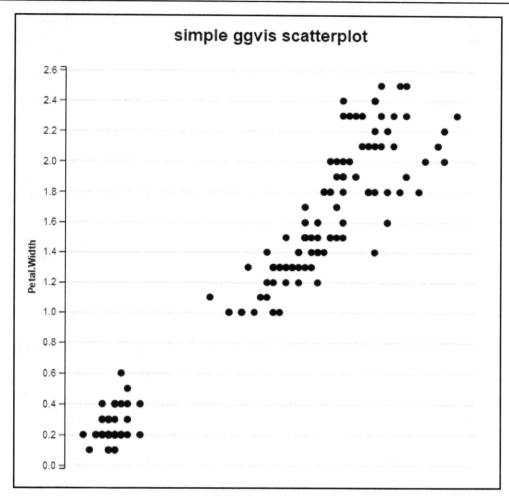

Figure 2.2 - titled ggvis scatterplot.

Now to the explanations.

How it works...

After running step 1, a new function named ggvis_title() is available in the environment. Four arguments are named, two with default values. Additionally, there is ellipsis (. . .), meaning that more arguments can be added if named. Feel free to modify and adapt this function to better fit your needs.

The object inputted with the function `function()` (kek) holds the new function name. Inside the parenthesis come the arguments: first one must be `vis`, so that the chaining process through the pipes keeps working, and then next comes `plot_title`. This last arguments has no default value and it may be declared with a string that will go into title.

Subsequent arguments are `title_size` and `shift`, both with default values. The first one adjusts the title size, while the second one shifts the title towards the top whenever inputted with positive values and shifts it down if the values inputted are negative.

Only naming arguments won't do it. We need to work those arguments inside `ggvis::add_axis()` function so that we get an invisible extra axis with a visible title. Also we make sure to not have any grid coming from this axis, neither visible ticks and labels.

There are two things to outline in step 2. One is the guessing process. Once we did not called for any geometry, `ggvis` is guessing `layer_points()` (point geometry). Two, the title was successfully added. Next, we are going to explore more about scatterplots. Just for a moment, let's forget about labels and titles, and focus on how we can have multiple colors and shapes altogether.

Plotting a scatterplot with shapes and colors

There are several aesthetics coming out from `geom_points()` that can be changed. Typing `?geom_point` into the R console will take you to the function documentation, which comes with a complete list of aesthetics understood by the function. The mandatory ones come in bold.

Names given are nothing but self-explanatory. Besides the mandatory x and y values, optional values range from `alpha` to `stroke`. For this particular recipe, we're settling for changes in the `shape` and `colours` arguments. Recipe also aims for similar results using both `ggvis` and `plotly`.

How to do it...

1. Change the `shape` and `colour` arguments to get a better result:

```
> library(ggplot2)
> sca1 <- ggplot(data = iris, aes(x = Petal.Length, y =
Petal.Width))
> sca1 + geom_point(aes(shape = Species, colour = Species))
```

Now each iris species is designated by a unique combination of shapes and colors:

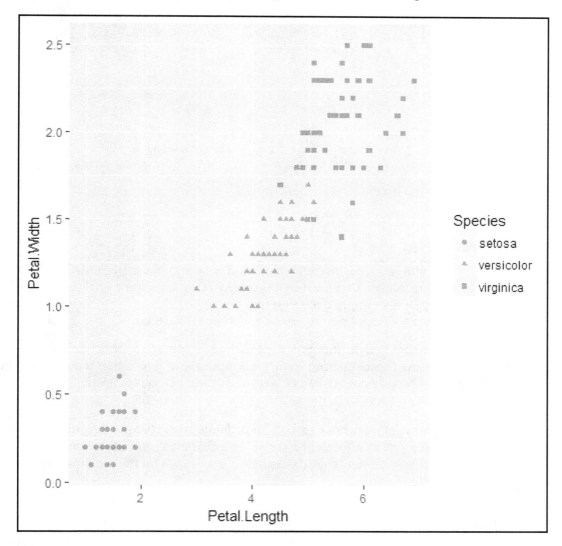

Figure 2.3 - Adding shapes and colors to a scatter plot.

2. `plotly` can also handle such a task:

```
> library(plotly)
> sca4 <- plot_ly(iris, x = ~Petal.Length, y = ~Petal.Width,
                  type = 'scatter', mode = 'markers', symbol =
~Species)
> sca4
```

3. Following code changes shapes and colors using `ggvis`:

```
> library(ggvis)
> sca3 <- ggvis(data = iris, x = ~Petal.Length, y = ~Petal.Width)
> sca3 >%> layer_points(shape = ~Species, fill = ~Species)
```

Explanations can be found on the next section.

How it works...

Step 1 defines `ggplot` with a set of different colors and shapes coming from the `Species` column in the data frame. Notice that most of it is asking for a scatterplot just like Recipe Plotting a basic scatterplot. By simply declaring two extra aesthetics (`shape` and `colour`) after the variable Species we've got points' colors and shapes tweaked.

It's important to outline that both arguments were named inside `aes()` function. We did this because values inputted were coming from a data frame variable. Other values could be named outside `aes()`. These aesthetics can be declared either by `ggplot()` or `geom_point()` function.

Step 2 conducts a similar change using `plotly`. To promote such change, the only requirement is to set the `symbol` argument after `~Species`; hence, each different value coming from that variable will refer to a different color and shape by the time the plot is drawn.

Next, step 3 does about the same using `ggvis`. To attach new shapes, trust `shape` argument. The colors are given by the `fill` argument. For both `ggvis` and `plotly`, variables coming from the data are named after the ~ sign. For `ggplot2`, arguments can be named after data frame variables by using `aes()` function.

Plotting a shape reference palette for ggplot2

Shapes are picked following a default scale when you input a variable to work as `shape` using `ggplot2`. You can always choose to tweak this scale to one of your preference. To do so you need to know which shapes are available and how you can call for them. This recipe simply draws the following shape palette:

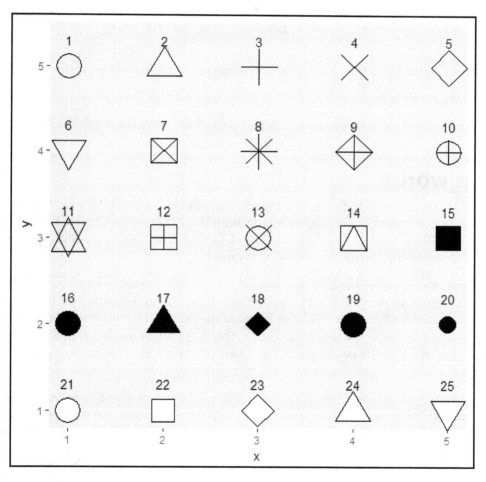

Figure 2.4 - ggplot2 shape palette.

It shows available points, plus the number used to call for them. Now let's explore the code that built it.

How to do it...

Draw a suitable data frame using `rep()` and `seq()` functions, them let's plot those using `geom_point()`:

```
> palette <- data.frame(x = rep(seq(1,5,1),5))
> palette$y <- c(rep(5,5),rep(4,5),rep(3,5),rep(2,5),rep(1,5))
> library(ggplot2)
> ggplot(data = palette,aes(x,y)) +
    geom_point(shape = seq(1,25,1), size = 10, fill ='white') +
    scale_size(range = c(2, 10)) +
    geom_text(nudge_y = .3, label = seq(1,25,1))
```

Function `geom_text()` is plotting the reference numbers related to each shape.

How it works...

First two lines draw the data frame to be used; the order chosen displays the shapes in regular reading orientation (left-right and top-bottom), as *Figure 2.4* shows. Following the data frame creation, `ggplot2` package is loaded. Unlike what had been done until now, the plot was not stored into an object but directly called.

Three arguments were tweaked by the `geom_point()` layer: `shape`, `size`, and `fill`. The first one was declared outside `aes()` (aesthetics function) and did called each shape by its number. The argument `size` is meant to increase the points size, but it will only do so if combined with the next layer, `scale_size()`. The `fill` argument is set to white; this way, the readers can see that the points from 1 to 20 are not affected by such an argument, while 21 to 25 are.

The layer `scale_size()` has the size range fixed, so the points size can be increased all together and not proportionally to one another, as `ggplot2` would do if this particular layer was skipped. Finally, `geom_text()` added text to each point. Text given for each shape is telling the reference number of each of them. Argument `nudge_y` makes sure that text and points would not overlay each other.

Whenever you feel like points shapes should be more carefully thought consider consulting a guide similar to the one given by Figure 2.4 .Function `scale_shape_manual()` allows you to pick the shapes manually. A good way to start a scatterplot is to try the default settings and only then look for the necessity of a more manual approach.

There's more...

Points shapes given by `ggplot2` come from R base graphics. Another way to look at them is to enter `?pch` in the console. Do not expect it to give you such a visual exemplification but rather a textual one.

Dealing with over-plotting, reducing points

There are mainly three techniques used to deal with over-plot. They are: (i) adopting smaller points,(ii) jittering data, and (iii) alpha blending. These are useful tools, not only to deal with over-plot but also to check if there is over-plotting.

However, these are not the only options; for example, alternative geometries can also be implemented. No matter how troublesome over-plotting may be there are good solutions available. There is not a single solution that is better for all the situations, so you must know a bunch of them.

This recipe advises how to apply a technique based on point size reduction using `ggplot2`, `ggvis` and `plotly`. In order to do so, we are trusting the `ggplot2::diamonds` data frame. Keep in mind that reducing points works better for cases where points are very close to each other but do not actually occupy the same coordinates.

How to do it...

1. Set `shape` to `'.'` in order to reduce points using `ggplot2`:

```
> library(ggplot2)
> sca5 <- ggplot(diamonds, aes(x = carat, y = price))
> sca5 + geom_point(shape = '.')
```

Result looks like the following:

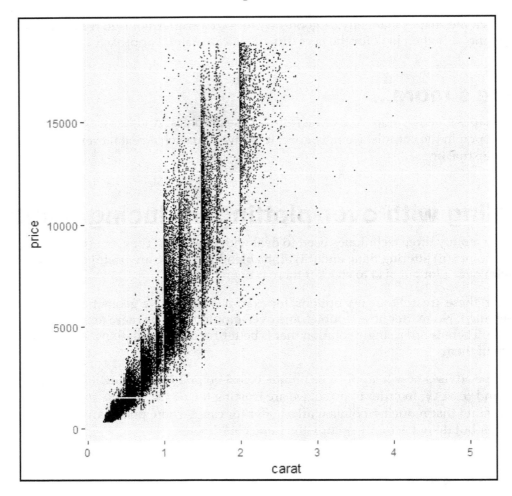

Figure 2.5 - Diamonds price versus cara with very small points.

2. `plotly` is also able to achieve similar results by declaring the `marker` argument:

```
> library(plotly)
> sca6 <- plot_ly(diamonds, x = ~carat, y = ~price, type =
'scatter',
                  mode = 'markers', marker = list(size = .8))
> sca6
```

3. Using `ggvis`, this change is done by the size argument:

```
> library(ggvis)
> sca7 <- diamonds %>% ggvis(x = ~carat, y = ~price)
> sca7 %>% layer_points( size := .5)
```

Explanations on sight, sailors!

How it works...

Step 1 demonstrates how to reduce points using `ggplot2`. Oddly, the argument used was `shape` and not `size`. Actually, the shape `'.'` replaces circles with really small dots. This reference is even smaller than point number 20. Adjusting the size argument is also an option but requires the addition of `scale_size()` along with the range argument, as the last recipe did.

Look at step 2 to understand how to change points size using `plotly`. Argument `marker` is able to change a bunch of marker properties, input it with a list and name the properties do you want to change as list's elements. In order to reduce points this step had named `size` as a list element which value was set to 0.8.

Step 3 shows a tricky detail about reducing points with `ggvis`. Simply declaring the `size` argument into `layer_points()` by using an equal signal won't do it. Declare it using `:=` (not scaled) signal instead of = (scaled). The colon along equal signal tells `ggvis` (only `ggvis` work this way) that the number inputted must no be re-scaled.

There's more...

Dealing with over-plotting may not be difficult using `ggplot2`, `ggvis` and `plotly`, but it's not a bed of roses. Each method can be associated with downsides. A clear downside of reducing points is that more the sizes are reduced, less the shapes are recognizable; thus, very difficult to work out this aesthetic. On the other hand if there is too much over-plotting shapes become unrecognizable no matter the size.

Dealing with over-plotting, jittering points

Size reduction is never an option when there are too many points sharing the exact same coordinates; it simply is not the right tool for the job. A clear option therefore is to jitter the data, that is, add a little noise to the data so that the points move around a little bit and the over-plotting kind of wears off.

Two points must be highlighted here. Jittering may be a good way to adjust the plot but not to adjust the data, so do not use jittered data for modeling and always be honest when transformations of that nature take place. Second point is that as long it may work pretty well when many points share coordinates. Although, if too many points are only close enough but do no share same coordinates there is a chance that jittering will work very badly.

Now let's go back to the iris data set and demonstrate how this technique can be applied using ggplot2, ggvis and plotly.

How to do it...

1. With ggplot2, set potion = 'jitter' in order to obtain the jitter:

```
> set.seed(100)
> library(ggplot2)
> sca1 <- ggplot( iris, aes( x = Petal.Length, y =
Petal.Width))
> sca1 + geom_point( position = 'jitter',
                     aes(shape = Species, colour = Species))
```

The jittered plot is shown by following image:

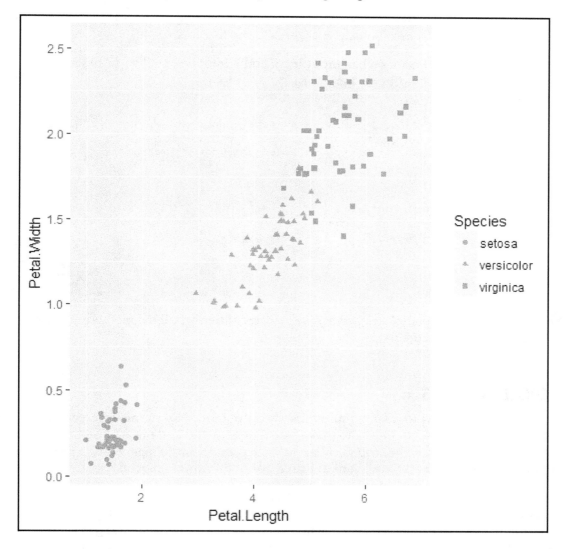

Figure 2.6 - Iris data set stacked with noise.

2. Create some vectors to jitter the data set variables later:

```
> jx <- rnorm(length(iris$Petal.Length), mean = 0, sd = .2)
> jy <- rnorm(length(iris$Petal.Width), mean = 0, sd = .06)
```

3. Apply these vectors when inputting x and y into the plot_ly() function, in order to achieve jitter using plotly:

```
> library(plotly)
> sca8 <- plot_ly(iris, x = ~Petal.Length + jx, y = ~Petal.Width +
jy,
                  type = 'scatter', mode = 'markers', symbol =
~Species)
> sca8
```

4. Does the same using ggvis:

```
> library(ggvis)
> sca3 <- ggvis( data = iris)
> sca3 %>% layer_points( x = ~Petal.Length + jx , y = ~Petal.Width
+ jy,
                         shape = ~Species, fill = ~Species)
```

While new vectors helped plotly and ggvis achieve jittering, all the methods avoided making any changes in the data.

How it works...

Figure 2.6 (section How to do it...) represents the output given by running the code from step 1. It starts with set.seeds() to make sure that both you and me achieve the very same result; function sets the seed number used for pseudo random generation processes. Call this function whenever you want to turn a "random" process reproducible.

Then, after drawing the regular ggplot2 scatter, the only thing needed to add jitter to the points was to operate position = 'jitter' inside the geom_point() layer. Another way to go is to replace geom_point() with geom_jitter(), and skip the position argument. For some occasions, that would be a better way, as it enables a great deal of arguments resulting in more control over the jittering process.

Step 2 uses the function `rnorm()` to create the objects `jx` (jitter x) and `jy` (jitter y). Both are designed to work as little noises. Function `rnorm()` is creating a vector of numbers "randomly" (pseudo-randomly) sorted from a normal distribution with given `mean` and standard deviation (`sd`).

 Normal distributions are not the only ones that can be generated. Functions `rt()`, `rpois()` and `rbinom()` respectively generates student, poisson and binomial distributions. There are more options available.

Steps 3 and 4 are analogous to each other. While step 3 is adding the noises (`jx` and `jy`) to variables inputted as x and y using `plotly`, step 4 does about the same but using `ggvis` instead. By doing this jitter technique was applied using both `plotly` and `ggvis`. Noises were stored in separated vectors and the data frame remais unchanged.

Dealing with over-plotting, alpha blending

Another popular technique is known as alpha blending. It consists on making points translucent, this way the audience gets to know if points are stacked or not. Between all the techniques demonstrated so far, alpha blending must be the most popular one. This recipe teaches how to apply alpha blending using `ggplot2`, `plotly`, and `ggvis`.

How to do it...

1. Set the `alpha` parameter to apply alpha blending to `ggplot`:

```
> library(ggplot2)
> sca1 <- ggplot( iris, aes( x = Petal.Length, y = Petal.Width))
> sca1 + geom_point( alpha = .5 ,
                        aes(shape = Species, colour = Species))
```

The following figure 2.7 shows alpha blending working:

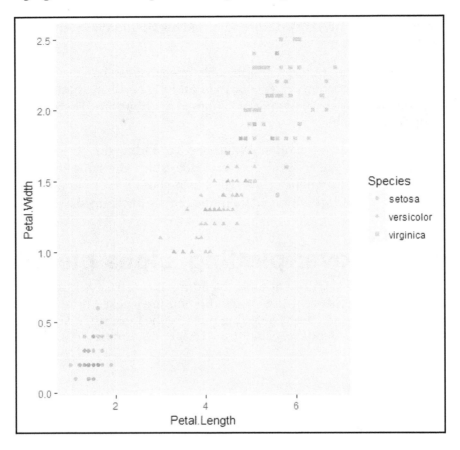

Figure 2.7 - alpha blending with ggplot2.

2. Setting `alpha` parameter with `plotly` will also apply alpha blending:

```
> library(plotly)
> sca9 <- plot_ly( iris, x = ~Petal.Length, y = ~Petal.Width,
>                  type = 'scatter', mode = 'markers', alpha = .5,
symbol = ~Species)
> sca9
```

3. `ggvis` applies alpha blending when `opacity` argument is set:

```
> library(ggvis)
> sca3 <- ggvis(iris, x = ~Petal.Length, y = ~Petal.Width)
> sca3 %>% layer_points(opacity := .5, shape = ~Species, fill =
~Species)
```

Notice that opacity had to be declared using : = instead of =.

How it works...

Step 1 demonstrates that by simple setting the `alpha` parameter to 0.5, the blending is implemented using `ggplot2`. Values under one and greater than zero make sense. Smaller values stand for more transparency. Try quite a few values and check how illustration responds to them. Lower values may be more suitable if there are too many points stacked.

Step 2 is doing about the same but using `plotly` package instead. Here we hold no novelties, the exactly same argument used to apply alpha blending using `ggplot2`, `alpha`, is now used to apply alpha blending to a `plotly` figure. Both works the same way, try values between zero and one.

Next step teaches the ways of accessing alpha blending through `ggvis`. Now the argument receives another name, `opacity`, and shall be declared using the : = operator instead of the simple =. Values accept here also range from zero to one.

There's more...

over-plotting is commonly associated with the point geometry. So far this chapter demonstrated three different ways to deal with it, bu these are not the only solutions. Another feasible solution is to set an alternative geometry that does not suffer with over-plotting, for example hexagonal heatmaps:

```
> library(ggplot2)
> sca5 <- ggplot(diamods, aes( x = carat, y = price))
> sca5 + geom_hex()
```

Resulting outcome is a hexagonal heatmap drawn over a diamonds data set; it's supposed to work as a little tease to what is going to be seen later in this book. There will always be downsides and upsides of choosing one over another. Each situation will call for one or more types of solutions. Now that you know a few, it's up to you to choose the one that suits you best.

Rug the margins using geom_rug()

Up till now, the chapter has focused on how to draw scatterplots and solutions related to over-plotting. Upcoming recipes, including this one, shall focus on enhancing scatterplots. If there is a bivariate relation to be displayed there is also two univariate distributions to show. How can they be used to improve the plots?

Answer lies in filling the margins with supplemental plots carrying representations of underlying univariate distributions. Still relying on the iris data set framework, this recipe introduces a simple solution, almost restricted to ggplot2. Let's rug plots in the margins with geom_rug().

How to do it...

1. Draw a scatterplot using ggplot2 and sum the geom_rug() layer:

```
> set.seed(50) ; library(ggplot2)
> rug <- ggplot(iris,
                aes(x = Petal.Length,
                    y = Petal.Width,
                    colour = Species))
> rug <- rug +
    geom_jitter(aes( shape = Species), alpha = .4) +
    geom_rug(position = 'jitter' , show.legend = F, alpha = .4)
> rug
```

The result is demonstrated by the following illustration:

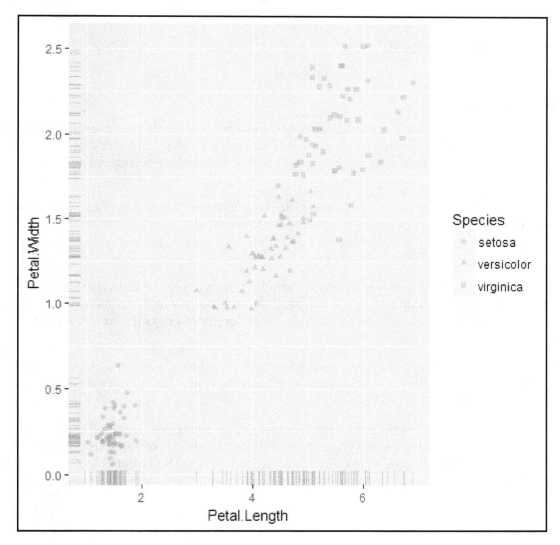

Figure 2.8 - Jittered scatterplot with rugs.

2. Using `plotly`'s `ggplotly()` function, this illustration becomes interactive:

```
> plotly::ggplotly(rug)
```

Let's see the nuts and bolts.

How it works...

First step begins by defining the seed generator, this way you get the same result I get from `geom_jitter()`. After loading `ggplot2`, the same step is creating and working an object called `rug`. It starts by receiving a `ggplot` with only some aesthetics declared and no geometry.

Aesthetics declared into `ggplot()` function are later inherited other ones, unless we change them. Subsequently, `rug` is receiving two geometries: `geom_jitter()` and `geom_rug()`. Calling `geom_jitter()` it's equivalent to `geom_point( position = 'jitter')`. Function `geom_rug()` is drawing rug plots in the margins.

Both rugs and points do suffer with over-plotting. Chosen solution was to combine jitter and alpha blending. Argument `alpha` had set the last technique for both geometries. Tweak `position` argument at `geom_rug()` function to ask for jittered rugs (points are already jittered once recipe used `geom_jitter()`).

Finally, calling `rug` will display the result. Note that the colors match for both points and rugs. Also notice that there are no legends to explain the rugs. That happened because we called `show.legend = F` inside `geom_rug()`.

Last step is conducting a simply coercion from a `ggplot` object to an interactive `plotly` one. Coercion may work for some geometries and not for others. For this particular one, it works. The only thing needed is to call `plotly::ggplotly()`. If no plot object is inputted, it shall display the last `ggplot` object called. It's a good practice to set `height` and `width` arguments.

Adding marginal histograms using ggExtra

Another way to go is to draw histograms or even density distributions in the margins. Drawing tailor made plots in the margins would require more code. On the other hand, if there is no need for greater customization ggExtra package can be used to spare many code lines. This recipe is demonstrating how to use ggExtra to easily draw histograms in the margins of a scatterplot.

Getting ready

In order to properly execute this recipe, the ggExtra package must be locked and loaded. Run the following code to make that happen:

```
> if( !require(ggExtra)){ install.packages('ggExtra')}
```

Once ggExtra is installed we can go on.

How to do it...

1. Draw a ggplot2 scatterplot like this:

```
library(ggplot2)
base_p <- ggplot(iris, aes(x = Petal.Length, y = Petal.Width,
colour = Species))
scatter <- base_p + geom_point( alpha = .5, aes(shape = Species)) +
   geom_rug(alpha = .5, sides = 'tr', show.legend = F) +
   theme(legend.position = 'bottom')
```

2. Load ggExtra and input the ggplot object into ggMarginal() function:

```
library(ggExtra)
ggMarginal(scatter, iris, type = 'histogram', bins = 150)
```

The result is shown by figure 2.9:

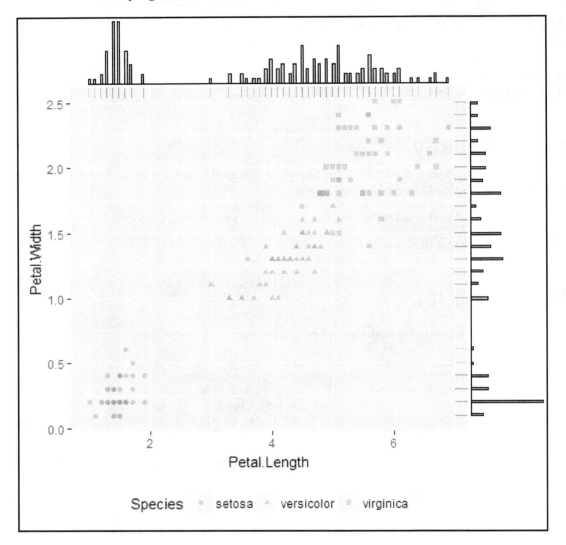

Figure 2.9 - Marginal histograms by the scatterplots.

How it works...

Before actually plot in the margins we need a core plot. Step 1 takes care of that. Final result is a rugged scatterplot, rugs are displayed in the top and right sides. Legends are relocated to the bottom. To move the rugs around, tweak `sides` argument coming from `geom_rug()`.

 Argument `side` has to be inputted with a string. This string may contain the initial letters referencing the sides that shall receive the rug plots. Include `'t'` for top, `'b'` for bottom, `'l'` for left and `'r'` for right (order does not matter). Most common combinations are `'tr'` or `'rt'` (top and right); `'bl'` or `'lb'` (bottom and left); and `'tblr'` (top, bottom, left and right)

Legends are moved to the bottom by setting `theme( legend.position = 'bottom')`. With that we're ensuring that the legends won't be in the way of the marginal histogram to be displayed on the right side.

Afterwards, step 2 draws the entire plot along with the marginals; it uses the `ggMarginal()` function coming from the `ggExtra` package. First argument accounts for the central `ggplot` object, next one holds the data frame. Argument `type` is picking the type of marginal plots, recipe had histogram chosen. Once we asked for `type = histograms`; argument `bins` is also available, it sets the number of bins to be displayed by each marginal histogram.

Drawing marginal histogram using gridExtra

If you seek a more tailor made result, there would be more code to do. The solution this recipe presents is to draw three plots and later arrange them into a 2x2 grid using the `gridExtra` package. Since it's a 2x2 grid there would be a blank space left to fill, let's move the legends there . This recipe works with `ggplot2`.

Getting ready

Package `gridExtra` must be installed:

```
> if( !require(gridExtra)){ install.packages('gridExtra')}
```

The recipe also requires a function to withdraw the legends from the plots:

```
> g_legend <- function(p){
>   tmp <- ggplot_gtable(ggplot_build(p))
>   leg <- which(sapply(tmp$grobs, function(x) x$name) == 'guide-box')
>   legend <- tmp$grobs[[leg]]
>   return(legend)}
```

This later solution was found as a StackOverFlow answer given by Luciano Selzer. Now we're ready for action.

How to do it...

1. Draw the center plot using `ggplot2` and extract the legend using the `g_legend()` function:

   ```
   > library(ggplot2)
   > main <- ggplot(iris, aes(x = Petal.Length, y = Petal.Width)) +
       geom_point(alpha = .5 , aes(shape = Species, colour = Species))
   > leg <- g_legend(main)
   ```

2. Still using `ggplot2`, draw a histogram to fit the top margin:

   ```
   > top <- ggplot(iris) +
       geom_histogram(alpha = .3, aes( x = Petal.Length, fill =
   Species)) +
       guides(fill = FALSE) + xlab('')
   ```

3. And another histogram to fit the right margin:

   ```
   > right <- ggplot(iris) +
       geom_histogram(alpha = .3, aes( x = Petal.Width, fill =
   Species)) +
       coord_flip() + guides(fill = FALSE) + xlab('')
   ```

4. Arrange them all using `gridExtra::grid.arrange()`:

   ```
   > library(gridExtra)
   > grid.arrange(top, leg, main + theme(legend.position = 'none'),
                  right, ncol=2, nrow=2, widths=c(4, 1), heights=c(1,
   4))
   ```

See figure 2.10 for the resulting illustration:

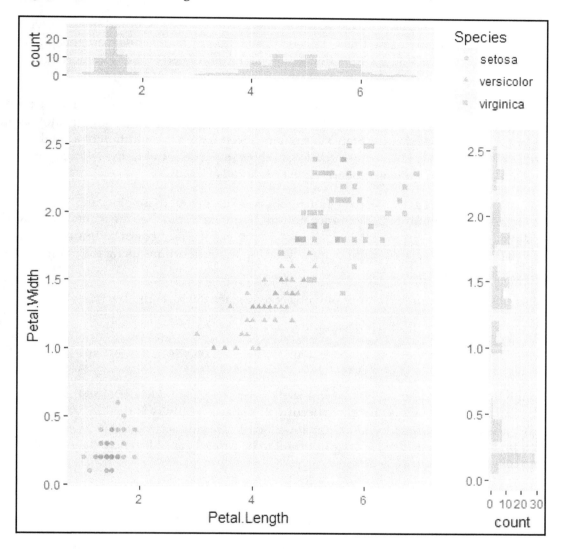

Figure 2.10 - Marginal histograms draw with gridExtra.

How it works...

Step 1 is drawing the scatterplot to fit figure's center. This ggplot is stored in an object called main. Also, we are using the g_legend() function to get legends from this plot and store it into an object called leg. Function g_legend() was created at the Getting ready section.

Step 2 draws the histogram that will fit the top margin. Function geom_histogram() asks for histogram geometry. Function guides() is used to turn off legends from this plot, while xlab('') erases the x-axis title. Step 3 is similar to Step 2 with the addition of a single fuction, coord_flip(). This is intended to flip the ggplot so it can fit the left margin. Note that because the plot was flipped, xlab() worked as ylab().

In the last step, the grid.arrange() function is used gather all these plots and legends into a single one, first four arguments account for them; main plot has the legends removed by adding theme(legend.position = 'none'). Next, the number of columns (ncol) and rows (nrow) are declared, right before declaring the proportions using the widhts and heights parameters.

It is also possible to create an empty plot object to replace the legends. Try the following:

```
> empty_plot <- ggplot()+geom_point(aes(1,1), colour="white") +
    theme(axis.ticks=element_blank(), panel.background=element_blank(),
          axis.text.x=element_blank(), axis.text.y=element_blank(),
          axis.title.x=element_blank(), axis.title.y=element_blank())
```

Although this recipe had used histograms to fit the margins, any kind of visualization coming out from ggplot2 is eligible to occupy this space-creativity is the limit. Also, here a 2x2 grid was used, but keep in mind that any kind of columns and rows can be set. When you arrange plots into grids it's very important to be careful about legends, they usually creates some distortions.

Crafting marginal plots with plotly

This recipe teaches how to make marginal plots using plotly. The way it's done is actually very similar to the way done with gridExtra, that is, by drawing a grid and arranging the plots in it. An advantage of using plotly is the interactivity that comes along with it. There is no need for supplemental packages; plotly as a stand alone can do it.

How to do it...

1. Use the `subplot()` function to arrange several `plotly`'s plots into a single grid:

```
> library(plotly)
> marg_plot <- subplot(
    plot_ly(data = iris, x = ~Petal.Length, type = 'histogram',
          color = ~Species, alpha =.5),
    plotly_empty(),
    plot_ly(data = iris, x = ~Petal.Length, y = ~Petal.Width, type
= 'scatter',
          mode = 'markers', symbol = ~Species, color = ~Species,
alpha = .5),
    plot_ly(data = iris, y = ~Petal.Width, type = 'histogram',
          color = ~Species, alpha = .5),
    nrows = 2, heights = c(.2, .8), widths = c(.8,.2), margin = 0,
    shareX = TRUE, shareY = TRUE
  )
> layout(marg_plot, showlegend = F, barmode = 'overlay')
```

Sail for explanations, fellow marooner!

How it works...

After loading `plotly`, the whole figure is stored in the object `marg_plot`. It uses `subplot()` function to arrange the plots into a grid. First inputs shall account for the plots to fit into the grid. Order here does matter, the first plots inputted shall fit the top spaces into the grid, last ones shall fit the bottom.

Following this orientation, the first plot inputted was the upper margin histogram (top-right). Next one was an empty `plotly` plot created with `plotly_empty()` function. Subsequently came the scatter plot and only then the left margin histogram. Once all these plots were inputted into `subplot()`, argument `nrows` is deciding how many rows the grid will have and indirectly the number of columns.

Next, the arguments `heights` and `widths` took care of the proportional sizes to be displayed by the columns and rows. Parameter `margin` brought the plots closer to each other, while `shareX` and `shareY` were set to `T` (`TRUE`), thus all all the plots were sharing the same axes.

Plot was then called using the `layout()` function. The parameters picked by this function had the legends removed and bars were set to overlay each other. Similar to `grid.arrange()`, `subplot()` is able group any kind of plots crafted with `plotly`, even plots made with `subplot()` can be inputted, be creative.

Adding regression lines

Regression lines are used to describe trends, it's not usual to have regression lines stacked with scatterplots. They can be drawn using `ggplot2`, `ggvis`, and `plotly`. For the first two, adding regression lines will only require calling a function or two, to do the same using `plotly` might require more lines of code.

This recipe's intention is to add regression lines to the scatterplots made from `iris` data frame. **Ordinary least squares** (**OLS**) regression lines will be grouped by species. Drawing un-grouped regressions requests for fewer code, so once you have mastered how to group them, it's not difficult to work the other way around.

How to do it...

1. Load `ggplot2` and call for the `geom_smooth()` layer:

```
> library(ggplot2)
> scatter <- ggplot(data = iris,
                    aes(x = Petal.Length, y = Petal.Width)) +
    geom_point(alpha = .5, aes(colour = Species, shape = Species))
> scatter +
    geom_smooth(method = 'lm', se = F, show.legend = F,
                aes(group = Species))
```

Resulting illustration would look like the following figure 2.11:

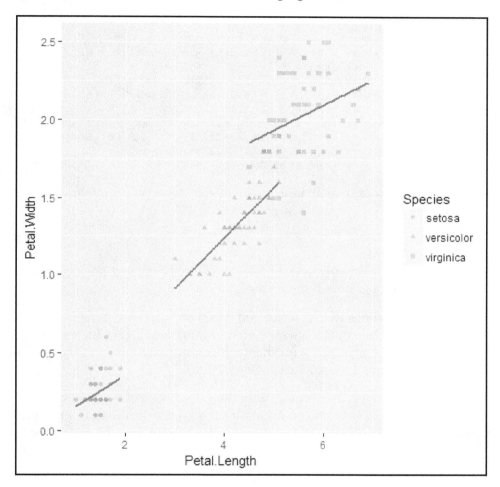

Figure 2.11 - scatterplot with grouped regression lines.

2. For ggvis, call layer_model_predictions() along with the group_by() function:

```
> library(ggvis)
> ggvis( iris, x = ~Petal.Length, y = ~Petal.Width, opacity := .5)
%>%
>   layer_points( shape = ~Species, fill = ~Species) %>%
group_by(Species) %>%
>   layer_model_predictions( model = 'lm', stroke = ~Species)
```

3. Using `plotly`, combine `add_lines()` with the `lm()` function to achieve a similar result:

```
> library(plotly)
> plot_ly(iris, x = ~Petal.Length, y = ~Petal.Width,
        showlegend = F, alpha = .5, color = ~Species) %>%
    add_markers(showlegend = T, symbol = ~Species) %>%
    add_lines(data = iris %>% filter(Species == 'setosa'),
            y = ~fitted(lm( Petal.Width ~ Petal.Length))) %>%
    add_lines(data = iris %>% filter(Species == 'versicolor'),
            y = ~fitted(lm( Petal.Width ~ Petal.Length))) %>%
    add_lines(data = iris %>% filter(Species == 'virginica'),
            y = ~fitted(lm( Petal.Width ~ Petal.Length)))
```

Following section holds some explanations.

How it works...

Step 1 draws regression lines using `ggplot2`. After loading `ggplot2` package, first step is drawing a scatterplot. Plot is stored into an object called `scatter`.

Regression lines would be colored based on `Species` variable if aesthetic `colour`, `shape` or `fill` were declared into it `ggplot()` instead of `geom_point()`. Calling for them with exception of `shape` aesthetic into `geom_smooth()` would also color the lines.

After the scatterplot is drawn, it's summed with the `geom_smooth()` layer to draw the regression lines. The `group` aesthetic declared into this layer asks for a unique regression for each species. There are a bunch of useful arguments available at this particular layer; consult them by typing `?geom_smooth()`.

For this recipe, three arguments are directly called for: `method`, `se`, and `show.legend`. The first one is inputted with `'lm'`, so that the lines are based on the linear model (there are others available). Next argument is set to `F` (FALSE), so that the confidence interval isn't drawn. The last one makes sure that the regression lines wouldn't be present in the legends.

Step 2 draws a similar plot using `ggvis`. After calling `layer_points()`, pipes (`%>%`) were used to group data by variable `Species` and then draw regression lines with `layer_model_predictions()`. Arguments `model` and `stroke` are respectively picking the prediction model and line colors.

Step 3 draws regression lines using the `plotly` package. The function `plot_ly()` is used to initialize the `plotly` object, it does not draw anything yet. Next function, `add_markers()`, is drawing the points. Argument `show.legends` asked for legends to explain the points.

Following `add_markers()` function there are a series of `add_lines()` functions. There is one for each `Species` showed by data. All of them work in a very similar way. First, data is filtered with respect to certain species using the `filter()` function. By doing this, the recipe groups the data manually. Next, the fitted values coming out from the linear model are inputted as `y`. The linear models were adjusted using the `lm()` function. The fitted values were rescued using the `fitted()` function. To draw a single ungrouped regression line would be much simpler. Don't you filter data and call a single `add_line()` function.

Adding quantile regression lines

There is another very useful kind of regression, quantiles. Drawing them under the `ggplot2` package it's not challenging; it has a whole quantile dedicated function, `geom_quantile()`. Drawing them using `ggvis` and `plotly` is also possible, but demands way more code.

This recipe draws 20 percent, 40 percent, 60 percent, and 80 percent quantile regression lines in a diamonds' carat versus price scatterplot. Drawing are amde using `ggplot2` and `plotly` respectively.

Getting ready

Quantile regressions come from the `quantreg` package; make sure to have it installed:

```
> if( !require(quantreg)){ install.packages('quantreg')}
```

Even `ggplot2` relies on `quantreg` to fit quantile regressions.

How to do it...

1. Load `ggplot2` and use `geom_quatile()` to draw quantile regression lines:

```
library(ggplot2)
ggplot( diamonds, aes( carat, price)) +
  geom_point(shape = '.') +
  geom_quantile(quantiles = c(.2, .4, .6, .8),
                colour = 'blue', size = 1) +
  ylim(0, max(diamonds$price))
```

Result is shown in the following image:

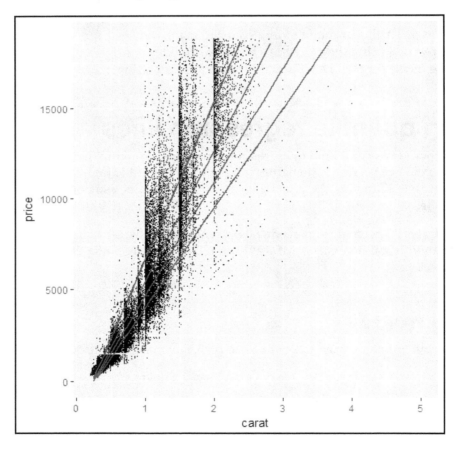

Figure 2.12 - A scatterplot with quantile regression lines.

2. Before trying a similar result on `plotly`, start by fitting the quantile regression:

```
library(quantreg)
q20 <- fitted(rq( price ~ carat, data = diamonds, tau = .2))
q40 <- fitted(rq( price ~ carat, data = diamonds, tau = .4))
q60 <- fitted(rq( price ~ carat, data = diamonds, tau = .6))
q80 <- fitted(rq( price ~ carat, data = diamonds, tau = .8))
```

3. Now it's possible to rely on `plotly` to draw quantile lines:

```
> library(plotly)
> c = I('black')
> plot_ly(ggplot2::diamonds, x = ~carat, y = ~price, type =
'scatter',
>          mode = 'markers', marker = list(size = .8)) %>%
>     add_lines(y = ~q20, color = c, marker = NULL) %>%
>     add_lines(y = ~q40, color = c, marker = NULL) %>%
>     add_lines(y = ~q60, color = c, marker = NULL) %>%
>     add_lines(y = ~q80, color = c, marker = NULL) %>%
>     layout(yaxis = list(range = c(0,20000)), showlegend = F)
```

Let's see how the events unfolded.

How it works...

Beginning with step 1, `geom_quantile()` is used to draw quantile regression lines with `ggplot2`. Argument `quantiles` must be inputted with a vector describing which quantiles may be drawn. Arguments `colour` and `size` pick lines' colors and sizes respectively. Also, it is important to outline the function `ylim()`, which limits the graph range so that the lines won't go to infinity and beyond.

Note that `geom_point`'s points were reduced using the reference `shape = '.'`.

Next, step 2 shows how to fit quantile regressions using the `quantreg` package. Function `rq()` adjusts the regression, argument `tau` rules the desired quantile. Function `rq()` is inputted into `fitted()` function, this way we get only the fitted values from quantile regression.

 Do not forget that diamonds data frame comes from `ggplot2`.

Finally, step 3 draws about the same lines using `plotly`. Right after loading the package, an object called `c` (color) is created. This is object is supposed to work later as a shortcut for the color black. Afterwards, `plot_ly()` function draws the scatterplot.

Subsequently, several `add_lines()` functions are chained by `%>%`, each function adding a specific quantile line. Note how our earlier `c` object is calling for the black color while it saves some space; also notice how markers are removed by setting `marker = NULL`.

In the end, `layout()` is called in order to set the limits of the y axis, thus avoiding lines going far far away. Brewing similar results with `ggvis` would require a little bit more code but definitely can be done. Here lies a challenge for the reader. Now let's craft a publish-quality scatterplot.

Drawing publish-quality scatterplots

Drawing a publication quality scatterplot doesn't require stacking up all that we've seen until now. It's usually the other way round. Telling a good history means sticking with the right tools and not deploying unnecessary ones. Unnecessary usually is synonymous to mixed signals. The history you need to tell with your plot may be a short or long one, may request few or many devices. This decision is up to you, but there are general things to look for that improves almost any scatterplot.

All graphics brought until now by this chapter may be considered good results if those were made only for exploratory purposes. However, on the other hand, they can be considered unfinished work when it comes to publish quality standards-there is still a pretty run to make.

Jeff Leek stresses that defaults in `ggplot2` are *pretty enough that might trick you into thinking the graph is production ready by using only defaults*. Each context will request a different amount of work to craft a publishing quality plot, but as Jeff Leek stands for, there at least a few things to look for that would improve almost any plot:

- Give complete information (measure included) in legends and labels

- Check spelling

- Grow labels bigger (increase font size)

- Grow axes bigger (include more breaks)

These are very basic, yet important points to visit when you seek expository quality. It is hardly reasonable to avoid any of them. The first thing to do in order to start is to brew a graphic using only defaults. Storing it into a variable and taking a good look at it is always a good way to begin.

This recipe's goal is to draw a nice exploratory graph that tells that different iris species hold different petal length and width relations, and turn it into a publication quality illustration. To the mission!

Getting ready

Let's stick with a plot similar to the one displayed by Figure 2.11 (Recipe Adding regression lines, How to do it... section), calling only a few tweaks, like a different default theme and `stroke` and `fill` aesthetics. This plot will be stored by an object called `core_plot` and will work as our departure point for this recipe-it can be considered a good exploratory figure but not a publication one.

```
> library(ggplot2)
> core_plot <- ggplot( data = iris, aes(x = Petal.Length, y = Petal.Width,
>                                        colour = Species, shape = Species,
fill = Species)) +
>   geom_point(alpha = .5, stroke = 1.5) +
>   geom_smooth(method = 'lm', se = F, show.legend = F) +
>   theme_minimal()
> core_plot
```

After running this code, following is the output we get:

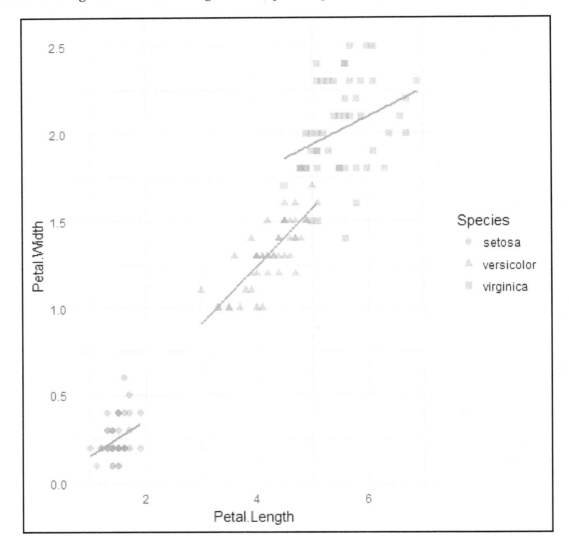

Figure 2.13 - the so called core_plot.

Now we have a few steps to go through.

How to do it...

1. Make sure that axes labels stand for full names by using the `xlab()` and `ylab()` functions:

```
> h1 <- core_plot + xlab('petal length (centimeters)') +
    ylab(' petal width (centimeters)')
```

2. Pick better shapes, and inside and outside colors using the `scale_*_manual()` functions:

```
> h2 <- h1 +
    scale_colour_manual(values = c('setosa' = 'magenta4',
                            'versicolor' = 'darkorange4',
                            'virginica' = 'steelblue4'),
                name = 'Iris species') +
    scale_fill_manual(values = c('setosa' = 'magenta',
                            'versicolor' = 'darkorange',
                            'virginica' = 'steelblue'),
                name = 'Iris species') +
    scale_shape_manual(values = c('setosa' = 21,
                            'versicolor' = 22,
                            'virginica' = 24),
                name = 'Iris species')
```

3. Grow the axes bigger, while accordingly labeling each break with `scale_*_continuous()`:

```
> h3 <- h2 +
    scale_x_continuous(labels = 1:7, breaks = 1:7, minor_breaks =
0) +
    scale_y_continuous(labels = sprintf('%.2f',seq(0,2.5,.25)),
                    breaks = seq(0,2.5,.25),
                    minor_breaks = 0)
```

4. Resize the text and relocate the legends using `theme()`:

```
> h4 <- h3 +
    theme(legend.justification = c('left', 'top'),
          legend.position = c(.65,.25),
          legend.background = element_rect(color = "black",
                                           size = 1,
                                           linetype = "solid"),
          legend.text = element_text(size = 13),
          legend.title = element_text(size = 13),
          axis.text = element_text(size = 15),
          axis.title = element_text(size = 15))
> h4
```

Finally, we have got something that can be considered publication quality:

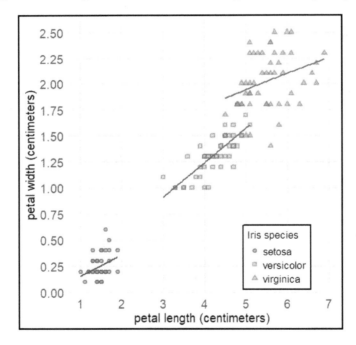

Figure 2.14 - Publication quality scatterplot.

How it works...

The entire plot is designed in a very interactive/layered way. Our `ggplot` begins with `core_plot` object going all the way through `h1`, `h2`, `h3`, and finally `h4`. Readers may like to call them separately to see the changes taking place. Do not feel intimidated. A publication plot does require more code but it's not difficult to understand it, and once you have created your routine, they are not that difficult to craft.

First step is a very short one, it simply relies on `xlab()` and `ylab()` to make axes and titles account for complete information (measure units included). Next, step 2 manually picking points' shapes and colors (inside and contour). All this is done by the `scale_*_manual()` functions.

Values bring the reference thing (`color`, `shape`, or `fill`) that we want to modify. Each vector element is named after a `iris$Species` level. The `name` argument sets the legends' titles. If two or more functions do not display matching `name` arguments, there will be two or more separated legends.

Step 3 grows the axes using `scale_*_continuous()`, once both the axes display continuous variables. Arguments `labels` and `breaks` must have the exact same length. First one labels each break while the second picks the breaks.
At `scale_y_continuous()` function a little trick was deployed-the `sprintf()` function was used to make sure every label showed two digits after the dot (`%f.2`).

Also, `minor_breaks` was set to zero so there won't be minor breaks. Last step can be considered lengthy but not difficult. The layer `theme()` conducts a wide range of changes, but all the argument names are very intuitive. This step resizes texts, relocates the legends to fit inside the figure, and creates a rectangle behind legends.

These are pretty much basics of what almost every `ggplot` must go through in order to be seen as publication material. Each case shall display its own nuts and bolts, so be creative. This closes for now the speech about scatterplots; can't wait to see you in the next chapter. Following section gives some useful links.

See also

- Color guide used to pick colors manually: `http://sape.inf.usi.ch/quick-reference/ggplot2/colour`

- Jeff Leek, Roger Peng, and Rafa Izarry blog: `https://simplystatistics.org/`

3
Plotting a Discrete Predictor and a Continuous Response

In this chapter, we will cover the following recipes:

- Installing the car package and getting familiar with data
- Drawing simple box plots
- Adding notches and jitters to box plots
- Drawing bivariate dot plots using ggplot2
- Using more suitable colors for geom_dotplot
- Combining box with dot plots
- Using point geometry to work as dots using ggvis, plotly, and ggplot2
- Crafting simple violin plots
- Using stat_summary to customize violin plots
- Manually sorting and coloring violins
- Using the ggjoy package to replace violins
- Creating publication quality violin plots

Introduction

Often you may find yourself in a spot where you are willing to investigate the relationship between two variables, just like the Chapter 2, *Plotting Two Continuous Variables* did. The tools covered there are more suited for the continuous versus continuous paradigma, but sometimes you are stuck with a discrete versus continuous paradigma. If that is the case, this chapter may have what you're looking for.

This chapter introduces box, dot, and violin plots. Besides the mainly used functions to build them under `ggplot2`, `ggvis`, and `plotly` supervision, it also addresses some nuts and bolts that are usually related to this kinds of visualizations. Little tweaks that greatly improve the outcomes are also advised.

 Two little disclaimers here. Sometimes, I may use categories as a pronoun for discrete values; I'm aware that they are not the same thing. Second disclaimer: by the time this chapter was written, `plotly` did not had functions to draw violins, nor did `ggvis`.

For `ggvis` and `plotly` packages, dot plots were achieved by using some sort of "hacks"; we will soon get to them. For that reason, the readers are going to see a lot more of `ggplot2`, only because this package is more mature. It's possible that some update had brought an easy way to design violin plots using `ggvis` or `plotly`, always look for updates. Now let's meet the data we're going to use a lot here.

Installing car package and getting familiar to data

Before getting our hands dirty, let's conduct a brief data examination. The `iris` data set could be used from the beginning to the end of this chapter, as it displays simultaneously discrete (`Species`) and continuous variables (`petal lengths/widths`, `sepal lengths/widths`), but let's get some fresh air.

Data set `Salaries` coming from the `car` package shows information about nine-month salary for professors in a college in the U.S. between 2008 and 2009. It holds exactly the kind of data that we need. This recipe will look for `car` package among the already installed packages. If it's already installed, recipe proceeds to a quick data exploration, otherwise it installs `car` at the first place.

How to do it...

We proceed with the recipe as follows:

1. Use an `if` statement to check and install the `car` package:

```
> if(!require(car)){ install.packages('car') }
```

2. Load the package and use `?` to call for data set documentation:

```
> library(car)
> ?Salaries
```

3. Check both the first row and the data set object type:

```
> head(Salaries)
> class(Salaries)
```

How does it works...

The first step performs that package check and installation thing introduced in `Chapter 2`, *Plotting Two Continuous Variables*. Conditional if statement will only run `install.packages()` if `require(car)` is NOT (`!`) true. Next, step 2 loads the package (`library()`) and asks for the `Salaries` data set documentation (`?Salaries`). Last step simply checks the first few rows by calling `head()`, while also checking if `Salaries` is already a data frame by using the `class()` function.

If, by any chance, you have found conditional so much useful that you going to use it a lot, consider making a function out of it.
Try: `check_install <- function(package_name) { if( !require(package_name) ) { install.packages( paste(package_name) ) }}`

There is more

Fortunately, `Salaries` already is a `data.frame` type object, a requirement for the `ggplot2` plots. For those not yet familiarized with `Salaries`, there are 397 observations on 6 variables and several are categorical, thus discrete variables like `rank`, `discipline` and `sex`. One continuous variable called `salary` accounts for the nine-month salary in dollars.

Remaining variables fit in a grey area between discrete and continuous variable. They are years since PhD (`yrs.since.phd`) and years of service (`yrs.service`). One could argue that as time referring variables they are continuous, cause time is continuous. Other would argue that they are represented by integers so they may be discrete.

Truth is that even continuous variables can be grouped into discrete ones. Think of it, instead of having weight measured in kilograms (continuous) you could have a variable for 'weights more than 10 kilograms' (discrete). There and back again, it's time to talk about visualizations.

See also

- For more data sets coming from packages, consult `https://vincentarelbundock.github.io/Rdatasets/datasets.html`

Drawing simple box plots

Box plots are simple, yet a very popular way to plot continuous versus discrete variables. Information covered by these plots usually account for median, first, and third quartile intervals, plus outliers. Among other visuals displayed here, it may be considered a simple one, once distribution format remains hidden. Sometimes less means more and simple means better.

If there is neither the need to highlight the distribution format nor investigate it, there is no reason to go further than box plot, otherwise you may send mixed signals to your audience. That would be like trying to hit a fly with a .50 bullet-you would probably miss it badly. This recipe teaches how to draw simple box plots using `ggplot2`, `ggvis`, and `plotly`.

Getting ready

Previous recipe had `car` package installed. If you did not run the previous recipe, you can simply run the following code:

```
> if( !require(car)){ install.packages('car') }
```

Now our data set will be available.

How to do it...

Here is how we draw simple box plot using `ggplot2`:

1. Begin by calling `geom_boxplot()` to draw box plot using `ggplot2`:

```
> library(ggplot2)
> box1 <- ggplot(data = car::Salaries,
                  aes( x = rank, y = salary))
> box1 + geom_boxplot( outlier.alpha = .4 )
```

Resulting graphic looks like the following figure 3.1 (alpha blending is applied to the outliers):

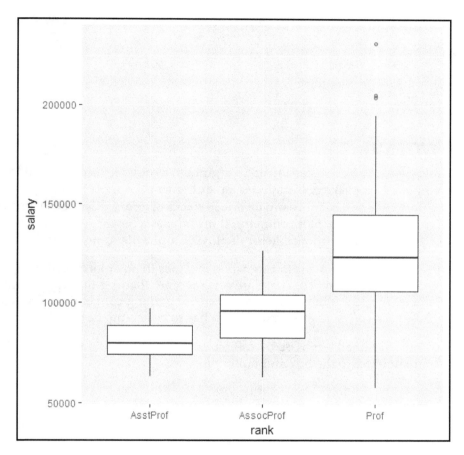

Figure 3.1: Simple ggplot2 box plot

2. Similar one can be drawn by `plotly`:

```
> library(plotly)
> box2 <- plot_ly(data = car::Salaries, y = ~salary, x = ~rank,
                   type = 'box', marker = list(opacity = .4))
> box2
```

3. Using `ggvis`, calling for alpha requires a little bit more code:

```
> library(ggvis)
> box3 <- ggvis(data = car::Salaries,
                x = ~rank, y = ~salary)
> box3 %>% layer_boxplots(opacity := .4) %>%
    layer_boxplots(size := 0)
```

Let's check the explanations.

How it works...

In step 1, calling `car::Salaries` as the `data` argument avoids the need to load the whole package. Having the `car` package installed is a requirement though. Object named `box1` stores base `ggplot`. Proximate line is stacking `geom_boxplot()` function to `box1`; therefore adding the box plot geometry. It introduces a new argument, `outlier.alpha`, responsible for deploying alpha blending to the outliers only.

The outliers can be a source of overplotting when it comes to box plots; adding alpha blending to them is a good practice. There are several other features that can be deployed to outliers only and all of them follow the point.separeted naming convention. Try setting the argument `outlier.shape = 3` as an example; it has to be set into `geom_boxplot()`.

You can flip any `ggplot` by calling `coord_flip()`. It's a very useful function to flip the box and violin plots.

Next step teaches how to draw similar box plot using `plotly`. Two very important arguments are `type` and `marker`. First one was set to `'box'`; hence picking the box plot geometry. Second argument added alpha blending to outliers, notice that it had a list inputted and alpha argument is now called `opacity`.

This result is now interactive. Besides the compatibility with web applications, it also displays accurate information when mouse is hovered over graphical elements. Step 3 finally draws a similar box plot using `ggvis`. This was done a little bit differently than the regular way so alpha blending could affect outliers only.

It starts by assigning basic aesthetics mapping to a `ggvis` object called `box3`. It has the data frame from which the plot will be drawn on `data` argument, plus x and y variables. Afterwards, function `layer_boxplots()` is stacked twice with `box3`. The first functions adds boxes with alpha (`opacity := .4`), second one is drawing only the boxes.

Problem is that the whole box receives the alpha to, hence resulting in a weird visual. A solution is to add another box plot overlaying this one, but now erasing the outliers. To proceed this way set argument `size := 0`. Now we have got ourselves a `ggvis` box plot which alpha blending seems to affect only outliers.

If you happen not to care about the outliers, you can call:

```
> box3 %>% layer_boxplots()
```

Now that you know the very basic of drawing box plots, let's see how to improve the ones coming from `ggplot2`. When it comes to displaying distribution information, box plots are commonly labeled as simple visualizations. This is not a problem but a characteristic, yet box plots can be worked to display additional information. Next recipe shows how to add notches and alternatively apply jitters to outliers.

Adding notches and jitters to box plots

A very useful feature/trick regarding box plots are notches. They are easily achieved by `ggplot2`; however, when the book was written, this was neither true for `ggvis` nor `plotly`. It adds little more information about distribution. Notches usually indicate the 95 percent confidence interval around the median, proven to be very useful in suggesting skews and making simple comparison between groups.

In addition to teaching how we can add notches to box plots, this recipe will also demonstrate how to apply jitter the outliers. Jittering is a feasible response to over-plotting that may come with outliers.

Getting ready

Having the `car` package is a requirement here:

```
> if( !require(car)){ install.packages('car')}
```

Now that we are locked and loaded, let's code.

How to do it...

We proceed as follows to add notches and jitters to box plots:

1. Load the packages and use `boxplot.stats()` to separate the outliers:

```
> library(ggplot2) ; library(car)
> out_data <- Salaries[match((boxplot.stats(Salaries$salary))$out,
                       Salaries$salary),]
```

2. Add `geom_jitter()` along with `geom_boxplot()` to draw a box plot with jittered outliers:

```
> set.seed(50)
> box1 <- ggplot(Salaries, aes( x = rank, y = salary))
> box1 + geom_boxplot( notch = T, outlier.shape = NA ) +
    geom_jitter( data = out_data, height = 0, width = .2)
```

Following, figure 3.2 shows a notched box plot with jittered outliers:

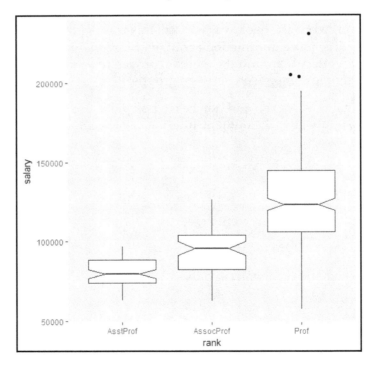

Figure 3.2 Notched and jittered box plot

Move on to the next section for explanations.

How it works...

First step starts by loading both `ggplot2` and the `car` package. We need both to create a data set for outliers. A new object (`out_data`) is created to hold only the outliers. A selective call on `Salaries` is handled by brackets. The function `match()` is used to pick only the rows containing outliers, those that are returned by `boxplot.stats(Salaries$salary)$out`.

> Brackets [ ] can be added after a vector/data frame/list name to select a range within dimensions (rows, columns, atributes). Data frames have two dimensions (`[ <rows> , <columns> ]`).

Basically, this particular step filtered `Salaries` data frame based on the `salary` variable. Only the rows containing outliers according to `boxplot.stats()` parameters were selected.

Next step takes care of drawing the box plot. Once we add pseudo-random noise to points, it begins by calling `set.seed()` so that the result can be perfectly reproduced. In the following lines the basic aesthetics mapping were stored into a `ggplot` object named `box1`.

Proximate lines sum it with the box geometry by calling `geom_boxplot()`. Besides asking for boxes, this last function also demanded those to be notched (`notch = T`) and erase outliers (`outlier.shape = NA`). Function `geom_jitter()` is also stacked in order to plot jittered outliers.

Note how the earlier designated `out_data` is fits `data` argument by the last function. A more tailor made control on the outliers is handled by arguments `height` and `width`. First one controls how much noise can be added vertically, while the second one draws the analogous limits horizontally.

Data frame and stats manipulations had played a major role in this recipe. This manipulations are often required when there is a desired for more customized results. Now let's check bivariate dot plots.

Drawing bivariate dot plots using ggplot2

Dot plots are commonly used to plot univariate discrete distributions. Dots are stacked and each dot represents a fixed number of occurrences. However, that is not the only usage. They can also represent bivariate and multivariate relations. `ggplot2` has a function fully dedicated to draw dot plots, but there are alternatives. They can also drawn by using `geom_point()` or `geom_jitter()` instead, as later recipes will demonstrate. They can also be seen as supplemental devices to box and violin plots.

This recipe teaches how to use the fully dedicated function, `geom_dotplot()`, in order to create simple dot plots. It also highlights an important aspect of dot plots built this way, **proportions**.

Getting ready

Data will come out from the `car` package:

```
> if( !require(car)){ install.packages('car')}
```

Once it's ready, the recipe is good to go.

How to do it...

Let us get started with drawing bivariate dot plots using `ggplot2`:

1. Use `geom_dotplot()` to draw a simple box plot:

```
> library(ggplot2)
> box1 <- ggplot(car::Salaries, aes( x = rank, y = salary))
> box1 + geom_dotplot(binaxis = 'y', dotsize = .3, stackdir =
'center')
```

As result, we get the following figure:

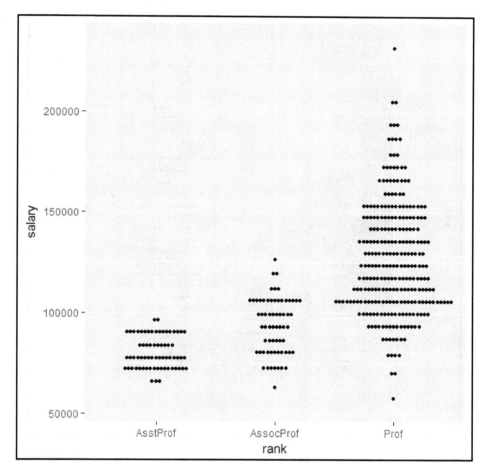

Figure 3.3 Simple ggplot2 dotplot.

2. A third aspect can be visualized by picking `aes(fill)`:

```
> box1 + geom_dotplot(binaxis = 'y', dotsize = .3,
>                     stackdir = 'center', aes(fill = sex))
```

Following figure shows that sex can now be visualized as graphic:

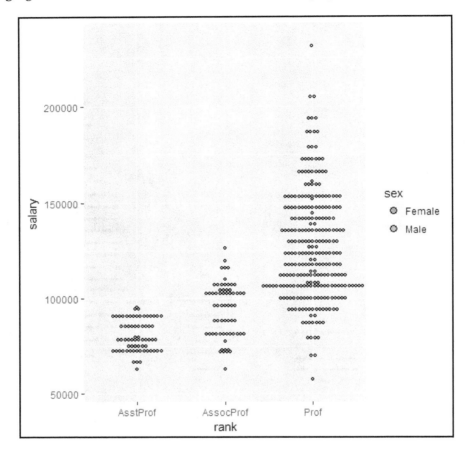

Figure 3.4 Dot plot with colors attached.

There are now some nuts and bolts to go through.

How does it work...

As a result from running step 1, we get a basic dot plot made via `geom_dotplot()`.
Argument `binaxis` receives a string telling the axis to bin dots along. Here the
`dotzise` argument was also changed, so dots from different ranks wouldn't overlay one
another. This argument is very susceptible to image proportion/size. Try exporting figure
with different widths and heights to see how the plot behaves. Last named argument
was `stackdir` (stack direction) and it tells the dots to be centered.

 Figure 3.4 sizes aer 528x528. Usually, your images have to fit a specific
size. A good practice is to preview the image before actually exporting it.
The parameter `dotsize` must be adjusted so it fits your sizing needs and
not the other way round.

The next step only adds `aes(fill = sex)` to `geom_dotplot()`, thus coloring the dots
according to the sex displayed by each observation. Still, note that for the colored output,
one color almost overlays another. This is an actual issue on GitHub (tydeverse/ggplot2,
issue #1096). There is a way to contour it, as the next recipe shall stress. For now, let me tell
about two other arguments not used yet.

There is more

Another important argument is called `method`. By default, `'dotdensity'` is set, hence the
maximum bin width can be set by adjusting the `binwidth` argument. Alternatively, one
could set the method to `'histodot'`, thus `binwidht` would pick bin width itself (not the
maximum). Now let's see a recipe that demonstrates how to contour the overlaying colors
issue.

Using more suitable colors for geom_dotplot

Speaking about `ggplot2` dot plots, there is a sort of a hacking solution to avoid colored
points to overlay one another: manually setting up a vector of colors. However, creating
such a vector wouldn't be enough, it has to be ordered properly or else a very wrong result
shall be outputted. This recipe sticks with the `Salaries` data set framework in order to
demonstrate how dots can be colored this way.

Getting ready

If you are not sure that you have `car` package installed, run the following code:

```
> if( !require(car)){ install.packages('car') }
```

Time to get hands dirty.

How to do it...

Following steps demonstrates an alternative way of setting colors with `geom_dotplot()`:

1. Pick the colors to fill the dots and store them into objects:

```
> color1 <- 'deepskyblue1'
> color2 <- 'darkred'
```

2. Create and reorder a vector with colors representing the `'Male'` and `'Female'` values coming from `Salaries$sex`:

```
> library(car)
> color_fill <- ifelse(Salaries$sex == 'Male',color1,color2)
> color_fill <- color_fill[with(Salaries,order(rank,salary))]
```

3. Assign `color_fill` to the `fill` parameter in order to properly color the dots:

```
> library(ggplot2)
> dot1 <- ggplot(Salaries, aes( x = rank, y = salary))
> dot1 + geom_dotplot(binaxis = 'y', dotsize = .32,
                      stackdir = 'center',colour = color_fill,
                      fill = color_fill)
```

Following illustration (Figure 3.5) demonstrates that colors are not overlaying one another anymore:

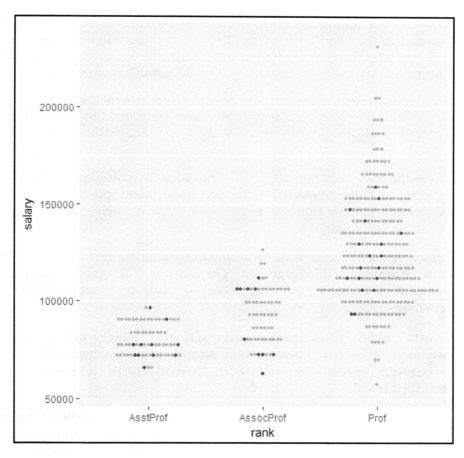

Figure 3.5: Another color solution.

Let's try to understand this code.

How it works...

The recipe begins with a very simple step. It simply creates objects (`color1`, `color2`) to hold color names. By separating them, we ensure that the code becomes more readable. Also, let me stress that the selection of colors plays a very important role here. There are way more dots for males than there is for females. Picking darker colors for females and lighter ones for males will make these fewer observations much more visible.

This color selection is strategical as it makes easier to visualize female observations. Even for exploratory figures the color selection can play a very important role. A well made color selection do contribute to insights. It's a good thing to spend some time picking the right colors.

Next step creates the color vector (`color_fill`) and sorts it accordingly. As we want to color dots with respect to the `sex` variable, this vector's elements must be colors matching values coming from `Salaries$sex`. To create such a vector, the `ifselse()` function was used.

It gets a condition as the first argument, returning the second argument if the condition is meet, otherwise returning the third argument. The way it was designed, `ifselse()` is checking upon each value coming from `Salaries`' sex variable, returning `color1` for `'Male'` observations and `color2` for `'Female'`.

For variables with only two possible values, using a single `ifelse()` function may be be the easiest way to go. If there are three ore more possible values, many `ifselse()` functions can be chained to get a vector of colors. Alternatively,it's also possible to create a function to handle this task.

This step also reordered the color vector (`color_fill`). Skipping it wouldn't stop you from plotting, but if you check the data, the result would be very wrong. So don't you ever skip this step. The vector was reordered based on the x and y variables respectively. This is the same way `geom_dotplot()` reorders inputted `data`, color vector must obey this same order to fill the right dots.

Finally, step 4 reaches the dot plot. After drawing the basic aesthetic mappings under `box1`, `geom_dotplot()` is stacked to add the dot geometry. Aesthetics `colour` and `fill` are declared outside `aes()`. Object `color_fill` is fitting arguments.

Combining box with dot plots

Box and dot plots can be combined in order to achieve a brand new visualization. Still employing the `car::Salaries` data set framework, this recipe demonstrates how to bring them under the `ggplot2` and `plotly` labels. Audience gets more detailed information when boxes and combined with dots.

Getting ready

Again, we need the `car` package locked and loaded:

```
> if( !require(car)){ install.packages('car') }
```

Data frame `Salaries` will come from `car` package.

How it works...

Now let's combine box and dot plots:

1. Combine `geom_boxplot()` and `geom_dotplot()` to reach the desired effect:

```
> library(ggplot2) ; library(car)
> dot1 <- ggplot(Salaries, aes( x = rank, y = salary))
> dot1 + geom_boxplot(outlier.size = 0) +
    geom_dotplot(binaxis = 'y',
                 dotsize = .3,
                 stackdir = 'center',
                 fill = 'red', alpha = .5)
```

Following image (Figure 3.6) shows boxes displayed beneath the dots:

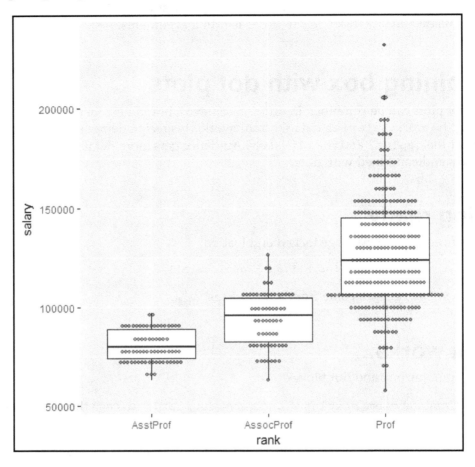

Figure 3.6: Dot and box geometry combined.

2. `plotly` can achieve similar result by combining parameters `type = 'box'` and `boxpoints = 'all'`:

```
> library(plotly)
> box2 <- plot_ly(data = Salaries, x = ~rank,
                  y = ~salary, type = 'box',
                  boxpoints = 'all',
                  marker = list(color = 'red',
                                opacity = .2))
> box2
```

Check the result in the following graphic (Figure 3.7):

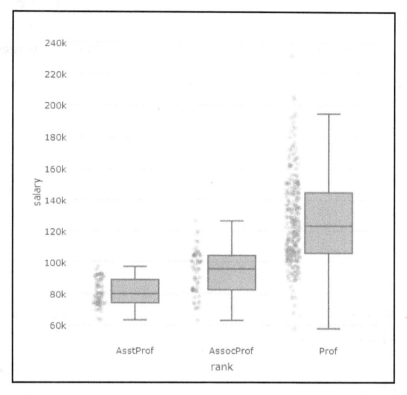

Figure 3.7: plotly's dot and box combination.

How it works...

Number one step simply stacks geom_boxplot() with geom_dotplot(). Two points are important to reinforce here. First, geom_boxplot() must be called before geom_dotplot(). This order is very important. Second, outliers coming from the boxes have to be erased. Do this by inputting outlier.shape = NA into the function geom_boxplot().

Other than that, all that we have already seen about dot plots may work here too. For example, you could set different colors to work in the dot plot just like we did with the Recipe *Using more suitable colors for geom_dotplot*. Other geometries could replace dot one to achieve a different vis. Feasible options would be geom_point() and geom_jitter().

Step 2 draws an alternative plot with `plotly`. It's combining the box geometry with points. After declaring the `data`, `x`, and `y` arguments, such result is achieved by declaring `type = 'box'` along with `boxpoints = 'all'`.

In order to reach points properties, call the `marker` parameter. These properties must be called inside a list object. Recipe tweaked markers' `color` and alpha (`opacity`) properties. Points are horizontally jittered; this can be controlled by the `jitter` argument. The values might range from 0 (no jitter) to 1 (maximum jitter).

Another important argument available is `pointpos`. Accepted inputs range from -2 to 2. When this argument is set to -2 the points are plotted at the left side of the boxes; a value of 2 will display the points at the right. Pick zero if you want to make points overlay the boxes.

See also

- Recipe *Using more suitable colors for* `geom_dotplot`

Using point geometry to work as dots using ggvis, plotly and ggplot2

Dot plots can be seen as binned scatterplots. Once you realize it, you also realize that the point geometry coming from all three packages (`ggplot2`, `plotly`, and `ggvis`) can be used to draw sort of dot plots (not actual dot plots). `ggplot2` can do this very easily. For `ggvis` and `plotly`, there are few key steps to follow:

1. Coerce the categories into numbers, so x will behave as continuous.
2. Add some little noise to x but not to y.
3. Draw a scatterplot using x and y.
4. Relabel the x-axis in order to reference categories.

This recipe is using `runif()` to create the noise and some tricks to re-label the ticks. Next section tells the requirements.

Getting ready...

Skip to the next section if you are sure about having `car` package installed. If you don't please run the following code:

```
> if( !require(car)){ install.packages('car')}
```

Having the `car` package installed is still a requirement.

How it works...

Following steps are crafting alternative visualization to dot plots using `ggvis`, `plotly`, and `ggplot2`:

1. Coerce the `Salaries$rank` categories into integers, plus add some jitter to them:

```
> set.seed(10)
> library(car)
> dt <- Salaries
> dt$rk <- 3 + runif(length(dt$rank),
                  max = .2, min = -.2)
> dt$rk[dt$rank == 'AssocProf'] <- dt$rk[dt$rank == 'AssocProf'] -
1
> dt$rk[dt$rank == 'AsstProf'] <- dt$rk[dt$rank == 'AsstProf'] - 2
```

2. Using `ggvis`, trust `layer_points()` to add the points and `add_axis()` to take care of adjusting the labels:

```
> library(ggvis)
> dt %>% ggvis(x = ~rk, y = ~salary) %>%
    layer_points(opacity := .3) %>%
    add_axis('x',values = c(1,1), title = '',
            properties = axis_props(labels = list(text =
'Assistant Professor'))) %>%
    add_axis('x',values = c(2,2), title = '',
            properties = axis_props(labels = list(text =
'Associated Professor'))) %>%
    add_axis('x',values = c(3,3), title = 'Rank',
            properties = axis_props(labels = list(text =
'Professor')))
```

Final result looks like the following image:

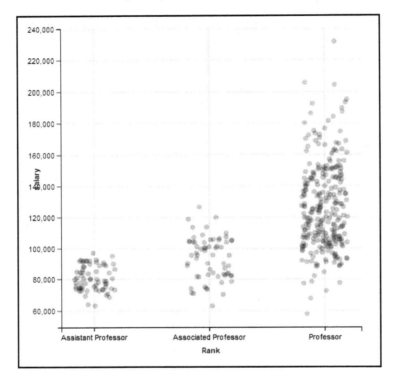

Figure 3.8: Plotting points with ggvis

3. `plotly` can also draw similarly; `layout()` takes care of the x-axis labels:

```
> plot_ly(dt, x = ~rk, y =~salary , type = 'scatter',
        mode = 'markers', alpha =.4) %>%
  layout(xaxis = list(tickvals = c(1,2,3),
                     ticktext = c('Assistant Professor',
                                  'Associated Professor',
                                  'Professor')))
```

4. `ggplot2` can do the same using `geom_jitter()`; jittered data is not needed:

```
> library(ggplot2)
> ggplot(Salaries, aes(x = rank, y = salary)) +
    geom_jitter(alpha = .4, height = 0,
                width = .3)
```

Let's see how these unfolded.

How it works...

Recipe begins with data manipulation. The first step starts by setting seed (set.seed()) once pseudo random processes are about to be called; this makes the example reproducible. After loading the car package, the Salaries data set is separated into an object called dt.

The three following lines are translating the categorical variable rank into numerical values. A specif range of values were "randomly" generated for each category and stored into a new column called rk. Relation between numerical ranges and categories are explained below:

- Assistant Professors: from 0.8 to 1.2
- Associated Professors from 1.8 to 2.2
- Professors: from 2.8 to 3.2.

Step 2 finally draws our *"dot plot"* using ggvis. Trusting the adjusted data (dt), layer_points() is deployed to reach for points geometry; the rk variable is inputted instead of rank. Notice the opacity argument setting up alpha blending. Afterwards, add_axis() is called in order to properly name the labels.

There is one add_axis() function for each label (3 labels, 3 functions). We're actually plotting several x-axes with custom text displayed by the tick discriminated at values argument. By ggvis version 0.4.3, inputting a single value into this argument would sometimes prevent the package from properly rendering the figure; duplicating the tick reference into a vector solved this problem.

Each add_axis() function carries a single tick reference while text is set by labels' properties. Also, notice how the axis title was renamed. To do this the title argument was inputted with empty strings (' ') at each add_axis() function with exception of the last one, which was inputted with the proper proper name string ('Rank').

Discriminating several ticks by the values argument while setting several texts by properties won't work. All the texts are going to be displayed at once at every single tick set on values. This is the reason we need one add_axis() function for each label we're willing to customize.

Step 3 draws a similar plot using `plotly`. Using the `plot_ly()` function along with the manipulated data, `type` was set to `'scatter'` along with `mode = 'markers'`, creating the "dot" visual. Pipe operator led to `layout()`, which took care of relabeling the x-axis. This last function was inputted with a list under `xaxis` argument in order to rework the x-axis. Parameter `tickvals` picked the ticks values while `ticktext` set up the names to be displayed.

Last step uses `ggplot2`. Plot is initialized with `ggplot()` using the original data set. Function `geom_jitter()` is then stacked to display the jittered points. This last function sets `height = 0` so that the points won't move vertically while `width = .2` controls the amount of movement (noise) added horizontally. It also sets alpha blending. Colors here could be simply added by declaring `aes(colour = sex)` inside `ggplot()` or `geom_jitter()`.

There is more

This approach is quite similar to dot plots but it is not a complete equivalent. While on dot plots the points are stacked, giving the audience quite a good idea about the format displayed by the distribution, the points plotted here are only jittered enough to deal over-plotting. It's quite hard to get an accurate idea on distribution format. On the other hand, points set this way are always honest about the values coming from the continuous variable, dot plots rarely are.

Crafting simple violin plots

To visualize data and its distribution format, violin plots may be the way to go. Some data scientists love them, others hate. Still they play a role of major importance in data visualization and it's good to know how to brew them and the whole utility belt that comes along. There are alternatives though, as we are going to discuss later.

Again, until first half of 2017, both `ggvis` and `plotly` R's libraries does not dispose of a dedicated functions and types to draw violin plots, thus making relatively difficult to obtain such a viz using those packages. `ggplot2` has a fully dedicated function, `geom_violin()`. Current recipe is teaching how to use this function. Make sure to have `car` package installed.

How to do it...

Let's get started with the recipe:

1. Draw the base aesthetics under an object:

    ```
    > library(ggplot2)
    > base <-ggplot(car::Salaries,
                    aes(x = rank, y = salary))
    ```

2. Call geom_violin() to draw a simple violin plot:

    ```
    > base + geom_violin()
    ```

Following figure is the output obtained by the preceding code:

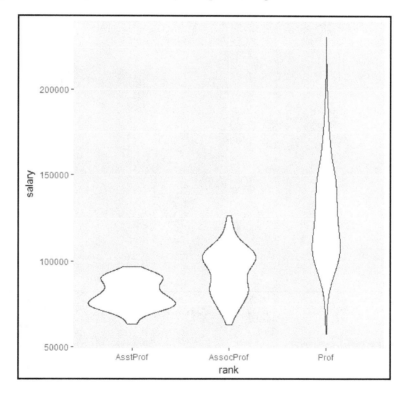

Figure 3.9 Simple violin plot.

3. To enhance it, you can `fill` the inside and add a box plot:

```
> base + geom_violin(fill = 'steelblue1') +
    geom_boxplot(outlier.shape = NA, width = .1)
```

Following figure demonstrates the result:

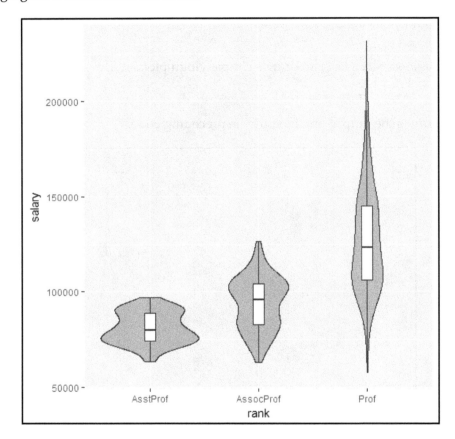

Figure 3.10: Violins and boxes combined

Keep going on for explanations!

How it works...

First step simply draws the very basic aesthetics into an object called base, to be used by following steps. Step 2 draws a very simple violin plot, while next step introduces a useful argument and a possible combination.

In step 3, the fill argument is used to color the insides of the violins. Color 'steelblue1' is picked. Next, geom_boxplot() is stacked in order to draw boxes inside the violins. For this intent, it is very important to erase the outliers by setting outliers.shape = NA and reduce boxes' widths with the help of the width argument.

Drawing violin plots using ggplot2 is very simple. Yet more complexity can be called to sum up some extra information, and some useful tricks can be deployed to improve plots. The following recipes are taking care of it.

Using stat_summary to customize violin plots

Think about some summarized information you want to display inside your violin. Maybe you want to show the median along with the interval given by plus and minus one standard deviation. Or maybe you want just the median to be displayed. That is possible and not difficult.

You can either create new a function that summarizes the information to be displayed into your violins or use an already existing function. This recipe teaches how that can be done and also how to draw quantiles inside your violins.

Getting ready

Make sure the Hmisc and car packages are already installed:

```
> if( !require(Hmisc)){ install.packages('Hmisc')}
> if( !require(car)){ install.packages('car')}
```

To the drawing now!

How it works...

We can start using `stat_summary` to customize violin plots as follows:

1. Create a basic violin plot with quantiles:

```
> library(ggplot2)
> violin <- ggplot(car::Salaries, aes(x = rank, y = salary)) +
    geom_violin(draw_quantiles = c(.25,.75), size = 1,
              fill = 'steelblue1')
```

2. Use `stat_summary()` to plot the median:

```
> violin +
    stat_summary(fun.y = median, geom = 'point', shape = 24,
               fill = 'darkslategray1', size = 4, stroke = 1.5)
```

Following figure (Figure 3.11) exhibits the result:

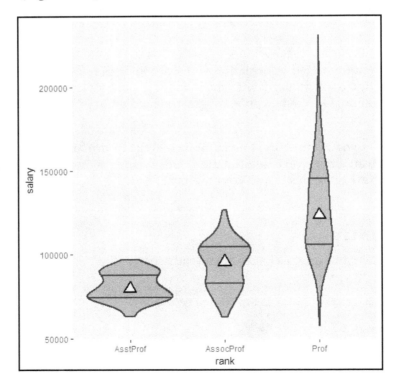

Figure 3.11: Violin summarizing the median.

3. Still using `stat_summary()`, change `fun.data` and `geom` to reach alternative visualization:

```
> violin +
    stat_summary(fun.data = mean_sdl, fun.args = list(mult = 1),
                 geom = 'pointrange', color = 'darkslategray1',
                 size = 1)
```

Following illustration (Figure 3.12) shows the result:

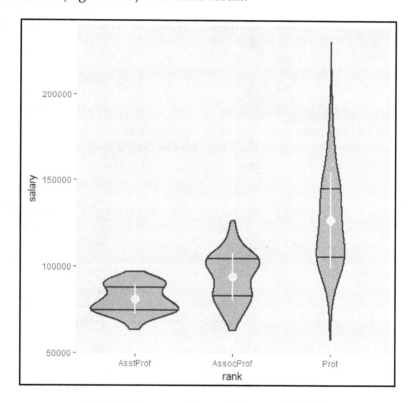

Figure 3.12: Point range summarizing mean plus/minus one standard deviation.

Next section explains what is happening.

How it works...

The very fist step draws the violin plot that is going to work as the base for the others. This one is stored under an object called `violin` object. Geometry is called by `geom_violin()`. Pay attention to the `draw_quantiles` argument-it draws quantiles on 25 percent and 75 percent marks for each violin.

Any number of quantiles can be draw. Besides this argument, `fill` is also called to color the insides while the `size` parameter takes care of increasing lines' size. This violin shall be stacked with `stat_summary()` later to summarize selected information into the violins.

Next steps were designed to introduce the way summary function and violin geometry can be combined. However, keep your mind open-combining them with violins is not the only option.

Step 2 stacks `violin` object along with `stat_summary()`. To use this function, we first define the function (`fun` parameter) to perform summary computation. This one aimed for median, so the recipe inputted `fun = median`, referencing base `median()` function. Do not forget to suppress the parenthesis and do not input a string there.

Next argument picks the geometry to display such information. Point geometry was picked by setting `geom = 'point'`; hence, all the aesthetics related to points are made available. We manually set the `shape`, `fill`, `size`, and `stroke` aesthetics. The resulting figure showed a violin plot with little triangles displaying the median.

Function `median()` returns a single value, but it's possible to input `stat_summary()` with any available function that do return either a single value or a data frame with a single row. If a data frame is returned it must have three columns: `y`, `ymin`, and `ymax`. Function `stat_summary()` at step 3 is inputted a function that returns a data frame.

 The function inputted at step 3 wraps `Hmisc::smean.sdl()` function; that is why we must have `Hmisc` installed.

In Step 3, `stat_summary()`'s `fun` argument is set to `mean_sdl`. It returns three values instead of one, so point geometry won't work well here; thus, this step picked `geom = 'pointrange'`. If your function has some arguments you want to set, it can be done with `fun.args`. Declare it as a named list; the names must account for the arguments you desire to change, while the elements are the actual values to fit in. For example, this step tweaked `mult` parameter to 1.

There is more...

One option is to design your own function to fit the `fun` argument. Make sure it returns either a single value or a data frame with one row and three properly named columns (y,ymin, and ymax). The following pseudo code gives a clue about how it can be done:

```
> hand_made_fun <- function(y){
  y <- <some computation>
  ymin <- <some computation>
  ymax <- <some computation>
  return( data.frame( y= y, ymin = ymin, ymax = ymax))
  }
```

`stat_summary()` will input your y variable into the selected function. It's possible to have more arguments but the first one must be the one to receive your y variable. Another possibility is to have three different functions for each computation. Then instead of naming fun, you name arguments `fun.y`, `fun.ymin`, and `fun.ymax`, each one returning single values.

Also, consider wrapping existing functions so the y, ymin and ymax values are properly outputted. Now let's learn a few more tricks to enhance our violins.

Manually sorting and coloring violins

It may have passed unnoticed, but until now all our boxes and violins were well ordered-*higher* ones came after the *lower* ones. This is very helpful when it comes to getting insights whenever we conduct data exploration, or presenting plot to the audience; but what if the data is not ordered?

This recipe teaches how we can put violins in order (also works for other binned visuals, like boxes). Filling each violin with different colors can also be done, recipe covers that too. In order to do all this, let's create fictional data frame.

Getting ready

1. Begin by checking if `gridExtra` and the `dplyr` package are already installed:

```
> if( !require(gridExtra)){ install.packages('gridExtra')}
> if( !require(dplyr)){ install.packages('dplyr')}
```

2. Forge a fictional data frame:

```
> set.seed(10)
> y1 <- rnorm(1000, mean = 2)
> y2 <- rnorm(400, mean = -1.5)
> y3 <- c(rnorm(500, mean = 1.5, sd = .7), rnorm(500, mean = -0.5,
sd = .7))
> y4 <- rt(200, df = 500) + .75
> y5 <- rpois(1000, lambda = 4)
> y <- c(y1,y2,y3,y4,y5)
> x <- c( rep('x1', length(y1)), rep('x2', length(y2)), rep('x3',
length(y3)),
          rep('x4', length(y4)),rep('x5', length(y5)))
> fiction <- data.frame( x = x, y = y)
```

This data frame holds variables x and y. The first one is supposed to work as group while the second one accounts for our continuous variable. Now we are ready to plot.

How to do it...

Following we're creating sorted and unsorted violins to compare them:

1. Draw an unsorted and uncolored violin plot for comparison:

```
> library(ggplot2)
> p1 <- ggplot(data = fiction, aes(x = x, y = y)) +
    geom_violin() +
    theme_minimal() +
    ggtitle('Not sorted/colored')
```

2. Reorder the data set (`fiction2`) and create a vector referencing colors (`col`):

```
> col <- c('darksalmon',rep('gray',3),'royalblue3')
> library(dplyr)
> fiction2 <- fiction %>% mutate(x = reorder(x, y, median))
```

3. Design a new plot with the reordered data, while individually filling the violins:

```
> library(dplyr)
> p2 <- ggplot(data = fiction2,
              aes(x = x, y = y)) +
    geom_violin(aes(fill = x), show.legend = F) +
    scale_fill_manual(values = col) +
    theme_minimal() +
    ggtitle('Sorted/colored')
```

4. Using `gridExtra` plot both of them side by side for comparison purposes:

```
> gridExtra::grid.arrange(p1,p2, ncol = 2)
```

Resulting plot looks like the following image (Figure 3.12):

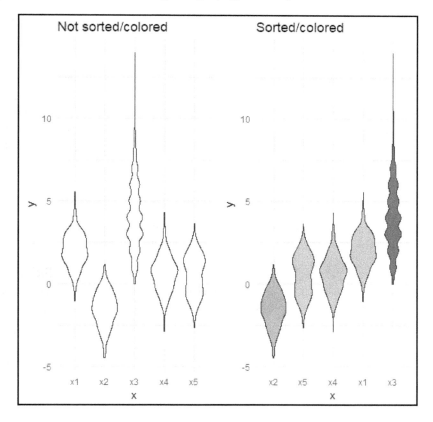

Figure 3.13: Coloring and sorting bins.

Comparison handled by `gridExtra` gives a clear idea about the improvement. Let me explain the code.

How it works...

First step creates a very simple violin plot; violins are not sorted yet. Note that the default theme is changed by `theme_minimal()` and a title is added (`ggtitle()`). This plot was made and stored as an object named p1, so that the results could be compared later.

Next step creates a vector holding color names under an object called `col`, plus it combines `dplyr::mutate()` function with `reorder()` to reorder fiction$x factor levels based on fiction$y medians. Data frame with reworked x variable is stored into an object called `fiction2`.

Step 4 designs a colored violin plot with the bins sorted. The sorting is done by simply inputting the reworked data frame (`fiction2`) into `ggplot()`'s data argument. To color the violins, the recipe starts by setting `aes(fill = x)`, while asking for legends to not be shown (`show.legend = F`) inside `geom_violin()`.

To manually pick the colors, the recipe stacks `scale_fill_continuous()` and declares our previously created vector of color names (`col`) as the `values` argument. Notice that the colors sequence follow the same sequence from x variable levels; you can check them by entering `levels(fiction2$x)`.

Functions `theme_minimal()` and `ggtitle()` were stacked to change default theme and add a title. This plot was stored by an object called p2. Finally, the last step uses `gridExtra` to plot both plots (p1 and p2) side by side, so we can compare the results. Reordering bins is not only a good practice for violins, but also for bar charts, box, and dot plots.

It may not be done when data already follows some indispensable logic, like chronological. Basically, reordering is done by changing a variable into a factor of customized levels. Now let's check an alternative for violin plots.

Using joy package to replace violins

As Rafael Irizarry would argue, violin plots display distributions that are at the same time vertical and mirrored, not a way most people are used to recognizing a distribution format. So why we not to plot distributions in a way most people are used to recognize? People from ggjoy package heard this appeal.

This package is ggplot2 supplement. Following code demonstrates how to brew the so called joy plots.

Getting ready

Make sure to have devtools installed once you get ggjoy from GitHub. Also, we are using fiction data set created at Recipe *Manually sorting and coloring violins*. If you do not have it in you environment, you may want to go back and rerun the *Getting ready* section. dplyr is also required:

```
> if( !require(devtools)){ install.packages('devtools')}
> if( !require(ggjoy)){ devtools::install_github('clauswilke/ggjoy')}
> if( !require(dplyr)){ install.packages('dplyr')}
```

These three packages plus ggplot2 are going to draw a joy plot.

How to do it...

Following code is crafting a joy plot:

- After loading ggjoy, call for geom_joy() to handle the plot:

```
> library(ggplot2); library(ggjoy); library(dplyr)
> ggplot(data = fiction %>% mutate(x = reorder(x, -y, median)),
        aes(x = y, y = x)) +
    geom_joy(scale = .8, fill = 'steelblue1')
```

As result we got ourselves a joy plot (Figure 3.14), enJOY it:

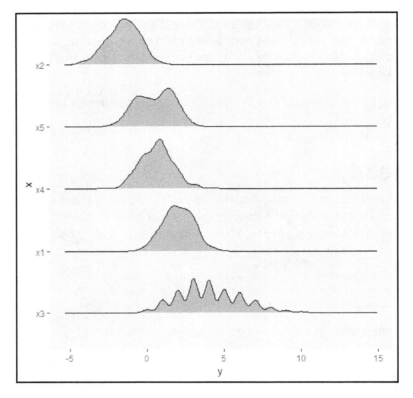

Figure 3.14: Joy plot.

Let's check the nuts and bolts.

How it works...

After loading all the required packages, `ggplot2`, `ggjoy`, and `dplyr`, recipe initializes the `ggplot` while reordering the x factor levels. Notice two things. One - we cut the middle guy; reordering was done directly into `data` argument and not stored into a separated data set. Code gets more objective but a little bit less readable. Two - instead of reordering the levels in an increasing way, we did quite the opposite by giving `y` a minus signal. Let me highlight it for you:

```
data = fiction %>% mutate(x = reorder(x, -y, median))
```

Afterwards, the basic aesthetics mapping were drawn. Also, note how the recipe set `aes(x = y, y = x)`. That is because our continuous variable (`fiction$y`) must be inputted into the horizontal axis (x) while categories (`fiction$x`) must fit into our vertical axis (y). Inputting the reverse shall result in warnings and no plot.

Function `geom_joy()` is stacked next. The argument `scale` is called to resize the distributions, so one does not overlay the one above it. The argument `fill` is also available, so we can fill the insides. Now that you know how to craft both violin and joy plots, you can decide which faction o rather join.

See also

- Check out Rafael Irizarry's opinion on violin plots and ggjoyat `https://simplystatistics.org/2017/07/13/the-joy-of-no-more-violin-plots/`

- Meet pirate plots at `https://sakaluk.wordpress.com/2017/02/03/15-make-it-pretty-diy-pirate-plots-in-ggplot2/`

Creating publication quality violin plots

As stated by the previous chapter, default `ggplot2` configurations are not publication ready. It's not difficult to name at least four general changes that may take place to achieve publication quality. These would be:

- Give legends complete information (measure unity included).

- Check the legend labels.

- Grow the labels bigger.

- Grow the axes bigger.

It's also important to give colors and theme a careful thought. For the moment, let's consider using theme_* functions from ggplot2 like theme_minimal() and theme_classic(). Chapter 9, *Using Theming Packages* is going to introduce you to a set of theme packages that shall give you a handful of alternatives.

The very first step to craft publication quality plots is the deployment of a some what crude version of all features we judge essential to transmit the core idea. For this recipe, the goal is to develop a high quality violin plot drawn upon our old friend, the car::Salaries data frame. Let's see how we can go from the crude version a publication quality one.

Getting Ready

Do not forget the car package:

```
> if( !require(car)){ install.packages('car')}
```

Fasten your seat belts now.

How to do it...

Let us start with creating publication quality violin plots:

1. Draw a basic plot to work as the departure point:

```
> library(ggplot2) ; library(car)
> hq_1 <- ggplot(Salaries, aes(x = rank, y = salary)) +
    geom_violin( fill = 'wheat2', colour = 'coral1',
                 size = 1.2) +
    stat_summary( geom = 'errorbar', fun.y = mean,
                  aes(ymin = ..y.., ymax = ..y.. , colour = sex),
                  width = .7, size = 1.5) +
    theme_minimal()
```

If you happened to call `hq_1`, the following illustration (Figure 3.15) would be seen:

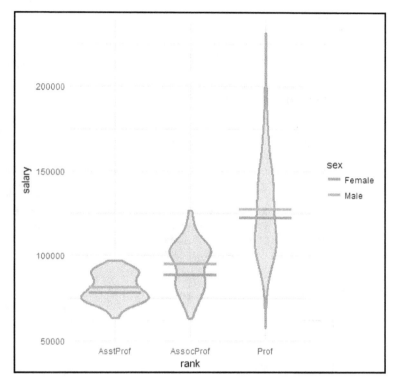

Figure 3.15: Basic plot, departure point

2. Correct the axes' titles:

```
> hq_2 <- hq_1 + xlab('') +
    ylab('9 Months Salary (US$ 1,000.00)')
```

3. Grow more breaks into the y-axis and rework all the axes labels:

```
> hq_3 <- hq_2 +
    scale_y_continuous(breaks = seq(50000,225000,25000),
                       labels = seq(50,225,25),
                       minor_breaks = 0) +
    scale_x_discrete(labels = c('Assistant\nProfessor',
                                'Associated\nProfessor',
                                'Professor'))
```

4. Manually set the bar's colors while renaming legends' title:

```
> hq_4 <- hq_3 +
    scale_colour_manual(
      values = c('Female' = 'red',
                 'Male' = 'navyblue'),
      name = 'Mean Salary')
```

5. Reposition the legends while resizing several texts:

```
> hq_5 <- hq_4 +
    theme(legend.justification = c('left', 'top'),
          legend.position = c(.05,.95),
          legend.background = element_rect(color = "black", size =
1,
                                           linetype = "solid"),
          legend.text = element_text(size = 14, face = 'bold'),
          legend.title = element_text(size = 14, face = 'bold'),
          axis.text = element_text(size = 15, face = 'bold'),
          axis.title = element_text(size = 13, face = 'bold'))
> hq_5
```

By calling `hq_5` in the last line, we see the final result:

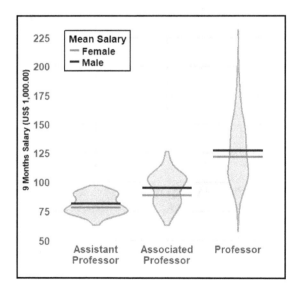

Figure 3.16: Publish quality violin plot.

Let's discuss each step.

How it works...

The recipe begins by creating hq_1, going all the way through hq_2, hq_3, and hq_4, to finally reach hq_5. This last plot (hq_5) is the one we call publication material. Feel free to call them in sequence in order to check what changes each step has made.

Primary step loads car and ggplot2 packages before drawing a crude version of our final plot (hq_1). It has all data-related features that we look for already. Violin geometry is added by geom_violin(), while stat_summary() takes care of representing the mean salaries given to men and women. Also, theme_minimal() is stacked by this step.

In the sequence, function xlab() was stacked to erased x-axis title; labels within this axis are pretty self-explanatory. Function ylab() was stacked to rename the y-axis title; now the axis' name displays complete information (including measure unity). All these changes can be found under the hq_2 object.

Proximate step greatly relies on the scale_*_*() functions. For the y-axis, scale_y_continous() grows more breaks, picks the new labels, and removes minor breaks. For the x-axis, scale_x_discrete() has the labels renamed to accomplish the complete rank names.

Step 4 manually picks the colors to fit the error bars arranged by stat_summary(). Same step also changed legends' title. The argument values is responsible for holding the colors reference. Colors are given by a vector; elements' names are related to values coming from sex variables.

To end, step 5 addresses several texts' size changes and also relocates the legends. After this step, legends can be seen inside the plot area; every text had its size increased, so it's easier to see them all. All these steps had made changes that generally can improve almost any simple violin plot made with ggplot. Although be aware there different situations may request different measures.

See also

- Check color reference palette at http://sape.inf.usi.ch/quick-reference/ggplot2/colour

4
Plotting One Variable

In this chapter, we will cover the following recipes:

- Creating a simple histogram using `geom_histogram()`

- Creating a histogram with custom colors and bins width

- Crafting and coloring area plots using `geom_area()` and more

- Drawing density plots using `geom_density()`

- Drawing univariate colored dot plots with `geom_dotplot()`

- Crafting univariate bar charts
- Using `rtweet` and `ggplot2` to plot twitter words frequencies

- Drawing publish quality density plot

Introduction

There are two general ways in which one variable plots are often used:

- As chief car of a single variable investigation
- To support multiple variables investigations

However, it certainly does not stop there. A wonderful usage of single variable plots is to make visual stands for hypothesis acceptance paradigmas as well to visualize Monte Carlo simulations results. In fact there are some stories about 1938 nobelist, the physicist Enrico Fermi. Before running experiments he would address Monte Carlo approximations to predict outcomes. Fermi reported the predictions to his friends; as the story goes, his predictions were remarkably accurate.

Think about it, Fermi was making Monte Carlo approximations before computacional power was a thing. This chapter is about to demonstrate how to run a simulation and make visual stands from it. Why not to predict and report your research results? Why not to run Morte Carlo simulations and summarize it graphically? It's very geek-cool and a well advised practice to cultivate.

Histograms, density, and area plots are all good friends with finances, physics, biology, and many more fields of knowledge. It's essential to master those visualizations. Few people may underestimate single variable visualizations, but it's a rookies mistake. Many times this visuals carries nothing but the synthesis coming from tons of information. A good example of that are the histograms and density plots used to summarize results from Monte Carlo simulations.

Creating a simple histogram using geom_histogram()

Histograms are simple graphical representations on continuous variables distributions. Brewing them using `ggplot2` is actually very easy, mainly done by `geom_histogram()`. Making interactive histograms is equally easy and can be made using both `plotly` and `ggvis`. For the first few examples we're heading back to year 1890. By this time the early efforts to measure light speed at air were paying off.

Getting ready

This first example carries data from `HistData` package. The frame chosen is called `Michelson`, after the brilliant scientist Albert A. Michelson. The following code makes sure that this data set is available, while it also introduces you to the data:

```
> if( !require(HistData)){ install.packages('HistData')}
> ?HistData::Michelson
```

Reaching data documentation by typing `?Michelson` will tell you that the data frame does not hold the actual light speed measures, but the measures subtracted by 299,000 kilometers/s. This data frame is an optimal candidate for histograms. It has . `ggplot2` has the tools to draw a histogram, and it's also makes it possible to remove bias without changing the data.

How to do it...

Histogram drawing can be done either by `ggplot2`, `ggvis` and `plotly`. The last two are more suited if you need html outputs, the first one generally culminates in lighter PNG files.

1. Instead of loading the whole `HistData` package only store the data frame into an object named `dt`:

```
> dt <- HistData::Michelson
```

2. Using `ggplot2`, call `geom_histogram()` to craft a histogram:

```
> libary(ggplot2)
> gg2_Mich <- ggplot(data = dt,
                     aes(x = velocity + 299000))
  gg2_Mich + geom_histogram()
```

The resulting histogram looks like the following:

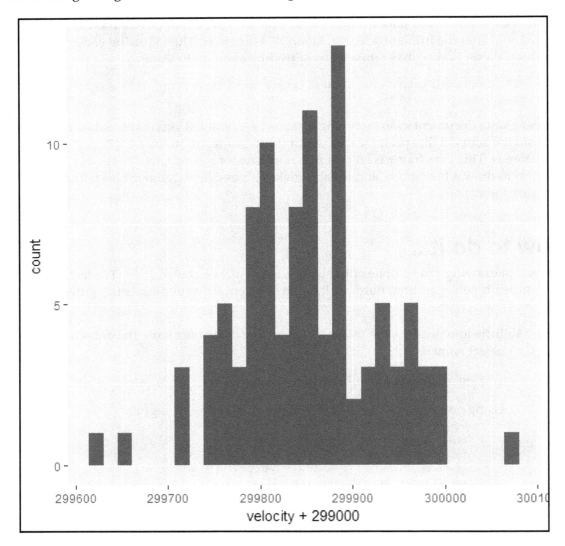

Figure 4.1 - ggplot2 histogram.

3. Using `ggvis` function `layer_histograms()` are the ones responsible for drawing histograms:

```
> library(ggvis)
> ggv_Mich <- ggvis(data = dt,
                    x = ~velocity + 299000)
  ggv_Mich %>% layer_histograms()
```

4. Speaking about `plotly`, setting `type = 'histogram'` is enough to give the originate histograms:

```
> library(plotly)
> pl_Mich <- plot_ly(data = dt,
                     x = ~velocity + 299000,
                     type = 'histogram')
  pl_Mich
```

Keep ahead for explanations.

How does it work...

Step 1 is only storing `Michelson` data frame (from `HistData` package) into an object called `dt`, that is short for data. Since the data frame is the only thing we need from `HistData`, this step is an alternative to loading the package and calling data for its actual name, `Michelson`. A clear upside here is that calling `dt` instead of `Michelson` requires less letters to be typed plus kind makes code more readable.

Step 2 is drawing a `ggplot2` histogram. Bias is removed by adding a constant to the x aesthetic. After initializing the `ggplot` and mapping basic aesthetics into an object called `gg2_Mich`, `geom_histogram()` is summed to attach the histogram geometry.

Notice the outputted message, it tells us that the number of bins were assigned by the default. This is a very important aspect of any histogram, one can pick those manually by declaring argument `bins` or `binwidth`. While the first is directly deciding the number of bins the second is deciding the range of each bin based on your x variable.

If you seek to draw an histogram using `ggvis` look at Step 3. It also removes the bias at the same time x variable is declared. To finally draw the histogram the pipe operator (`%>%`) chains `layer_histograms()` function. Bins size can be manually set by `width` argument.

Step 4 is drawing `plotly`'s histogram, the bias is also removed. The geometry is picked at `plot_ly()` function's `type` argument. To designate a manual number of bins is slightly more complicated. We first have to turn off the algorithm that automatically pick the bins. Do this by declaring `autobinx` (or `autobiny` for bins located by the y-axis) to false. Afterwards we have to decide where the bins shall `start`, `end` and the intervals between each bins (`size`), this properties may be declared as a list inputted into `xbins` or `ybins`, depending on the axis holding the binned values.

Next recipe is demonstrating how to customize bins colors based on the x-axis . We're going to experiment with those feature while we exploring simple Monte Carlo simulations and the Hypothesis Acceptance Paradigma. All this will be done while relying on a context loved by statisticians: the games of chances.

Creating an histogram with custom colors and bins width

This recipe meant to introduce and explain several useful arguments available at `geom_histogram()`. To spice things up, a problem context based on the game of chances is adopted. It is an optimal scenario to explain how histogram features can work both to display Monte Carlo simulations and aid hypothesis decisions. Once this context is explained, extrapolating it to challenges of your own won't be difficult.

In order to keep the focus on what matters, let's elaborate a very simple paradigma, design a game, and simulate it over and over again. The game rules can be summarized as following:

- Initial bet is fixed on $75
- Player decides before hand the number of rounds he is going through
- For each round, a fair coin is tossed (fifty-fifty chance for each outcome)
- Tail means current balance (positive or negative) is increased by 20 percent
- Head subtracts 17 bucks from the current balance

Our player wants to have visual aid from a histogram. He wants to know what the odds would be if he settles for 30 tosses, this recipe aims to simulate this game 200 times and plot the results as histograms.

Getting ready

Game simulation will be drawn by a function. To do that we relying on three features:

- A for loop taking care of rounds
- rbinom(), a pseudo-random binomial distribution generator, working the tosses
- conditional if and else computing results from each round

Following code block is creating a function named game_on() intended to handle simulations. Same code also sets a pseudo-random generator while creating a data frame based on 200 simulations:

```
> game_on <- function(rounds = 30){
    balance <- 75
    for(i in 1:rounds){
      coin <- rbinom(1,1,prob = .5)
      if(coin == 1){ balance <- balance*1.2}
      else{balance <- balance - 17}
      }
    return(balance)
  }
> set.seed(10)
> simulations <- data.frame(x = sapply(rep(30,200),FUN = game_on))
```

Data frame called simulations is carrying the outcomes from each one of the 200 simulations.

 Use the sapply() function to apply a function (FUN argument) to each element from the inputted vector.

Following section demonstrates to how visualize this data set.

How to do it...

Now let's settle for manual number of bins and use more than one color in the same histogram.

1. To aid hypothesis acceptance determine critical values that would make player want or not to play while creating a new variable at the data frame:

```
> simulations$Play <- 'Yes!'
> nos <- simulations$x <= 75*1.2
> simulations$Play[nos] <- 'No!'
```

2. Besides drawing a colored histogram, using ggplot2 we also can draw a vertical line to enhance visualization:

```
> library(ggplot2)
> gg2_game <- ggplot(data = simulations,
                     aes( x = x, fill = Play))
> gg2_game +
    geom_histogram(binwidht = 40,
                   colour = 'black') +
  geom_vline( aes( xintercept = 75*1.2),
              linetype = 'dashed', size = 1)
```

Following image (Figure 4.2) exhibits the outcome:

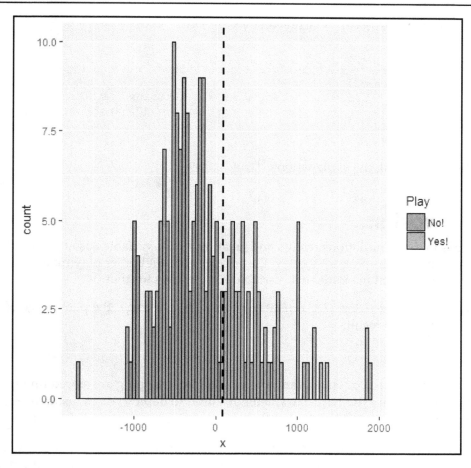

Figure 4.2 - Colored ggplot2 histogram.

3. Colored `ggvis`'s histograms can also be made:

```
> library(ggvis)
> ggv_game <- ggvis(data = simulations,
                    x = ~x, fill = ~Play)
  ggv_game %>%
    group_by(Play) %>%
    layer_histograms(width = 40)
```

4. A similar result can be achieved by `plotly`:

```
> library(plotly)
> pl_game <- plot_ly(data = simulations, x = ~x, type =
'histogram',
                 color = ~Play, autobinx = FALSE,
                 xbins = list(size = 40, start = -2000, end =
2000))
 pl_game
```

Next section is handing the explanations.

How it works...

Initial Step is taking simulations results and creating a new variable based on whether our player would had desired or not to play. Our player will not bother playing if he has at least a 20 percent increase on his initial bet, variable `Play` stands for that.

> Try `mean(simulations$Play == 'Yes!')` to get the percentage of positive results.

Step 2 is drawing a `ggplto2` histogram. Basic aesthetics mapping are stored under `gg2_game` object. Notice the `fill` parameter, it's used to deploy colors inside the bins, for this particular case accordingly whether that was a desired or not result for our player.

Right next `geom_histogram()` and `geom_vline()` are stacked with `gg2_game` to create our histogram. The earlier function demands the histogram geometry, `binwidth` declares the width of bins while `colour` asks for the contour color on the bins. Last function sets a dashed vertical line by the value considered critical by our hypothetical player.

Third Step is drawing a similar histogram, without the vertical line, using `ggvis` package. To color this one the `fill` argument is also required plus it's required to stack a `group_by(Play)` function before calling `layer_histogram()`. This last function also picks the bin width by declaring the `width` argument.

Last Step is designing a `plotly` colored histogram. Whole histogram is designed and stored into a variable named `pl_game`, `plot_ly()` function is handling all the work. Argument `color` takes care of the coloring task, `type = 'histogram'` asks for the histogram geometry while the combination of `autobinx` and `xbins` arguments does manually picks bins width.

This recipe had demonstrated how we can run simple simulations but mainly how to draw colored histograms with manually picked bins widths using both `ggplot2`, `ggvis` and `plotly`.

Crafting and coloring area plots using geom_area() and more

Area plots are wild cards. They can properly represent either one or two variables. In economics for example, area plots are a very popular way to display government expenditures or a country importations versus exportation. When it comes to plotting single variable can be seen as alternatives to histograms.

This recipes is rescuing the data frame built by Recipe *Creating a histogram with custom colors and bins width* in order to demonstrate how to craft area plots with `ggplot2`, `ggvis` and `plotly` packages.

Getting ready

Once this recipe relies on simulations data frame created by Recipe *Creating a histogram with custom colors and bins width* make sure to have it into your environment or else obtain it by running that recipe. Code needed can be found at sections *Getting Ready* and *How to do it...* (first step only).

How to do it...

Both `ggplot2`, `ggvis` and `plotly` are able to draw area plots, although the last two require some computation to be done before plotting.

1. To draw area plots under the `ggplot2` library stack `geom_area()` function:

```
> library(ggplot2)
> gg2_game <- ggplot(data = simulations,
                     aes(x = x, fill = Play))
> gg2_game +
    geom_area(stat = 'bin', colour = 'black') +
    geom_vline( aes(xintercept = 75*1.2),
                linetype = 'dashed', size = 1)
```

Figure 4.3 results from the first step:

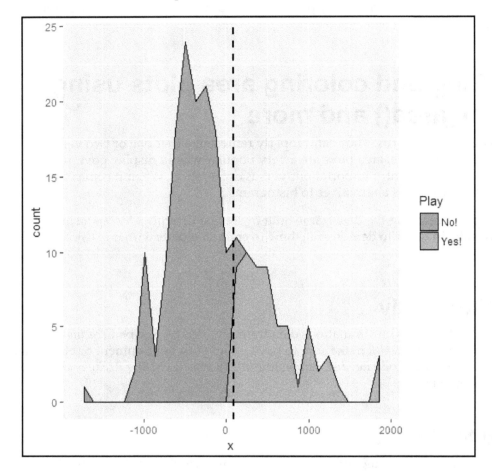

Figure 4.3 - ggplot2 area plot.

2. Before calling the area plots (`layer_ribbons()`) with `ggvis` we first group data set by the variable about to set the colors while running computations with `compute_bin()`:

```
> library(ggvis)
> simulations %>%
    group_by(Play) %>%
    compute_bin(~x) %>%
    ggvis(x = ~x_, y = ~count_, fill = ~Play) %>%
    layer_ribbons(y2 = ~0)
```

3. Speaking about `plotly` the same steps bearing the computation must go on in the first place. Inside `plot_ly()` the combination of `type`, `mode` and `fill` parameters makes sure we got an area plot:

```
> library(plotly) ; library(ggvis)
> simulations %>%
    group_by(Play) %>%
    compute_bin(~x) %>%
    plot_ly(x = ~x_, y = ~count_,
            type = 'scatter', mode = 'lines',
            fill = 'tozeroy', color = ~Play)
```

Following section is carrying the explanations.

How it works...

Primary step is drawing an area plot using `ggplot2`. This drawing is very similar to the histograms, main difference is that to obtain area plots we got `geom_histogram()` replaced with `geom_area()`. This last function usually works with `ymin` and `ymax` aesthetics but in order to represent single variable we tweaked `stat` argument to `'bin'`.

We also had `fill` argument demanding color changes plus another geometry was stacked (`geom_vline()`) to add a vertical line. Afterwards, Step 2 is drawing a similar plot using `ggvis`. We start by chaining `simulations` data frame with `group_by()` and `compute_bin()`.

Last function is doing about the same thing `stat = 'bin'` had done for `ggplot2`. After this lines we've got ourselves a suited data frame to draw the area plots the way we wanted to. The new variables from this data set are _x and _count.

This two variables are then inputted into `ggvis()` which is stacked with `layer_ribbons(y2 = ~0)` to create the area plot. Step 3 is borrowing `group_by()` and `compute_bin()` from `ggvis`, so it begins by loading not only `plotly` and also `ggvis`. Although `ggvis` is already loaded, it's good to reinforce from where these functions are coming from.

Lines from 2 to 4 are simply crafting the same data frame used by previous step. Function `plot_ly()` is then inputted with `_x` and `_count` as x and y while the combination of `type = 'scatter'`, `mode = 'lines'` and `fill = 'tozeroy'` are responsible for creating the area plot geometry; `color` argument is simply filling it accordingly with `Play` variable.

Drawing density plots using geom_density()

Another alternative to histograms are the density plots. Those are usually seen as a visual more related to the academic environment; accurate interpretations are only obtained by being familiar to the statistical concept of densities. On the other hand shallow interpretations can be easily grasped by anyone.

For an instance let's go back to the Iris data set in order to plot the petal's length kernel density estimates discriminated by species. This can be done using `ggplot2`, `ggvis` and `plotly`. Until the fist half of 2017 `plotly` would require computation to be directly done before actually plotting. This recipe is about to demonstrate it all.

How to do it...

Upcoming steps are demonstrating how to breed density plots using `ggplot2`, `ggvis` and `plotly`.

1. To craft a density plot using `ggplot2` stack the function `geom_density()`:

```
> library(ggplot2)
> gg2_petal <- ggplot(data = iris,
                  aes(x = Petal.Length,
                      fill = Species))
  gg2_petal +
    geom_density(alpha = .5) +
    xlim(.75, 7.5)
```

Following illustration (Figure 4.4) demonstrates the resulting image:

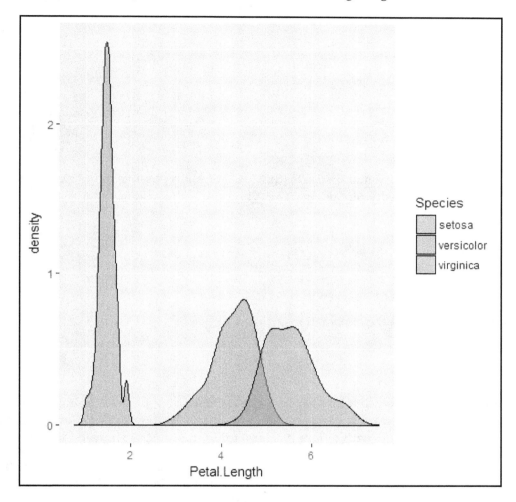

Figure 4.4 - ggplot2 density plot.

2. `ggvis` does about the same work by stacking `layer_densities()`:

```
> library(ggvis)
> ggv_petal <- iris %>%
    group_by(Species) %>%
    ggvis(x = ~Petal.Length, fill = ~Species)
> ggv_petal %>% layer_densities()
```

3. Before drawing the density plot using `plotly` we need first to store the estimates on data frames, base R functions can handle the task:

```
> dt <- split(iris, iris$Species)
  dens <- function(a){
    data.frame(
      density(a$Petal.Length)[1:2]
    )
  }
> dt1 <- dens(dt$setosa)
> dt2 <- dens(dt$versicolor)
> dt3 <- dens(dt$virginica)
```

4. With recently created data sets (`dt1`, `dt2`, `dt3`) it's possible to use `add_trace()` to create a density plot using `plotly`:

```
> library(plotly)
> pl_petal <- plot_ly(data = dt1, x = ~x,
                    y = ~y, type = 'scatter', mode = 'lines',
                    fill = 'tozeroy', name = 'setosa')
> pl_petal %>% add_trace(data = dt2, name = 'versicolor') %>%
    add_trace(data = dt3, name = 'virginica')
```

Ahead it's possible to see the explanations.

How it works...

First Step is drawing a density plot using `ggplot2`. Object `gg2_petal` is being set by `ggplot()`, it holds the data and basic aesthetics mapping. The `fill` aesthetics demands different density estimates (with different colors) for each `Species` showed by data.

Later by this same step the `geom_density()` asks for the density geometry. This function is also responsible for computing the kernel density estimate to be draw. On the behind of scenes computations are done by base `density()` function. Alpha blending (`alpha`) is also set, this is a good practice when there is more than one density curve.

Step 2 is drawing the density plot with `ggvis`. Once there is computation to be done by `ggvis`' functions, it's necessary to group `Species` variable in order to make sure that `fill` parameter will work. Density geometry is attached by the function `layer_densities()`.

In Step 3 different kernel density estimates for each species available on data set are being crafted. It begins by splitting `iris` data frame into a list, then a function wrap is created (`dens()`) to estimate the kernels and return the results as data frames. In the sequence the estimates are computed and stored into separated objects: `dt1`, `dt2` and `dt3`.

Subsequent step is plotting those estimates using `plotly`. This about the same we've done on the previous recipe to draw area plots but with density data. Plus we're also calling argument `name` in order to set densities with their actual species names. Once version 4.7.0 of `plotly` lacked a function that would do the computation itself we had to do this before plotting.

See also

- Mathias Grenié sample code to color quantiles, at `https://gist.github.com/Rekyt/f2ee61aa39c8b7684965`
- StackOverflow on how to color density plots based on x value, at `https://stackoverflow.com/questions/36652977`

Drawing univariate colored dot plots with geom_dotplot()

Univariate dot plots account for very simple and very objective visualizations. They can represent either continuous or discrete variables and are a good way to display how small samples are distributed. These plots are also an alternative to histograms, specially when there is only very few observations.

For the this recipe, we're going to use continuous data in order to explain how to manage the `binwidth` parameter whenever calling for a `ggplot2` dot plot. There are two things that are good to know about dot plots breed using `ggplot2::geom_dotplot()`. First thing is that these plots are very sensible to plot measures (height and width). Second is that the y-axis hardly is meaningful. Now let's get to know our data.

Getting ready

To demonstrate how to plot univariate dot plots using `geom_dotplot()`, the data to be used will come from the DAAG package. Data set name is `anesthetic` and it's telling if a patient moved (`move`) or not when an incision was made after maintaining certain level of anesthetic (`conc`) agent for 15 minutes. Following package is checking if DAAG is installed while also taking a first look at data:

```
> if(!require(DAAG)){ install.packages('DAAG')}
> library(DAAG)
> ?anesthetic
> anesthetic
```

There are very few observations (30); hence, a very suitable data set for dot plots. Following sections is discussing different ways to work out dot plots.

How to do it...

Now let's see how we can draw a colored dot plot while dealing the axis and proportions issues.

1. A basic dot plot can be draw using `ggplot2` with `geom_dotplot()` function:

```
> library(ggplot2)
> dot <- ggplot(data = DAAG::anesthetic,
                aes(x = conc,
                    fill = factor(move))) +
    geom_dotplot(binwidth = .2,
                 stackgroups = T,
                 binpositions = 'all')
```

2. To erase labels and titles from the y-axis stack a `scale_y_continuous()` function. Also use `coord_fixed()` to deal the proportions issue:

```
> dot +
    scale_y_continuous(name = NULL,
                       breaks = NULL) +
    coord_fixed(ratio = 1.4)
```

Following image (Figure 4.5) exhibits the resulting dot plot:

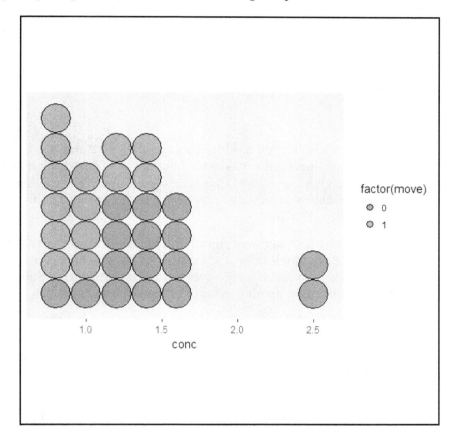

Figure 4.5 - ggplot2 dot plot.

Now let's check how this codes had worked and an alternative.

How it works...

Step 1 is drawing a basic dot plot, there are several important arguments to go through. While drawing the basic aesthetics mapping with `ggplot()`, `fill` argument is asking for different colors for different values for move `variable`. Skip this argument if those are unwanted features. Dot plot geometry is being called by `geom_dotplot()`.

This last function comes with a series of important arguments. To begin with, binwidth is ruling dot's range. Once concentration (conc) variable is increasing by 0.2 at least, this was the same amount inputted into this argument. This way each unique concentration value would be represented by a unique column of dots.

 Here increasing binwidth would mean dots with a wider range of concentrations (conc) grouped under the same column.

Function geom_dotplot() is also inputted with stackgroups = T and binpositions = 'all'. Combining both arguments recipe makes sure that no dot from different color would overlay another. If you happen to skip those arguments and pay careful attention you will notice that some points went missing. You shall find the missing points if you set alpha = .5 then.

The whole ggplot designed by first step was stored into an object named dot. If you happen to call it, a very basic dot plot will be displayed. Vertical axis bears no meaning while the figure is very sensitive to sizes changes, small heights would crop some dots, on the other hand greater heights might result in a lot of unused space.

This issues are addressed by Step 2. It sums dot object with scale_y_continuous() to erase breaks, labels and titles coming from y-axis. Trick is done by setting name and breaks arguments to NULL. It also stacks coord_fixed(ratio = 1.4) to make sure the plot will respond well to different sizings.

One downside of setting coord_fixed() it's the great deal of blank spaces displayed on figure's outside. An alternative to it is search for a dot size (dotsize) that suits your image size requirements. The following code demonstrates a dotsize input that suits well a 528x528 image:

```
> library(ggplot2)
> ggplot(data = DAAG::anesthetic,
         aes(x = factor(conc),
             fill = factor(move))) +
    geom_dotplot(binpositions = 'all',
                 stackgroups = T,
                 dotsize = 6) +
    scale_y_continuous(name = NULL,
                       break = NULL)
```

Figure 4.6 carries the result. Important to outline that x aesthetic was inputted with `factor(conc)` and not `conc` itself. This way we got unique columns for each concentration while not needing to tweak `binwidth` argument. Concentrations with zero observations are not displayed by the figure, so after the column at the 1.6 concentration mark there is leap to the 2.5 concentration mark, this can be misleading. Check the figure:

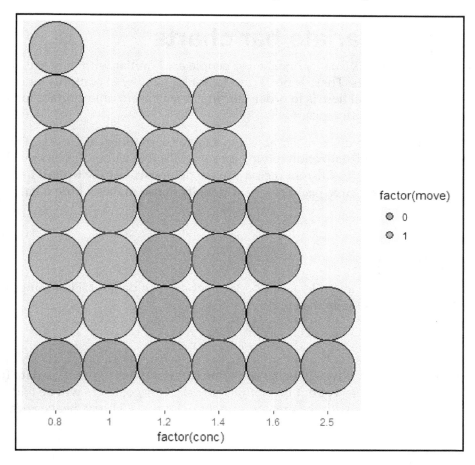

Figure 4.6 - alternative way to dealing sizing issues.

This is the general way that dot plots are draw using `ggplot2`'s `geom_dotplot()` method. Dots can be replaced with emojis, See also section is pointing a package capable of doing it.

See also

- Are you sick of points? Use emojis instead! Check `ggChernoff` package at `https://github.com/Selbosh/ggChernoff`

Crafting univariate bar charts

Bar chats are very popular visualizations, most people are familiar with it; hence, they know to interpret bar charts. There is no excuse to not know how to craft this kinds of visualizations. A trick detail here is to order the bars, it may seem unimportant for some people but it makes total difference.

The trick here is to turn the discrete variable into a factor with reordered levels. This should be done with almost any visualization relying on some discrete values. It works well for `ggplot2`, `ggvis` and `plotly`. Current recipe aims to demonstrate how to craft bars with custom order using all the three packages. Additionally it also makes a little data computation.

Getting ready

To achieve such goal we're about to adopt `Ecdat::Journals` data set. First things first, make sure that `Ecdat` is already installed:

```
> if(!require(Ecdat)){install.packages('Ecdat')}
> if(!require(dplyr)){install.packages('dplyr')}
```

We also will require `dplyr` package to handle some computations. `Journals` data frame is bearing a series of information about Economic Journals. Our goal here will be to draw bars representing the publishers with the greater number of journals. Hurry, heave ahead!

How to do it...

Let us start crafting univariate bar charts:

1. Filter data based on the top 5 publishers (`Journals$pub`) that appear the most, also turn `pub` variable into a factor with sorted levels:

```
> library(Ecdat)
> dt <- within(Journals,
```

```
      pub <- factor(pub,
                levels=names(sort(table(pub),
                                 decreasing=T)))))
> top5 <- levels(dt$pub)[1:5]
> dt <- dt[dt$pub %in% top5,]
```

2. Initialize a `ggplot` object and stack `geom_bar()` function to craft a `ggplot2` bar char. This visual can be improved using with `geom_text()`:

```
> library(ggplot2)
> gg2_eco <- ggplot(data = dt, aes(x = pub))
> gg2_eco + geom_bar(fill = 'white',
                color = 'darkblue',
                size = 1.5) +
    geom_text(stat = 'count' ,aes(label = ..count..),
            nudge_y = 1.5)
```

The resulting chart shows the publishers by the x-axis and the amount of economic journals hold by each of them by the y-axis, just like following illustration (Figure 4.7):

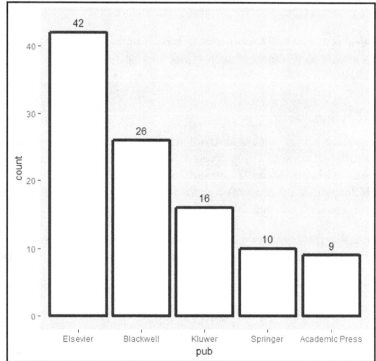

Figure 4.7 - ggplot2 bar chart.

3. `plotly` will not do the count computation by itself, so `dplyr::count()` is called before actually drawing the bars with `plot_ly()`:

```
> library(dplyr)
> dt_pl <- dt %>% count(pub)
> library(plotly)
> pl_eco <- plot_ly(data = dt_pl, x = ~pub, y= ~n, type = 'bar',
                marker = list(color = 'white',
                                line = list(color = 'black', width =
1.5)))
> pl_eco
```

4. `ggvis` does the computation but it also displays the `levels` with no observations. Before plotting bars with `layer_bars()` the empty levels from `dt$pub` are being cleared:

```
> dt$pub <- factor(dt$pub, levels = top5)
> library(ggvis)
> ggv_eco <- ggvis(data = dt, x = ~pub)
> ggv_eco %>%
     layer_bars(stroke := 'black', fill := 'white')
```

These are the general ways of crafting univariate bar charts using `ggplot2`, `ggvis` and `plotly`, keep ahead so we can get some nuts and bolts cleared.

How it works...

Very first step is loading `Ecdat`, package from which `Journals` data set is coming from. Once it's loaded another data set (`dt`) is created. It took `Journals` data set and reordered `pub` variable `levels`. This variable was already a factor holding the publishers names as `levels`. What this step actually did was to reorder them with `factor()` function; `levels` were reordered using `sort()` function.

 Controlling factor `levels` is the way we can control the order which each level will be displayed by a plot made with `ggplot2`, `ggvis` or `plotly`.

If you happen to check dt$pub will you notice that the first levels are the ones with the greater number of observations. Operator %in% is then called to filter the data frame in order to displays only the observations accounting for the top 5 publishers (in number of journals).

Each package will interpret and show data in different ways as the following steps stresses. Step 2 is drawing the ggplot2 bar char. Plot is initialized with dt data and x variable, pub. These basic aesthetics mapping were stored into an object name gg2_eco.

Stacking it with geom_bar() will result in our univariate bar chart. Nearest function does the computation on how many observations displays the same discrete value - publisher's name - while allocating this info by the y-axis. Variable pub is a factor with lots of empty levels, those are not draw by geom_bar().

There are a bunch of arguments called by this function:

- fill - colors bar's inside
- color - colors bar's contours lines
- size - resize bar's contours lines

All these can be called inside aes() when there is the need to refer to a data set variable. These are not the only available parameters, try ?geom_bar() to meet many more.

There is another geometry stacked by this first step, geom_text(). A combination of stat = 'count' and aes(label = ..count..) arguments is writing the number of observations hold by each publisher at the respective bar. Parameter nudge_y is making sure that texts does not overlay bars. Usually geom_text() are able to improve this visualizations.

Step 3 is achieving similar results with plotly. Main difference here is that plot_ly() function won't handle the computation by itself; so dplyr::count() is doing it before we plot. Computation is stored at dt_p1 data frame. Here the bar geometry is attached by plot_ly()'s argument type. Parameter marker is inputted with lists to change inside and contours colors.

In the sequence, Step 4 is demonstrating how to draw a `ggvis` bar chart. Once we had `dt` filtered, `pub` variable has a total of 47 empty levels. `ggvis` will display this empty `levels` by the figure unless we erase them, so this is what the first line is doing. It's deleting `levels` with no observations.

We then initialize the plot with `ggvis()` while chaining `layer_bars()` to craft a bar chart. Arguments `stroke` and `fill` respectively customize the contours and inside colors from the bars. Notice that those are being declared using `:=` instead of only `=`. That means they account for absolute values and not relative ones.

There are much more to learn about bar graphs. Discussion gets deeper by `Chapter 5`, *Making Other Bivariate Plots*. Next Recipe is about to demonstrate how to scrap data from twitter while plotting it with `ggplot2`, either by drawing bar charts or lollipops plots.

Using rtweet and ggplot2 to plot twitter words frequencies

This section seeks the master for words of wisdom. We're about to scrap Hadley's twitter (`@hadleywickham`). Several packages are combined in order to bring achieve the upcoming visual. This recipe begins by doing the twitter scrap, filtering data and finally plotting it with `ggplot2`.

Getting ready...

Besides `ggplot2` there are four packages we require for this recipe. All of them can be downloaded and installed by the following code:

```
> if(!require(rtweet)){ install.packages('rtweet')}
> if(!require(rcorpora)){ install.packages('rcorpora')}
> if(!require(dplyr)){ install.packages('dplyr')}
> if(!require(tidytext)){ install.packages('tidytext')}
```

With the right tools (packages) the task can be easily handled.

How to do it...

Let us see how to use <kbd>rtweet and `ggplot2` to plot twitter words frequencies

1. Scrap tweets from Hadley's time line with `rtweet::get_timeline()`:

```
> library(rtweet)
> sept_2017 <- '907969109840756736'
> hadley_wisdom <- get_timeline(user = 'hadleywickham',
                                 n = 800,
                                 max_id = sept_2017)
```

2. Fill vectors with the words you're not interested in. This can be done both manually and with the help of `rcorpora` package:

```
> library(rcorpora)
> corpora_stop <- corpora("words/stopwords/en")$stopWords
> my_stop <- c('https','rt','t.co','hadleywickham')
```

3. Combine `dplyr` and `tidytext` packages to manipulate original data frame and count how many times a word were tweeted. Using brackets do a selective call on them to select only the most tweeted ones:

```
> library(dplyr);library(tidytext)
> dt <- hadley_wisdom %>%
    unnest_tokens(word, text) %>%
    count(word, sort = TRUE) %>%
    filter(!word %in% c(corpora_stop,my_stop))
> dt <- dt[1:10,]
```

4. Factor `dt$word` before actually drawing bars using `ggplot2`, so that an specific order is coerced:

```
> dt$word <- factor(dt$word,
                    levels = (dt$word[order(dt$n)]))
> library(ggplot2)
> ggplot(data = dt, aes(x = word, weight = n)) +
    stat_count() + xlab('') + coord_flip()
```

As result we got the following bar chart (Figure 4.8):

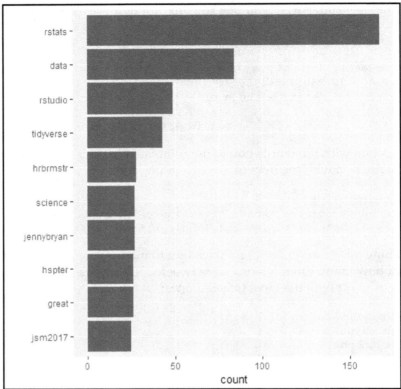

Figure 4.8 - ggplot2 bar chart.

5. Combine `geom_segment()`, `geom_point()` and `geom_text()` to craft an amazing lollipop plot:

```
> gg2_hadley <- ggplot(data = dt, aes(x = n, y = word))
> gg2_hadley +
    geom_segment(aes(yend=word, x=min(n)-3, xend=n-3),
                        linetype="dashed", size=0.1) +
    geom_point(size = 12, colour = 'lightblue') +
    geom_text(aes(label = n), size = 5)
```

The lollipop plot is showed by the following image (Figure 4.9):

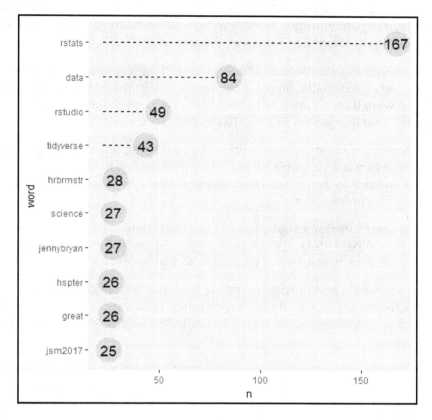

Figure 4.9 - ggplot2 lollipop plot.

Now let's check some explanations.

How it works...

Primary step is scrapping words from Hadley's twitter. This was done using `rtweet` package. After loading this package a character is set and store (`sept_2017`). This accounts for a twitter status id which tells how old a tweet is. In the sequence an object named `hadley_wisdom` is created to hold the data frame with twitter information.

Data frame is crafted by `rtweet`'s `get_timeline()` function. Here recipe inputted the `user` we're scrapping from, the number of tweets (n) and the older tweet we're looking for (`max_id`). The later argument is not mandatory, it was declared in order to make recipe reproducible, our input demanded for tweets later than 09-13-2017.

Step 2 is simply designing stop words. Those we're picked from `rcorpora` package stop words and also picked manually. Step 3 is turning text column into separated words with `tidytext`, those were then counted with the aid of `dplyr` package which also filtered unwanted words. Last line is selecting the 10 most tweeted words.

Fourth step is drawing a basic bar chart with `ggplot2`. It begins by turning word variable into a factor so that bars are properly sorted. Once data set has now the words and counts by itself there is no need to `ggplot2`'s functions to do the computation. Basic aesthetics are not only x but also includes `weight`.

To breed the bar chart functions `stat_count()`, `xlab()` and `coord_flip()` were used. The first one draw the bars (default geometry is bar), the second erased x-axis title while the last flipped the plot. Finally last step is giving life to a lollipop plot.

Basic aesthetics are now x and y. After mapping the basic aesthetics, `geom_segment()` is stacked to draw the stick; extra aesthetics are required (`yend` and `xend`). Points are added with `geom_point()`. Function `geom_text()` is called to write the number of observations inside of each point.

When we check the result we see that one of the most tweeted words is *hrbrmstr*. This accounts for twitter's user Bob Rudis. He made amazing contributions to R community, rely on his contributions plus he has several of his own. I encourage the reader to check some of his work by his GitHub profile and also to check his blog.

See also

- Bob Rudis's GitHub profile at `https://github.com/hrbrmstr`
- Bob Rudis's blog `https://rud.is/b/`

Drawing publish quality density plot

This Recipe aims to draw a publish quality density plot from `iris` data frame. It usually takes about 2 to 4 lines to craft a very good exploratory bar chart with `ggplot2`. Defaults are pretty good but don't fool yourself, there is much more to do in order to achieve publishing quality.

To begin with, generally axes must be grown and texts resized. Many times labels must be rewritten to display the correct name plus it's often good to rework colors. Following section shows how to code this changes with `ggplot2`.

How to do it...

Let us start with publish quality density plot:

1. Load `ggplot2` and draw a basic density plot:

```
> library(ggplot2)
> hq_1 <- ggplot(data = iris,
                 aes( x = Petal.Length, fill = Species)) +
    geom_density(alpha = .5, size = 1) + theme_classic()
```

2. Correct axes labels with `xlab()` and `ylab()` functions. Also correct legends while coercing a new color scale with `scale_fill_manual()`:

```
> hq_2 <- hq_1 + xlab('Petal Lenght (centimeters)') + ylab('Density') +
    scale_fill_manual(labels = c('Iris setosa','Iris versicolor','Iris virginica'),
                      values = c('coral','deepskyblue','springgreen'),
                      name = 'Iris species')
```

3. Add `scale_*_continuous()` to grow axes bigger plus extend figure limits:

```
> hq_3 <- hq_2 +
    scale_y_continuous(labels = sprintf('%1.1f', seq(0,3,.2)),
                       breaks = seq(0,3,.2)) +
    scale_x_continuous(labels = sprintf('%1.0f', seq(0,8,1)),
                       breaks = seq(0,8,1), limits = c(0,8))
```

4. Stack `theme()` functions to perform several changes, from legends replacement to texts resizing:

```
> hq_4 <- hq_3 + theme(legend.justification = c('left', 'top'),
                    legend.position = c(.55,.95),
                    legend.background = element_rect(color = "black",
                                                     size = 1,
                                                     linetype =
"solid"),
                    legend.text = element_text(size = 13, face =
'italic'),,
                    legend.title = element_text(size = 14),
                    axis.text = element_text(size = 15),
                    axis.title = element_text(size = 15))
> hq_4
```

Check following image (Figure 4.10) to see the final result:

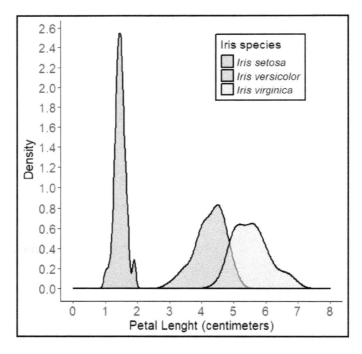

Figure 4.10 - Publish quality density plot.

Keep ahead for explanations.

How it works...

Recipe kicks-off by setting a simple density plot under `hq_1` object. Yet it bears some small changes that improve default visual. Inside `geom_density()` we got alpha blending called by `alpha` argument, hence solving the overlaying curves problem. This same function had contour lines increased by `size` argument. At the end it also had tweaked default theme to classic.

Second step is making x-axis label account for its full name (measure unit included) with `xlab()` function. Y-axis labels were also reworked, `ylab()` is doing that. Colors scheme, legends' titles and labels were also reworked, all this under the same function: `scale_fill_manual()`. Argument `labels` is changing legends' labels; names of species must start with capital letter. Parameters `values` and `name` are respectively changing color scheme and legend's title.

Step 3 is growing axes bigger with `scale_*_continuous()` family functions. Breaks are grown by `breaks` parameter, a `seq()` function helped with this task. Combine the same sequence inputted into `breaks` inside `sprintf()` function to write `labels` with fixed number of digits after the dot. Increase x-axis limits with `limits` argument thus avoiding some curves to be cropped.

Last step is handling several themes changes under `theme()` function. From drawing a rectangle around legends to repositioning those inside the figure; from increasing several text sizes to changing legend's labels font face to italic once those represent scientific names.

These are general changes that could improve a `ggplot` from the exploratory level to the publishing level. There is no right or wrong way to do it and the needs widely vary depending on what kind of audience do you have, yet these changes might be able to cover several needs.

5
Making Other Bivariate Plots

In this chapter, we will cover the following recipes:

- Creating simple stacked bar graph
- Crafting proportional stacked bar graph
- Plotting side-by-side bar graph
- Plotting a bar graphic with aggregated data using `geom_col()`
- Adding variability estimates to plots with `geom_errorbar()`
- Making line graphs
- Making static and interactive hexagon plots
- Adjusting hexagon plot
- Developing publish quality proportional stacked bar graph

Introduction

There is a wide variability among bivariate plots. Even if we have seen some of them, there are still some popular ones remaining. Bars, for instance, can account for bivariate data in more than one way. Also, there are line graphs, very popular among economists. Not to talk about hexagons plots, just like the one we glanced at `Chapter 2`, *Plotting Two Continuous Variables*.

This chapter covers these kinds of visualizations, bivariate bar chars, line and hexagon plots. Most of the recipes found in this chapter are focused on `ggplot2`, yet some recipes are carrying `ggvis` and `plotly` codes.

Creating simple stacked bar graphs

Stacked bars are often settled to display how data is distributed across categories with respect to other categories. Using `ggplot2`, stacked bar plots can be simply handled by `geom_bar()` function; that would require nothing more than explicitly declaring the `fill` parameter. To demonstrate how `ggplot2`, `ggvis` and `plotly` can craft simple stacked bar plots we shall use `car::Salaries` data frame.

Getting ready

The data frame is `Salaries` from the `car` package. We also need the `plyr` package:

```
> if( !require(car)){ install.packages('car')}
> if( !require(plyr)){ install.packages('plyr')}
```

Make sure to have the internet connection before running above code.

How to do it...

After looking at the data, `ggplot2` can deploy stacked bars by naming the `fill` argument:

1. Call the `geom_bar()` function to make sure to have the bar geometry:

```
> library(ggplot2)
> gg2_sal <- ggplot( data = car::Salaries, aes(x = rank))
> gg2_sal + geom_bar(aes(fill = sex))
```

Check the following image (Figure 5.1) to see the result:

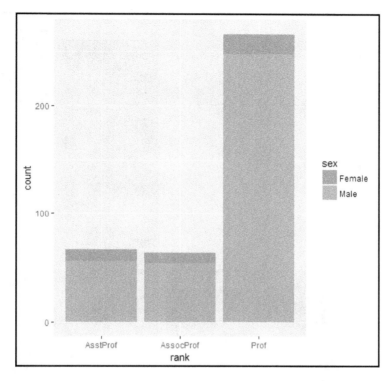

Figure 5.1: Simple stacked bar graph

2. Stacks can be reversed by adjusting the position argument:

```
> gg2_sal + geom_bar(aes(fill = sex),
                  position = position_stack(reverse = T))
```

3. ggvis can also draw a stacked bar graph:

```
> library(ggvis)
> ggv_sal <- ggvis(data = car::Salaries, x = ~rank)
> ggv_sal %>% group_by(sex) %>% layer_bars(fill = ~sex)
```

Following image (Figure 5.2) shows the result:

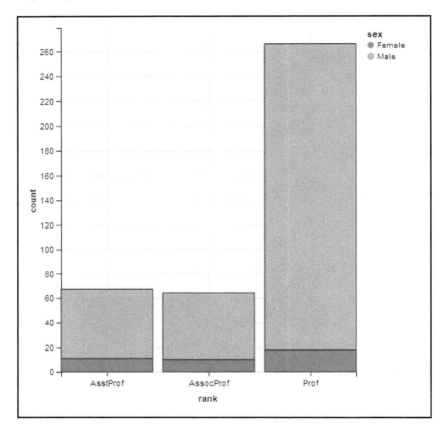

Figure 5.2: Simple ggvis stacked bar graph.

4. Split the data set and then compute the counts using the `plyr` package, before plotting with `plotly`:

```
> library(car)
> sal_male <- plyr::count(Salaries$rank[Salaries$sex == 'Male'])
> sal_fem <- plyr::count(Salaries$rank[Salaries$sex == 'Female'])
```

5. With the data ready, combine `plot_ly()` and `add_trace()` to the job:

```
> library(plotly)
> pt_sal <- plot_ly(data = sal_male, x = ~x, y = ~freq ,
                     type = 'bar', name = 'Male')
> pt_sal %>%
    add_trace(data = sal_fem, name = 'Female') %>%
    layout(barmode = 'stack')
```

Let's understand what happened.

How it works...

Step 1 stores a `ggplot` with the `rank` variable from the `Salaries` data frame named `gg2_sal` (ggplot2 salaries). Afterwards, this `ggplot` is called and summed with the `geom_bar()` layer. The only thing that is required to stack the bars is to set the `fill` parameter inside `aes()`. It could be set by `ggplot()`; it wouldn't make any difference.

Step 2 not only explicitly calls for stacks, but also tells that the default order must be reversed. It does so by setting the `position` argument with a function from the `position_*()` family. If we had stacked `coor_flip()` it would be good to reverse the stacks position.

Keep in mind the tricks used to reorder bars discussed in `Chapter 3`, *Plotting One Variable*. Any bar position (including stacks order) can be changed by manipulating factors. The order in which the bars show up is important and may be carefully chosen to deliver conclusions in an easy and intuitive way.

Stacked bars are also made available by `ggvis` and `plotly`. Step 3 demonstrates how to brew those using nothing but `ggvis`. The function responsible for calling bars is `layer_bars()`. Also, a `fill` argument handles the stacks, but it wouldn't work without the `group_by()` function.

Note how the order displayed by the bars is now different from the previous one. To change that, one can simply rely on the `factor()` function to change the levels' ordering:

```
> sal <- car::Salaries
> sal$sex <- factor(sal$sex, levels = c('Male', 'Female')
```

Do not forget to change the data argument from `car::Salaries` to `sal` after running the previous code. The bars can be reordered in a similar way by re-factoring `rank` instead of `sex`. Steps 4 and 5 are introducing the guns used to create stacked bar graphs with `plotly`.

Creating those visualizations with `plotly` does require more code once computations are not handled directly by `plotly`. Step 4 handles the computation. After loading the `car` package, `sal_male` and `sal_fem` stores the data frames about to be used. The first one holds `ranks` as a variable called `x` and counts as a variable named `freq`, only for male observations; the second does about the same, but for female observations.

Computation was done by the `count()` function from `plyr` package. Next, step 5 creates the bars. It begins by creating a bar chart (`pt_sal` object) with only male observations (`data = sal_male`). Argument `type = 'bar'` is asking for the bars. Following lines are chaining `pt_sal` with `add_traces()` and `layout()` to create stacked bar graphs.

Function add_traces() is inputted with sal_fem data frame to create the bars

This recipe taught us how to brew stacked bars using `ggplot2`, `ggvis`, and `plotly`. Stacked bar graphs are useful to display absolute values, but there is a bar plot specialized in the display of relative values. Plots of such kind are called proportional stacked bar plots and are covered by some of the following recipes.

Crafting proportional stacked bar

If you have to make a stand about proportions, proportional stacked bar graphs may be the way to go. Note that it works better when there are only few categories to analyze. If you have two continuous variables to display at both axes and still want to reinforce how proportions are changing among categories you shall call for proportional area plots instead.

Sticking with `car::Salaries` data frame, this recipes is demonstrating how to craft proportional stacked bar graphs. Codes are covering plots made with `ggplot2`, `ggvis` and `plotly`.

Getting ready

The only requirement that the recipes have the `car` , `scales`, and `plyr` packages installed. Try running the following code to check for them and install if they not there:

```
> if( !require(car)){ install.packages('car')}
> if( !require(plyr)){ install.packages('plyr')}
> if( !require(scales)){ install.packages('scales')}
```

To install a missing package, internet connection is required.

How to do it...

Proportional stacked bar are very useful visualization to make accurate observations about proportions. Following we can see how to code them:

1. Using `ggplot2`, proportionality can be called by the argument `position`:

```
> library(ggplot2)
> gg2_sal <- ggplot( data = car::Salaries, aes( x = rank))
> gg2_sal + geom_bar(position = 'fill', aes( fill = sex))
```

See the result in the following image (Figure 5.3):

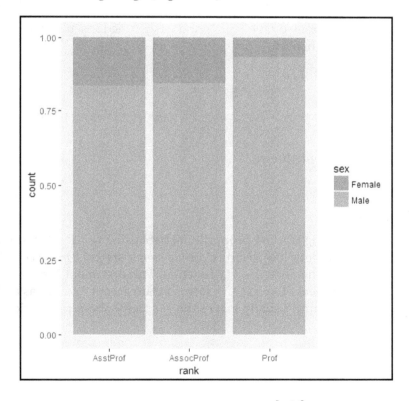

Figure 5.3: Proportional stacked bar draw by `ggplot2`.

2. In order to do the same using `ggvis`, a little computing using the `plyr` package must be done first:

```
> library(ggvis);library(plyr)
> car::Salaries %>% group_by(sex) %>% compute_count(~rank) %>%
  plyr::ddply(.(x_),transform,prop=count_/sum(count_)) %>%
  ggvis(x = ~x_, y = ~prop) %>% layer_bars(fill = ~sex)
```

3. In order to do the same using `plotly`, let us store the data created previously into two data frames separated by `sex` variable:

```
> sal_prop <- car::Salaries %>% group_by(sex) %>%
compute_count(~rank) %>%
             plyr::ddply(.(x_),transform,prop=count_/sum(count_))
> sal_prop_m <- sal_prop[sal_prop$sex == 'Male',]
> sal_prop_f <- sal_prop[sal_prop$sex == 'Female',]
```

4. With computing done by the `ggvis` and `plyr` functions, it's time to plot using the `plot_ly()` function:

```
> library(plotly)
> plot_ly(data = sal_prop_m, x = ~x_, y = ~prop, type = 'bar', name
= 'Male') %>%
    add_trace(data = sal_prop_f, name = 'Female') %>% layout(barmode
= 'stack')
```

Next section is explaining somethings.

How it works...

Step 1 in takes care of plotting stacked proportional bars using `ggplot2`. It demands only little coding and most of it looks like Recipe *Creating simple stacked bars*, except for the `position` argument in the `geom_bar()` function. This argument is now inputted with the string `'fill'`. A great deal of `geom_*()` functions do accept `'fill'` as an input to `position` argument. This input usually makes the geometry about proportions.

Argument `position` makes very easy to ask for proportions using `ggplot2`. Improvement can be delivered by Hadley's `scale` package. If you have already got it installed, there is no need to restart your R Session, but if that's not the case, do so and run the following code to improve the y-axis labels:

```
> if( !require(scales)){ install.packages('scales')}
> library(ggplot2)
> gg2_sal <- ggplot( data = car::Salaries, aes(x = rank))
> gg2_sal + geom_bar(position = 'fill', aes(fill = sex)) +
>   scale_y_continuous(labels = scales::percent_format())
```

The resulting plot displays the y-axis labels in the percentage format. Changes like that are very useful, keep `scales` package nearby. Check the result in the following image (Figure 5.4):

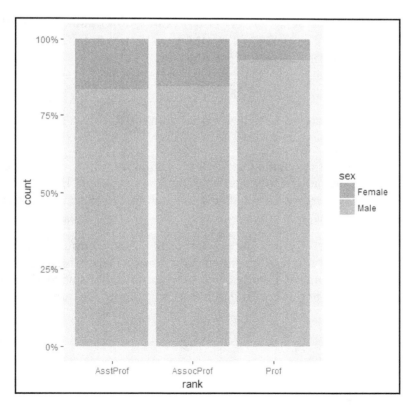

Figure 5.4 - combining ggplot2 with scales to throw the percentage format.

Step 2 gives life to an interactive graph using `ggvis`. It demands more code lines as computations must be done by `plyr` before plotting. After the package is loaded, the pipe line operator (`%>%`) is used to chain the functions that will compute the proportions.

Data (`car::Salaries`) is grouped by `sex` variable. Afterwards, grouped data is used to compute counts based on ranks; the `compute_count(~rank)` function handles it. Next pipe is handing those computations to a function coming from the `plyr` package.

The `ddply()` function calculates proportions for each rank variable (renamed to `x_` by `compute_count()`). Categories are named inside `.( )` function. More than one can be named but they must but comma separated then. The last argument's name (`props`) accounts for the new variable to be created. The input rules the computation.

 `.( )` is actually a function coming from `plyr`. It's similar to the usage of `~` by `ggvis`. Replacing `.()` for `~` would cause no trouble since `ggvis` is loaded. Failing to load `plyr` would cause `.()` to fail though. You can type `?.` into the console to know it better.

Finally, the data is inputted into the `ggvis()` function with the help of pipes. Bars are finally crafted by stacking `layer_bars()` function. Names set in both these functions are given by manipulated data and not by the original data set. Bars and stacks can be reordered with the help of `factor()`.

Step 3 does not actually plot but splits this same computation into two separated data frames. First we assign the data frame to an object called `sal_prop`. Later, brackets (`[ ]`) are used to select only those rows for which the `sex` column equals `male` and store it on the new `sal_porp_m` data frame.

An analogous process created the `sal_prop_f`; thus the same computation done by previous step is now stored into two separated data frames. Data is ready to be plotted, Step 4 takes care of it; the data set already carries the computations needed to draw proportions. It is important to outline here that the computation borrowed functions from `ggvis` and `plyr`.

See also

- Creating simple stacked bar graphs

Plotting side-by-side bar graph

Instead of stacking the categories, we could have chosen to display them side-by-side. You might recall one side-by-side bar graph coming from a blog, magazine or newspaper. These plots can be easily made with `ggplot2` and `plotly`, but `ggvis` was not there when this book was written. Check the *See also* section for more reference.

This kind of viz is good to show comparisons between categories across some other categories (or time). If you choose side-by-side bars instead of stacked ones you're probably choosing to highlight the variable displayed by colors over the one displayed by the x-axis. Let's see how `ggplot2` and `plotly` handle it.

Getting ready

Besides the usual `ggplot2` and `plotly` packages, `car` package is required once data frame is coming from it. We also need `plyr` to do some computation:

```
> if( !require(car)){ install.pacakges('car')}
> if( !require(plyr)){ install.packages('plyr')}
```

Running the preceding code is going to check local availability of such packages. If any answer is negative and the internet connection is fine, the missing package might get download and installed for you. Now you are ready to get your hands dirty.

How to do it...

Following steps are crafting side-by-side bar graphs using `ggplot2` and `plotly`:

1. We start by storing the `car::Salaries` data frame into a global environment object and changing the factor levels within the `sex` variable:

   ```
   > sal <- car::Salaries
   > sal$sex <- factor(sal$sex, levels = c('Male','Female'))
   ```

2. To plot a side-by-side bar graph using `ggplot2`, the `position` argument must be declared as a string (`'dodge'`):

   ```
   > library(ggplot2)
   > gg2_sal <- ggplot( data = car::Salaries, aes( x = rank))
   > gg2_sal + geom_bar( position = 'dodge', aes( fill = sex))
   ```

If you take a look at the previous recipe, only the `position` argument is replaced. Following illustration (Figure 5.5) shows the output:

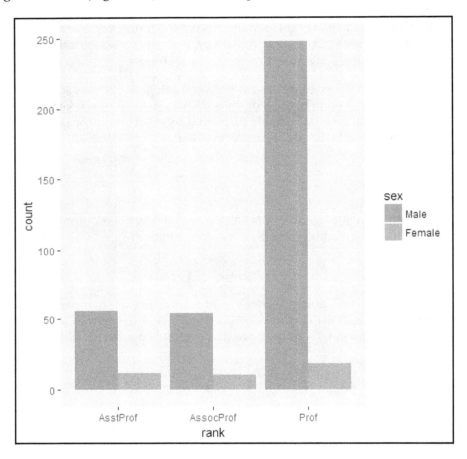

Figure 5.5: Side-by-side ggplot2 bar plot

Now it is time to brew a `plotly` version of the preceding illustration.

3. Before actually plotting it, let's split the data frame based on the `sex` variable and count how many of each `rank` do we have:

```
> sal_male <- plyr::count(car::Salaries$rank[car::Salaries$sex ==
'Male'])
> sal_fem <- plyr::count(car::Salaries$rank[car::Salaries$sex ==
'Female'])
```

The readers can go to the console and call both objects to see how the `plyr` package has handled these commands.

4. With the data prepared, the `pot_ly()` and `add_trace()` functions can be used to code the plot:

```
> library(plotly)
> pt_sal <- plot_ly(data = sal_male, x = ~x, y = ~freq ,type =
'bar', name = 'Male')
> pt_sal %>% add_trace(data = sal_fem, name = 'Female')
```

As result, we get an interactive bar plot that looks likes the following illustration (Figure 5.6):

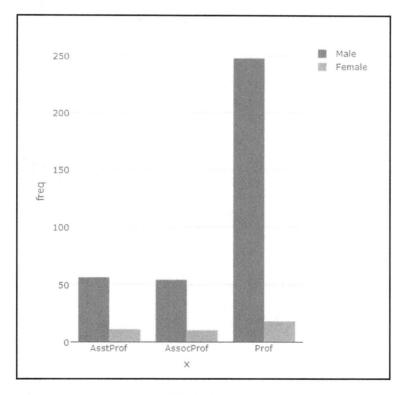

Figure 5.6: Side-by-side plotly bar plot

Let's see how the gears got together here.

How it works...

Mastering *Recipe Creating simple stacked bar graphs* make the understanding upon this one much faster and easier. The first code block begins by storing the `car::Salaries` data frame into a new object. Afterwards, it takes the new data frame and reorder levels from `sex` variable using `factor()` function.

It does so, this way the bars with the most counts can stand first. Next code block actually does the plotting. After loading `ggplot2`, it sets the basic coordinate mapping using `ggplot()` and stores them into an object called `gg2_sal` (ggplot2 salaries). Next thing to finish up plotting it is to add the bars function.

They are added by using + before summoning the `geom_bar()` function. Inside this function, the `sex` variable is picked for the `fill` argument. Call for it inside the `aes()` function. Also, the `position` argument is inputted with `'dodge'` (note that `' '` makes it a string). Our `ggplot` is then outputted.

Next step is manipulating data before we draw the `plotly` graphic. The data frame is split into two, this way we can craft the bars using `add_traces()` later. Package `plyr` is counting how many observations we do have for each `rank`. Computation is done separated for male (`sal_male` data frame) and female observations (`sal_fem` data frame).

Step 4 does about the same done by *Recipe Creating simple stacked bar graph* while crafting the `plotly` bar chart. The only difference is that it skips last pipe (`%>%`) and `layout()` function. By doing this, the default `barmode` (`'group'`) sets the side-by-side bars viz. Using `plotly` actually requires less code to brew side-by-side bar graphs than what is required to draw stacked ones.

See also

- GitHub questions about side-by-side `ggvis` bar plots at `https://stackoverflow.com/questions/28553760/ggvis-side-by-side-barchart-grouped-by-second-variable`
- Creating simple stacked bar graph

Plotting a bar graphic with aggregated data using geom_col()

This recipe is taking one step further into bar plots. We are sticking with the side-by-side grouped bars, but now we shall plot aggregated data on the y-axis (it could fit continuous data as well). Plotting aggregated data can feel a little more complicated than plotting continuous data once it requires aggregation. So it's a great opportunity to learn how to aggregate data and build data frames from it.

About the visuals this graph brings in, they are very good to show exactly how the variables perform across diverse categories and groups. For example, economists could use bar graphics with aggregated data to make stands about salary inequalities between U.S. college professors from different ranks and genders. Let us check what are the requirements to bring this example alive.

Getting ready

Besides `ggplot2`, the `car` package is needed in order to reproduce this recipe:

```
> if( !require(car)){ install.packages('car')}
```

Once this is ready, it's possible to move on and code the plot.

How to do it...

Following steps are telling how to craft bar graphs with aggregated data using `ggplot2`'s `geom_col` function:

1. We begin by using the `aggregate()` function to aggregate data into a new data frame:

```
> new_data <- aggregate(x = list( mean_salary =
car::Salaries$salary),
                        by = list(rank = car::Salaries$rank,
                            sex = car::Salaries$sex),
                    FUN = mean)
```

2. Call the `factor()` function to change the order in which the bars will be displayed later:

```
> new_data$sex <- factor(new_data$sex, levels = c('Male','Female'))
```

3. Use the `geom_col()` layer to display continuous values by the y-axis:

```
> library(ggplot2)
> gg2_bar <- ggplot(data = new_data, aes( x = rank, y =
mean_salary)) +
    geom_col(position = 'dodge', aes( fill = sex))
> gg2_bar
```

Calling `gg2_bar` at the end should result in something like the following image (Figure 5.6):

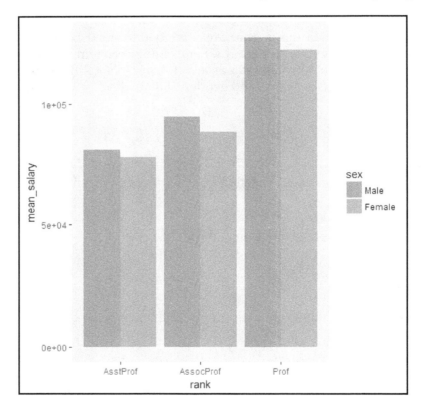

Figure 5.6: Bar graph with aggregated data.

Next section shows how the steps worked.

How it works...

Step 1 is an essential and a big step. It creates a new data frame that exhibits the mean salary for each combination of sex and rank available. The data frame is built by the base function `aggregate()`. The first and second arguments are declared as lists for which element's names are going to be columns' name at `new_data`.

The first argument takes the variable upon which computation will be made on. The next argument points out the grouping variables. All these will be coerced into factors. The last argument is declared after the name of the function that will carry on the computation. Do not name it with parenthesis.

Step 2 reorders factors' levels based on `sex` column. The function `factor()` does the trick by declaring the `level` argument in the desired order. Finally, step 3 loads `ggplot2`; draws the base coordinates and aesthetics using `ggplot()` (now the y argument is required!); calls `geom_cal()` to match the bar geometry along with the continuous y variable; and store all that into an object called `gg2_bar`. This object is then called to plot the result.

Adding variability estimates to plots with geom_errrorbar()

The previous recipe can be improved. One must request a sort of a variability analysis in addition the bar chart. We came to the conclusion 9-month salary was higher for men of every rank but what if maximum women salary were much higher than men or the minimum much lower.

`ggplot2` certainly has functions draw variability intervals; one of them is the `geom_errorbar()`. The device drawn by such function demands `ymin` and `ymax` aesthetics arguments. Variability intervals can fit information of any kind: standard deviations, minimum and maximum values. Limitations are given only by creativity.

Getting ready

To make it happen, our departure point is going to be the `new_data` object. Thus, we need to make sure that the `car` package is installed and run step 1 from *Recipe Plotting a bar graphic with aggregated data using geom_col()*. Next code block is doing both things:

```
> if( !require(car)){ install.packages('car')}
> new_data <- aggregate(x = list( mean_salary = car::Salaries$salary),
                    by = list(rank = car::Salaries$rank,
                        sex = car::Salaries$sex),
                FUN = mean)
```

Now follow the next steps to meet our destination.

How to do it...

Following steps are demonstrating how to draw error bars into a bar chart:

1. We begin by creating a column with maximum salary for each rank-sex category combination using `aggregate()`:

   ```
   > new_data$max_salary <- aggregate(list(max_salary =
   car::Salaries$salary),
                         list(rank = car::Salaries$rank,
                         sex = car::Salaries$sex),
   max)$max_salary
   ```

2. Now create a column with minimum salary for each rank-sex category combination with `aggregate()`:

   ```
   > new_data$min_salary <- aggregate(list(min_salary =
   car::Salaries$salary),
                              list(rank = car::Salaries$rank,
                              sex = car::Salaries$sex),
   min)$min_salary
   ```

3. The error bar can be called using the `geom_errorbar()` function:

   ```
   > ggplot(new_data, aes(x = rank, y = mean_salary, fill = sex)) +
     geom_col(position = 'dodge') +
     geom_errorbar(aes(ymin = min_salary, ymax = max_salary),
   position = 'dodge')
   ```

Produced graph would look like the following illustration (Figure 5.7):

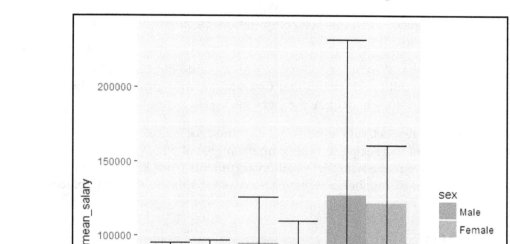

Figure 5.7: Bar plot with geom_errorbar()

Next section is explaining how `geom_errorbar()` is working.

How it works...

Much of what was done by this recipe resembles *Recipe Plotting a bar with aggregated data using geom_col()*. This recipe takes off from `new_data` data frame. Step 1 creates a new column called `max_salary`. New column holds maximum 9-month salaries values for each `Salaries$sex` and `Salaries$rank` combination. Function `aggregate()` is creating this new variable.

Step 2 does about the same, but it creates the `min_salary` column into the `new_data` data frame. This one carries the minimum 9-month salary observed for each `Salaries$sex` and `Salaries$rank` combination. With this last computation, all the required information is now hold by the data frame.

Step 3 finally draws the plot. We choose to set `fill = sex` into `ggplot()`; this way `geom_errorbar()` would understand that variables are also grouped by the `sex`. For this last function, it's mandatory to declare the `ymin` and `ymax` aesthetics.

These two were declared respectively as `min_salary` and `max_salary`, the columns created in the beginning of this recipe. It is also important to set `position` argument to `'dodge'`. By doing this we make sure that position arguments from `geom_col()` and `geom_errorbar()` are matching; hence, error bars are not displayed at wrong places.

There's more...

Many geometries can be called to show variability estimates and other kinds of intervals. A few useful options are: `geom_linerange()`, `geom_pointrange()`, `geom_errorbarh()` and `geom_crossbar()`. If you feel unfamiliar with some of them I encourage you to try some (or all) of them.

See also

- Recipe *Plotting a bar graphic with aggregated data using* `geom_col()`

Making line plots

Line graphs are very used both at the academy and industry. Needless to say, economists are mad about line graphs, and for a good reason. They are an easy choice when it comes to demonstrating a progression (for example, time-progression) of some continuous variable, let's say macroeconomic indicators.

Non-interactive line plots can be drawn by `ggplot2`. If there is some need to update the graphic with considerable frequency, interactive ones are a better fit and they can be crafted by `ggvis` or `plotly`. Plots made with these packages rapidly respond to data changes.

For this recipe, we're going to draw line graphs about the evolution of foreign trade (as percentage of Gross Domestic Product) of Finland and West Germany between 1965 and 1990. Both countries had chosen different economic paths. Let's see check their economic paths once we make sure to meet the requirements.

Getting ready

Before moving on, we need to install the `Zelig` package in order to make data available. We also need to filter data, following code does both:

```
> if( !require(Zelig)){ install.packages('Zelig')}
> library(Zelig)
> data(macro)
> macro <- subset(macro, country %in% c('Finland','West Germany'))
```

Make sure to have internet connection if you are not sure that the `Zelig` package is already installed.

How to do it...

Keep in mind that visualizing fewer lines is much easier than visualizing a bunch of them:

1. Load `ggplot2` and use `geom_line()` to get it done:

```
> library(ggplot2)
> ggplot(data = macro,
         aes(x = year, y = trade, colour = country)) +
         geom_line()
```

Outputted graph might be similar to the following figure:

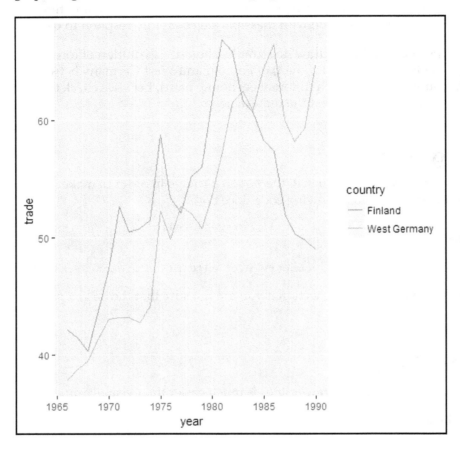

Figure 5.8: Line plot draw by ggplot2

2. To make it interactive, one can load `ggvis` and trust `layer_lines()` to the quest:

```
> library(ggvis)
> ggvis(data = macro %>% droplevels(),
        x = ~year, y = ~trade, stroke = ~country) %>%
    layer_lines()
```

3. Loading `plotly`, filter the data set and use `add_traces()` to draw lines for each country:

```
> library(plotly)
> plot_ly(data = macro[macro$country == 'Finland',], x = ~year, y =
~trade,
          type = 'scatter', mode = 'lines', name = 'Finland') %>%
    add_trace(data = macro[macro$country == 'West Germany',], name
= 'West Germany')
```

Let's move on to see how each step performs.

How it works...

As usual, step 1 begins by loading the `ggplot2` package. Next, base aesthetics are drawn: x, y, and `colour`. Only the first two are mandatory to the subsequent function, `geom_line()`, but for our proposes, `colour` can easily be taken as mandatory; missing it would result in a plot with two black lines and no clue about the country any of them represents.

For step 2, we are using `ggvis`. After loading the package, `ggvis()` draws the basic aesthetics. A little trick was done when declaring the `data` argument: with the help of a pipe (`%>%`), the `drop_levels()` function dropped the unused levels from the `macro` factor variables, so that they don't appear on the legends. The argument `stroke` sets the colors, while `layer_lines()` finally asks for the lines geometry.

Step 3 is plotting with `plotly`. It begins with `plot_ly()` drawing the lines for data related to Finland. This choice was made by filtering the data set for rows that match this country. The lines were selected by setting both `type = 'scatter'` and `mode = 'lines'`. A single pipe operator was then used to call for `add_traces()`. This last function had `data` filtered for West Germany and drew lines for this location.

Each step drew about the same figure for each package. It is important to remember that `ggvis` and `plotly` bring up interactive plots while `ggplot2` doesn't.

Making static and interactive hexagon plots

Hexagons can be seen as a mixture of scatterplots and heat maps. Instead of points like we would have in a scatterplot, we get exclusively hexagons. Instead of color gradients standing for a third variable like it would be in a heat map, colors tells how many points approximately each hexagon bears. Let me highlight that this is a huge simplification of the hexagon plots.

Also, think about the hexagon plots as feasible alternative to over plotting. Through this recipe, we will learn how to brew hexagon plots using `ggplot2`. In the end, it will coerce this static form to an interactive one by using the `plotly` package. To make the point about over plotting, current Recipe is using air pollution data (`robustbase::NOxEmissions`). We are plotting the log of hourly mean NOx ambient concentration (ppb) against the square root of wind speed (meters/second).

Getting ready

Data about pollution comes from the `robustbase` package. As some packages require, we must use the `data()` function in order to make our data set available:

```
> if( !require(robustbase)){ install.packages('robustbase')}
> library(robustbase)
> data(NOxEmissions)
```

The preceding code block ensures that the package is installed and loaded, and the data frame `NOxEmissions` is ready to go. Carry on to see how to actually plot a hexagon.

How to do it...

Current section is demonstrating how to create hexagon plots:

1. To plot a hexagon, there is no big trouble; add `geom_hex()` to your `ggplot`:

```
> library(ggplot2)
> ggplot(NOxEmissions, aes(x = LNOx, y = sqrtWS)) + geom_hex()
```

The resulting figure looks much like the one as follows:

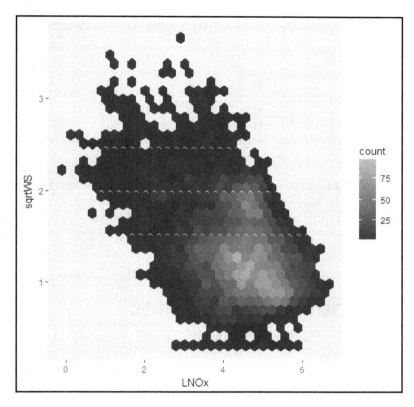

Figure 5.9: Hexagon plot made by ggplot2.

2. Convert it into the interactive form by calling `plotly`:

```
> plotly::ggplotly()
```

The result looks a tiny bit different from the previous one. Let's understand how it works.

How it works...

The first step loads `ggplot2` using the `library()` function. Afterwards, it draws the hexagon plot right away. Starts by entering the basic aesthetics mapping demanded (x and y) using the `ggplot()` function. Next, it uses `ggplot2`'s sum (`%+%`) and add the hexagon geometry. These are the only things to do in order to draw a simple `ggplot2` hexagon plot.

Step 2 coerces the earlier static plot into an interactive one. Instead of loading the whole package, recipe called for the function using the `<package>::<function()>` form. As the hexagon plot was the last `ggplot` plotted, the only thing needed to coerce it into a `plotly` plot is to simply call `plotly::ggplotly()`.

There is more...

The static form of this hexagon plot is more scale dependent than the interactive form. The white paths surrounding the hexagons may fade in and out based on the scales. Speaking for the interactive form, all hexagon borders are actually white.

This data fits nicely to the hexagonal geometry; the range from the variable inputted as `fill` is not that wide. Still, having an interactive data would help very much because one could discover how many points each hexagon bears by simply hovering the mouse over it. Remember that interactivity does not remain if you happen to export you figure into formats like PNG or JPEG.

Adjusting your hexagon plot

Previously, we learned how to give life to simple hexagon plots using `ggplot2` and coerce them into `plotly`. We took a bunch of default settings rather than customized ones. This recipe is going to show the readers some core parameters to tweak. We could, for example, resize the hexagons and/or choose different color scales and breaks.

Getting ready

In order to make the changes very clear, we're going to elaborate on the previous recipe, so the requirements from it still remain. There's no need to go back, as the following code will fulfill our needs if internet connection is available:

```
> if( !require(robustbase)){ install.packages('robustbase') }
> library(robustbase)
> data(NOxEmissions)
```

Let's roll.

How to do it...

Following code is changing hexagons size and colors:

1. We start the same way as in the previous case, but we set up the `binwidth` parameter and call for an object from the `scale_fill` group:

```
> ggplot(data = NOxEmissions, aes( x = LNOx, y = sqrtWS)) +
  geom_hex(binwidth = c(.2,.1)) +
  scale_fill_gradientn(colours = rainbow(7), breaks = seq(0,80,10))
```

Look at the following figure to see the result:

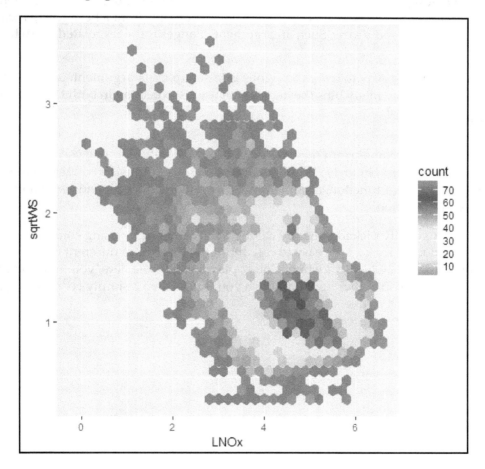

Figure 5.10: Elaborated hexagon plot

2. Once the plotting is done, we could coerce it into a `plotly`:

```
> plotly::ggplotly()
```

Move on to the next section for explanations.

How it works...

Just like the previous recipe, this recipe begins loading the package and mapping the basic aesthetics (x and y) using `ggplot()`. After the sum operator, function `geom_hex()` is calling for the hexagon geometry. Inside this function there is the `binwidth` argument. It receives a vector with two elements telling the increasing unit from a hexagon to the next respectively by the *x* and *y* axes. Such an argument changes the sizes related to each hexagon.

 Another way to resize hexagons is to set up `bins` argument. It more or less tells how many bins (hexagons) the user is expecting in both the directions (y and x).

Next function added comes from the `scale_fill_*()` family. The one used was `scale_fill_gratientn()`. While argument `colours` adjusted colors scheme by inputting a `rainbow()` function, argument `breaks` reworked the legends with a little help from the `seq()` function.

Colors can be manually picked either by calling their names or by using color generating function. Function `rainbow()` is easy to call. Input the number of different colors you are looking for inside `rainbow()` function. Colors play a major role here, you may want to careful pick them if you are willing to publish you figure. Step 2 simply coerces the `ggplot` illustration into a `plotly` one.

See also

- You can check `geom_hex()` documentation by entering `?geom_hex` into your console

- Working alpha along with these kind of plots may be hard; take a look at a feasible solution, if you feel like, at `https://stackoverflow.com/questions/13167531/`

- It's difficult to make hexagons' size account for some variable. Check an alternative at `https://gist.github.com/geotheory/5748388https://stackoverflow.com/questions/16894460`

Developing a publish quality proportional stacked bar graph

In order to develop a publish quality proportional bar graph, this recipe will produce a figure similar to the one produced at Recipe *Crafting a proportional stacked bar graph*. The only difference is that this time we will aim for publishing quality. The way we do this is by: manually setting color; reworking labels' content and sizes; and reworking legends and axes. Let's begin by looking at the requirements.

Getting ready

Apart from package `ggplot2` the only required package will be `car` package. Run the following code if you are not sure about having this last package already installed:

```
if( !require(car)){ install.packages('car') }
```

Do not forget that internet connection is needed. Now let's draw.

How to do it...

The bar proportional bar chart will be produced in a iterative way. After each step you can check the changes made by the step by calling the object created by the particular step (h<step number>):

1. We start by loading the library and creating the plot that will serve as the building ground:

```
> library(ggplot2)
> h1 <- ggplot( data = car::Salaries, aes(x = rank)) +
    geom_bar(position = 'fill', aes(fill = sex)) +
    theme_minimal()
```

2. Rework the labels by renaming them and displaying more values at the y-axis:

```
> h2 <- h1 + xlab('') +
    ylab('U.S. college composition of academics (in percent)') +
    scale_y_continuous(labels = sprintf('%.1f%%',seq(0,1,.125)*100),
breaks = seq(0,1,.125))
```

3. Change the colors related to the sex variable, and at the same time, rename the legends:

```
> h3 <- h2 + scale_fill_manual(labels = c('Female','Male'),
                    values = c('coral','deepskyblue'),
                    name = 'Sex')
```

4. Lastly, adjust the remaining themming features, such as text size and legends' layout:

```
> h4 <- h3 + theme(legend.background = element_rect(color =
"black",
                                        size = 1, linetype =
"solid"),
                legend.text = element_text(size = 13),
                legend.title = element_text(size = 13),
                axis.text = element_text(size = 13.5),
                axis.title = element_text(size = 15))
```

5. Call for the `h4` object to reach the final illustration (Figure 5.11):

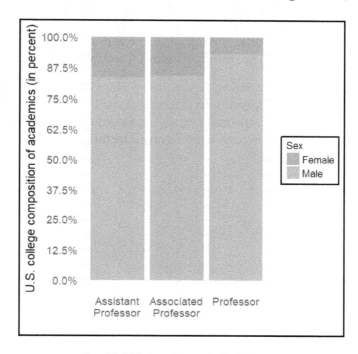

Figure 5.11: Publication quality proportional stacked bar graph

Following section answers the why and hows from this recipe.

How it works...

Starting with step 1, the base plot was created and stored by an object called `h1`. Besides the proportional stacked bar graph created using `geom_bar()` function with properly set `fill` argument, first step is also changing the default theme using `theme_minimal()` function.

Step 2 takes off from `h1`, erasing the x-axis-label by calling `xlab()` inputted with an *empty* string. The `ylab()` function is called to coerce the y-axis-label to its full description. Finally it stacks `scale_continuous()` function to grow the y-axis with more ticks and tweak labels to fit percent format. All these adjustments were then stored into an object called `h2`.

Instead of trusting `scales::percent_format()` with the task of
coercing values to the percentage format, we turned ourselves to a
combination of `sprintf()` and `seq()`. This way we could deliver a label
that always displays the first digit after the dot no matter what.
Function `scales::percent_format()` wouldn't do it.

Step 3 launches itself from `h2`, summing `scale_fill_manual()` to manually set colors to
the `sex` variable and rename the legends accordingly (First Letter Uppercase On Board). All
these changes are then stored into the new object, `h3`. Step 4 calls the `theme()` function with
a lot of parameters adjusted. These parameters draw a rectangle around the legends and
resizes some text.

6
Creating Maps

This chapter is going to cover the following recipes:

- Making simple maps - 1854 London Streets
- Creating an interactive cholera map using plotly
- Crafting choropleth maps using ggplot2
- Zooming in on the map
- Creating different maps based on different map projection type
- Handling shapefiles to map Afghanistan health facilities
- Crafting an interactive globe using plotly
- Creating high quality maps

Introduction

Finally, maps! If you think about maps single purpose is to take from location A to B I hope this chapter will change your mid. Maps are actually a wonderful way to display all sorts of information. Data journalists often use maps, a tendency created by Dr. John Snow whose creativity and efforts ended a cholera outbreak that happened in London by the nineteenths.

Maps can optimally display information that is somehow related to geography. This chapter shall create those using ggplot2, ggvis, and plotly. We will begin by drawing the John Snow cholera map, going all the way through Afghanistan map to an interactive globe showing the countries affected by the 2009 baking crises.

Making simple maps - 1854 London Streets

Plotting an entire country, district, lakes and forests can be seen as a task for polygons while plotting streets, roads, and rivers a quest for paths to handle. Really informative maps would request much more than this recipe is going to teach but we're getting there. This recipe is going to show you how to plot some 1854 London streets.

Do not get anxious, maps are pretty cool and there is plenty of stuff to learn. Step by step, this chapter will introduce you to a lot of useful ones. This recipe's intention is to show you how maps can simply be translated into paths (and polygons); later, we will be improving this very map to get a result very similar to the one that John Snow (the doctor, not the ranger) breed.

Getting ready

Besides the regulars (ggplot2, ggvis, and plotly), the king (the king being this recipe) demands the HistData package:

```
> if( !require(HistData)){ install.packages('HistData')}
```

For now, we're still relying on packages to bring data. As maps usually carry many nuts and bolts to go around, the later recipes will show you how to handle some; you might have to download and read shape files sometimes, we're doing this later but all done from the console. Now to the streets of 1854 London.

How to do it...

Let us get started with simple maps:

1. HistData is the package containing data; load it:

    ```
    > library(HistData)
    ```

2. Load ggplot2 and address geom_path() the street drawing:

    ```
    > library(ggplot2)
    > ggplot(data = Snow.streets) +
      geom_path(aes(x = x, y = y, group = street))
    ```

The outcome looks like the following illustration (Figure 6.1):

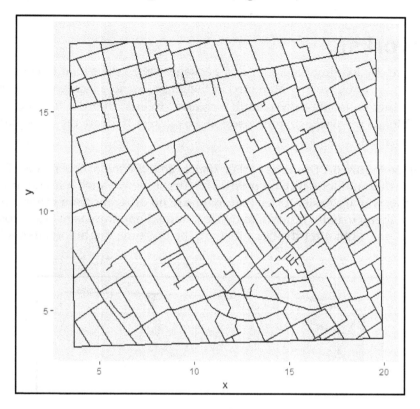

Figure 6.1: 1854 London streets drawn by ggplot2

3. To draw a similar image using `ggvis`, use `layer_paths()`:

```
> library(ggvis)
> Snow.streets %>% group_by(street) %>%
    ggvis(x = ~x, y = ~y) %>% layer_paths()
```

4. `plotly` can hand out the same using `add_lines()`:

```
> library(plotly)
> plot_ly(Snow.streets, type = 'scatter', showlegend = F) %>%
    group_by(street) %>% add_lines(x = ~x, y =~y)
```

Keep reading ahead for explanations.

How it works...

The recipe begins by loading the `HistData` package--step 1 does load it. Data is coming from `HistData`; for now, we are interested in the `Snow.streets` data frame. There are three variables that are going to be useful: `x`, `y`, and `street`. In order to make a `ggplot` out of them, step 2 loads the package, then uses `geom_path()` to draw the lines--setting `group = street` is essential.

The result will be Figure 6.1 from the earlier *How to do it Section* of this recipe. The default `ggplot2` theme does not look nice on maps. This first time we stick with default theme for a good reason--this way it's easier to see that maps are no different from other plots; `x` and `y` axes are always there, usually hidden. In order to hide them, the easier way would be to sum `theme_void()` right after the last function; the outcome might look like following map (Figure 6.2):

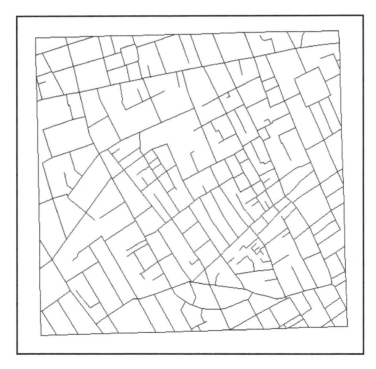

Figure 6.2: ggplot map with a void theme

Step 3 draws a similar map using only `ggvis`. Grouping is made by the `group_by()` function and `layer_paths()` takes care of the rest. Step 4 draw streets using `plotly`. It also uses the `group_by()` function and lines are demanded by the `add_lines()` function. This recipe demonstrated two things:

- The first footstep required to reproduce Snow's cholera map
- How maps can be easily seen as paths (and polygons) and also made out from those primitives

The next recipe will reproduce John Snow's map and demonstrate how to add points to inform the audience.

Creating an interactive cholera map using plotly

The hoover feature displayed by `plotly` makes this package a very attractive option when it comes to the creation of interactive maps. The previous recipe intended to show you how maps can be seem and made out from primitives like paths; now it's time to see how points can add useful information.

This particular recipe will make an interactive version of a graph made by Doctor John Snow. For those who don't know him yet, his graph showed the spatial relation between cholera deaths happening in 1854 London and water pumps; at the time, the general believe was that cholera spreads through the air. He fixed the outbreak by making the contaminated pump unavailable.

His map outlines the spatial relation between water pumps and deaths by cholera; hence, proving that cholera was spreading through water. This map made its way into the hall of fame; for some people, it is the first important application of data visualization dedicated to human health improvement.

For this particular recipe, our goal is to reproduce an interactive version of it. Red circles deployed are for each cholera death while blue diamond-shaped points represent water pumps. As the previous recipe, lines sign in for London streets.

Getting ready

We stick with the `HistData` package requirement:

```
> if( !require(HistData)){ install.packages('HistData')}
```

Once it is installed we can proceed to the plotting.

How to do it...

We start creating interactive map as follows:

1. Load packages to be used and initialize the `plotly` object:

```
> library(HistData); library(plotly)
> plot_ly(data = Snow.streets, type = 'scatter') %>%
group_by(street) %>%
```

2. Use `add_lines()` to draw the streets:

```
>   add_lines(x = ~x, y = ~y, hoverinfo = 'none',
        line = list(color = 'rgba(0, 0, 0, 1)'), showlegend = F) %>%
```

3. Rely on `add_markers()` to draw points related to each death caused by cholera:

```
>   add_markers(data = Snow.deaths, x = ~x, y = ~y, hoverinfo =
'none',
        marker = list(symbol = 0, size = 4, color = 'rgba(153, 0, 0,
1)'),
        name = 'cholera\ndeath') %>%
```

4. `add_markers` are also used to deploy points for water pumps:

```
>   add_markers(data = Snow.pumps, x = ~x, y = ~y,
        hoverinfo = 'text', text = ~label,
        marker = list(symbol = 2, size = 10, color = 'rgba(0, 0, 153,
1)'),
        name = 'water\npump') %>%
```

5. The proper use of `layout()` can hide the axis and add a title:

```
> layout(xaxis = list(visible = F), yaxis = list(visible = F),
title = '1854 London')
```

This final step leads to the following map (Figure 6.2) to be plotted:

Figure 6.3: John Snow's cholera map

Let's understand what happened.

How it works...

After loading `HistData` and `plotly` packages, step 1 initializes the `plotly` object using `plot_ly()` and additionally groups data using the `group_by()` function. This way, lines to represent streets can be easily drawn by the `add_lines()` function, yet not summoned.

Step 2 stacks `add_lines()` function. Inside this function, `hoverinfo = 'none'` demands that no information shall be displayed when the mouse is hovered, legends are hidden by setting argument `showlegend` to false, while color was picked by the `line` argument.

The `line` argument is able to adjust several parameters; we attained ourselves to `color`, nonetheless it should be declared inside a `list()` function. Colors were named after the RGBA system, which is the regular RGB system (Red, Green, Blue) plus a number representing alpha, so it is really RED-GREEN-BLUE-ALPHA.

Step 3 finally draw points in the map for each cholera death by the location it happened--the `add_markers()` function fulfilled this mission. Notice that this function uses another data frame: `Snow.deaths`. Hover information was removed. Several parameters were manually picked as `symbol`, `size`, and `color`. All these were set inside a `list()` declared at `marker` argument. The `name` argument is meant to set legend labels.

Step 4 also relies on `add_makers()` and requests a new data frame, `Snow.pumps`. Now hover information is selected as `'text'`; the `text` argument was picked after the data frame column named `label`, which designates each water pump name. Again, the `marker` argument is used in order to manually pick `symbol`, `size`, and `color` for these points. The `name` argument is also set.

Step 5 summons the `layout()` function to hide the axes and add a title. Similar to `line` and `makers` arguments, `xaxis` and `yaxis` has parameters assigned inside a `list()`, both set `visible` to false (F or FALSE). This is similar to call `theme_void()` while using `ggplot2`. Afterward, `title` receives a string that stands for the proper title.

Important to remember that the original output is actually interactive, so it's possible to hover the mouse around and get the names of each water pump. Although `plotly` is in many ways different from `ggplot2`, it's not hard to figure out how a similar plot could be made using the last--try it as an exercise.

Crafting choropleth maps using ggplot2

Choropleths are thematic maps, usually colored according to a third continuous variable. This recipe demonstrates how to brew these using `ggplot2`. This recipe crafts a choropleth displaying the 1985 USA states' **gross product** (GSP). The way I see it--there are at least four important things to check out from this recipe:

- How to use ggplot2 to get map data
- How to merge map data (coordinates and stuff) and other data in order to plot
- How to use polygons and colors to draw the map and make a choropleth
- How to manipulate the guide color bar

To the job!

Getting ready

Besides `ggplot2`, we need some data coming from `Ecdat`, and `dplyr` is used to manipulate data. Make sure to have both by running the following:

```
> if( !require(Ecdat)){ install.packages('Ecdat')}
> if( !require(dplyr)){ install.packages('dplyr')}
```

Let's roll.

How to do it...

Let us start with the choropleth:

1. `ggplot2` has a function called `map_data()`, which is just what we need to a create data frame with desired coordinates:

   ```
   > library(ggplot2)
   > us_map <- map_data('state')
   ```

2. Data about production comes from the `Ecdat` package; load the package and store data:

   ```
   > library(Ecdat)
   > us_prod <- Produc[Produc$year == 1985,]
   ```

3. Create a new column called `region`, whose name convention must match the one found at `us_map` data frame (all lowercase and space-separated), then use the `dplyr` package to merge coordinates with the `us_prod` data:

   ```
   > us_prod$region <- gsub('_',' ',tolower(us_prod$state))
   > merged_data <-
   dplyr::left_join(us_map,us_prod[,c('region','gsp')],by = 'region')
   ```

4. Combine several `ggplot2` functions to make a neat plot:

   ```
   > choropleth <- ggplot(data = merged_data) +
     geom_polygon(aes(x = long, y = lat, group = group, fill = gsp),
   color = 'black') +
     theme_void() + theme(legend.position = 'bottom') +
     scale_fill_continuous( guide = guide_colorbar(barheight =
   ```

```
unit(2,units = 'mm'),
                                        barwidth = unit(5,units =
'cm')))
> choropleth
```

Following map Figure (6.4) demonstrates the result:

Figure 6.4: 1985 US States GSP

Keep going to understand it.

How it works...

Step 1 uses a `ggplot2` function called `map_data()` to get USA map coordinates. We used it in order to create a data frame suited to plot USA states using `geom_polygon()`; data was stored by the recently created `us_map` object. It still lacks the data holding the GSP.

> `ggplot2::map_data()` is an important function. There are many ways to use it; I recommend you to enter `?map_data()` by the console to get to know it better.

Step 2 brings this data up using the `Ecdat` package and stores it in an object called `us_prod`. Perceive that a selective call was done using brackets--only data from 1985 was stored by this object. This data frame has the US state names but lacks the coordinates required to drawn them.

Pay attention to the name conventions used to tag the states across different data frames. The first one uses all lowercase and space-separated, the second uses all uppercase and underscore-separated. Step 3 deals with this plus merge both data frames together.

It starts by adjusting the name convention. A new column named `region` is created in the `us_prod` data frame. The `gsub()` function is used to replace underscore with spaces while `tolower()` applies lowercase to all letters. Afterward, dplyr's `left_join()` is used to merge `us_prod` with `us_map` data frame.

 Alternatively, the base function `merge()` could had been used to merge the two data frames, but would request some more code afterward because data might need to be reordered right after.

By the end of Step 3, the `merged_data` object is bringing all the needed information together. Although `ggplot2` is capable of stacking different functions using different data frames, this Recipe is going to fit a single geometry function to draw choropleth. Because of this, we need all the information fit the same data frame.

Step 4 actually creates the choropleth and adds some improvement to it. It begins assigning a value to the new object called `choropleth`. By the end, this object will be holding the entire map. The first function called to draw it is `ggplot()`, which initializes the `ggplot` object with the right data already set.

In the sequence, `geom_polygon()` draws the map. Aesthetic arguments have to be named accordingly--x carries the latitude, y the longitude, `group` holds the group given by the `map_data()` function, and `fill` bears the gsp given by the `Ecdat::Produc` data frame. This last aesthetics gives the map the choropleth aspect. Also, `color` is set to `'black'` so borders are signed by this color.

Then, `theme_void()` is used to erase axes and ticks while `theme()` is summoned with the `legend.position` argument declared in order to move legends toward the bottom. Next, `scale_fill_continuous()` is used to make legends longer and thinner at the bottom; not making legends longer would result in labels overlaying one another.

Notice that there is one gray space among the plot--actually two--but the second may be too little to see. This happened because `Ecdat::Produc` did not have observations for two districts: Tennessee and District of Columbia. You can easily notice this with the following code:

```
> setdiff(us_map$region, us_prod$region)
```

This is a useful code to reveal differences across data frames. Next, we will investigate how to zoom in on this map.

Zooming in on the map

If you want to analyze a specific region better, you might want to zoom in on the map. By doing this, a more detailed and better looking map is achieved. It's not hard to take the previous choropleth and zoom it. Although it's easy to obtain such a result, trusting the wrong tools leads to lame outcomes, so it's important to keep it straight.

With this recipe, we will zoom in on the tri-state area (New York, New Jersey, and Connecticut). Besides zooming in, we will outline them by coloring the outer states with grey. For now, go ahead and check the requirements.

Getting ready

This recipe requires the `choropleth` and `merged_data` objects created by the last recipe, *Crafting choropleth using ggplot2*, hence automatically requesting the same requirements from it. Having `ggplot2` installed, the `choropleth` object and `merged_data` in your environment would be enough.

How to do it...

We can zoom into the map as follows:

1. Manipulate data using the `%in%` operator to create data that will help establish coordinates to zoom in and also to set the states' color different from the tri-state:

```
> tri_state <- c('new york','new jersey', connecticut')
> long_lim <- merged_data$long[merged_data$region %in% tri_state]
> lat_ylim <- merged_data$lat[merged_data$region %in% tri_state]
```

2. Once the data is ready, take off from `choropleth` plot and use `coord_fixed()` to zoom in:

```
> library(ggplot2)
> choropleth +
    geom_polygon(data = outer,
                 aes(x = long, y = lat, group = group), fill =
'gray', color = 'black') +
    coord_fixed(xlim = c(min(long_lim),max(long_lim)),
                ylim = c(min(lat_lim),max(lat_lim)),
                ratio = 1.3)
```

The map coming from this code will look like the following one (Figure 6.5):

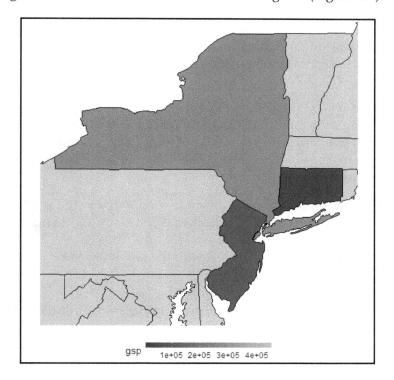

Figure 6.5: Zooming the Tri-State area

Besides zooming in, it also highlighted the tri-states by filling all the other ones gray. Proceed to the explanation.

How it works...

The first step deals with data manipulation. It starts by creating a vector (`tri_states`) with all the states within the chosen tri-state area (New York, New Jersey, and Connecticut); all of them following data set name convention (lowercase, space-separated). Not storing this vector into an object could work as well, but would make the code less readable and request more hand-work.

The same code block creates a vector with boundary longitudes (`long_lim`) for the tri-state area and the other vector with latitudes (`lat_lim`). These will be used later to delimitate the zoom area. A data frame (`outer`) containing data only for states diverse from the tri-state area was created--its purpose is to highlight the tri-states by drawing grey polygons (states) around them.

Step 2 begins by loading `ggplot2`. Next, it takes off from the `choropleth` object while the proximate function uses the `outer` dataset to fill other states with gray and, by doing this, highlights the tri-states area. The next layer is `coord_fixed()`, arguments `xlim` and `ylim` respectively account for the longitude and latitude limits. Notice how vectors `long_lim` and `lat_lim` were used to set limits.

This same layer also relies on another argument, `ratio`. By picking 1.3, this argument asks for the latitude: longitude ratio to stand still, always following 1:3, no matter the fuzz we made. This scaling feels fine and setting `coord_fixed( ratio = 1.3)` after a map is sometimes a good practice. Try your console with the following code:

```
> choropleth + coord_fixed(1.3)
```

Don't you agree that this is a prettier result than calling `choropleth` alone? Needless to name the argument, `ratio` is the first function argument. If you're calling in the right order, there is no necessity to name arguments, the reason I almost always do is to make code more readable. Next, we're sailing for the projection types, a subject related to map projection types.

See also

- The *Crafting choropleth maps using ggplot2* recipe

Creating different maps based on different map projection types

If you go back to Figure 6.4 (recipe *Crafting choropleth maps using ggplot2, How to do it...* section), several aspects from the map feel right, others might feel funny. This happened because the scale used was unusual; to be honest, scales were free and ruled by figure aspect ratio along with data. Ratio is related to the projection type--it's a source of distortion--and there are ways to set it stone still, one (not the best) already introduced at the end of the previous recipe .

This recipe's intention is to teach you how one or another projection type can be selected. Speaking about ggplot2, it has a whole function dedicated to this purpose. Projection types can widely vary and we are again taking off from the results obtained by the *Crafting choropleth maps using ggplot2* recipe.

Although fully understanding maps, scales, projections, and symbolization may seem complicated (yet very important), picking (and not choosing) one or another after the hard work is done is actually a very easy task--check how easy it actually is.

Getting ready

This recipe relies on the choropleth object created in the recipe *Crafting choropleth maps using ggplot2* to run smoothly. Make sure that it's loaded in your environment, otherwise, you might want to go back and run that recipe again.

How to do it...

We start the recipe as follows:

1. Use theme() to center align titles and subtitles coming out from the choropleth plot:

```
> library(ggplot2)
> choropleth <- choropleth + theme(plot.title = element_text(hjust
= .5),
                                    plot.subtitle =
element_text(hjust = .5))
```

2. Summon `coord_map()` to set the mercator projection:

```
> choropleth + coord_map() +
    ggtitle('US Map - mercator projection')
```

Following map (Figure 6.6) fits the mercator projection:

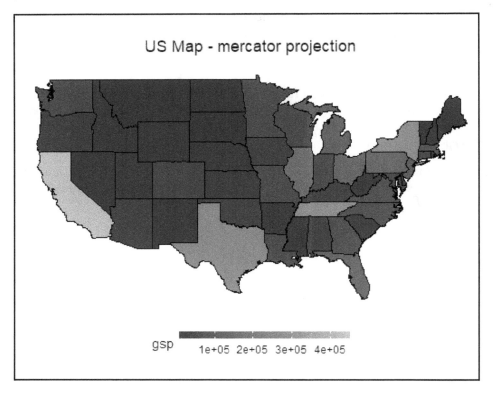

Figure 6.6: Choropleth adopting the mercator projection

3. Set `coord_map()`'s `projection` argument to choose a different map projection:

```
> choropleth + coord_map(projection = 'gilbert') +
    ggtitle('US Map - gilbert projection')
```

4. Conic projection also requires the latitude zero (`lat0`) to be informed:

```
> choropleth + coord_map(projection = 'conic', lat0 = 50) +
    labs(title = 'US Map - conic projection',
        subtitle = 'latitude zero = 50')
```

Conic projection feels very different from the mercator projection:

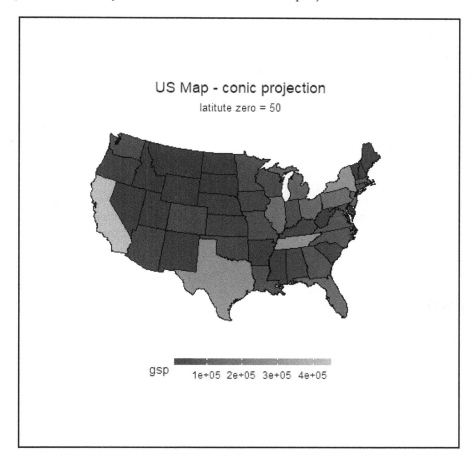

Figure 6.7: Choropleth made out using conic projection with latitude zero set for 50

Can you tell which states do benefit from each projection? Let's see how these unfolded.

How it works...

Step 1 simply alters the `choropleth` object with respect to the title and subtitle alignment. Using the `theme()` function, upcoming titles and subtitles may be now center-aligned instead of the default left-aligned. All the subsequently steps rely on `coord_map()` to pick the projections and `ggtitle()` or `labs()` functions to display an informative titles and subtitles.

Step 2 demonstrates that, by default, `coord_map()` adopts the mercator projection. Step 3 shows you how to adopt a different projection type; the `projection` argument is actually the first so there is no need to explicitly name it, inputting the string as the first argument is enough.

Step 4 shows you that some projections request extra arguments--those arguments highly influence the result so be careful about them. To know better about the map projections available enter the following code:

```
> ?mapproj::mapproject
```

This will lead you toward a more complete list with a handful of details on how each of them work. Picking the right projection is a very serious matter, there is no such thing as an even better projection and a bunch may satisfy your needs but a couple may be misleading and picking one of those means disaster.

See also

- The Crafting choropleth maps using ggplot2 recipe
- Check Rudis's (demi-god among mortals) talking about map projections' importance and how to handle them with R at https://rud.is/b/2015/07/24/a-path-towards-easier-map-projection-machinations-with-ggplot2/

Handling shapefiles to map Afghanistan health facilities

This recipe is wonderful because it's teaching so many things at once. The main goal is to teach you how to read and handle shapefiles. Additionally it also teaches how to download files directly from the console, how to create temporary files and directories, and reinforce the use of polygons and points to draw maps using `ggplot2`.

A little disclaimer: this code is big. However, do not feel intimidated by it, there is much to learn from this recipe. Much of it is not restricted to maps, it can be generalized to the handling of web-available data. Relying on data available on the internet makes your codes more reproducible and less local-file dependent. Upload your data and code. Tet the community help out. Now let's plot Afghanistan districts and highlight health facilities.

Getting ready

Make sure to have an internet connection. This is a not only a requirement for the packages we may need to install but also to get that. That will be downloaded directly from the console (that rocks). For this particular recipe, besides `ggplot2`, we require two other packages, `rgdal` to read shapefiles, and `broom` to turn sp objects into data frames:

```
> if( !require(rgdal)){ install.packages('rgdal')}
> if( !require(broom)){ install.packages('broom')}
```

If any of those packages are missing, above code will look after them.

How to do it...

Let us get working on the shapefiles:

1. Create a temporary file and directory to handle the downloads:

```
> url1 <-
'http://www.mapcruzin.com/afghanistan-shapefiles/district-boundarie
s.zip'
> url2 <-
'http://www.mapcruzin.com/afghanistan-shapefiles/health-facilities.
zip'
> tmp_file <- tempfile()
> tmp_dir <- tempdir()
```

2. Download and unzip the shapefiles them into the temporary directory:

```
> download.file(url1,tmp_file)
> unzip(tmp_file,exdir = tmp_dir)
> download.file(url2,tmp_file)
> unzip(tmp_file,exdir = tmp_dir)
```

2. Read shapefiles using the rgdal package:

```
> library(rgdal)
> districts <- readOGR(dsn = tmp_dir, layer = 'admin3_poly_32')
> health <- readOGR(dsn = tmp_dir, layer = 'all_bphs')
```

3. Load broom to turn sp objects into data frames and ggplot2 to draw the map. Also store an element_rect object :

```
> library(broom)
> library(ggplot2)
> bg <- element_rect(fill = 'lightgray')
```

4. Use polygons and points to draw the map:

```
> ggplot() +
    geom_polygon(data = tidy(districts),
            aes(x = long, y = lat, group = group),
            color = 'white', fill = 'lightblue', size = .1) +
    geom_point(data = data.frame(health@coords),
            aes(x = coords.x1, y = coords.x2),
            color = 'red', shape = 3) +
    theme_bw() +
    theme(panel.background = bg) +
    labs(title = 'Afganisthan\'s Health Facilities',
        subtitle ='source: www.mapcruzin.com')
```

The following plot (Figure 6.8) bears final output:

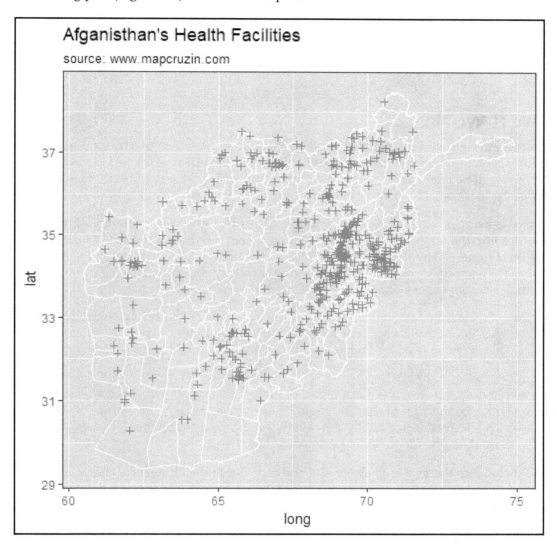

Figure 6.8 Afghanistan map made using ggplot2 (Publication year = 2000)

5. Delete the temporary files and directories:

```
> unlink(tmp_file, recursive = T)
> unlink(tmp_dir, recursive = T)
```

Now for the explanations.

How it works...

Do not feel intimidated by the lengthy code, we got this. Step 1 begins by storing the URLs that directs you toward the .zip archives holding the shapefiles. If you try to navigate these URLs you will be taken to MapCruzin website from which we got the shapefiles from. Temporary file (`tmp_file`) and directory (`tmp_dir`) were created to hold the data later.

Step two is using `download.file()` and `unzip()` functions to respectively download the shapefiles into the temporary file and then unzip them into the temporary directory.There are several reasons why this recipe done this way. Mainly, it does not touch the browser to do what we want to, secondly, it's not working directory dependent, so it's easier to reproduce and also does not stack your HD with data you may not miss later.

 Having data in a temporary file is not a safe approach. I personally advise you to have a secure protocol for data, at least for important data. It's good to have labeling / naming / filing conventions and good practices going on. Backup protocols are also well advised.

If we were reading from a .csv file, neither directory would be needed nor a temporary file. A simple open connection to the file would be enough, but due to the nature of shapefiles the easier way to read is to actually download the .zip archive. Shapefiles (`.shp`) sometimes require more than one file to be properly read.

Step 3 introduces the `rgdal` package, the one carrying the reading task. The `readOGR()` function does this. The `dsn` argument receives the path toward the shapefiles (and all the other related files); the `layers` argument displays the filename without the extension.

Step 4 is loading `broom` and `ggplot2` package. The first one will lend `tidy()` function to turn `districts` object into a data frame. The second one will be used to draw the map. This same step is creating and storing an `element_rect` object called `bg`. Later this object will be used as a kind of shortcut to paint the map background with gray.

Step 5 is drawing the map. Function `geom_polygon()` is used to draw Afghanistan districts. Health facilities are draw with `geom_point()`. Additionally, a nicer theme is being picked with `theme_bw()`, `theme()` function is painting the background color and `labs()` is writing title and subtitle. These functions order are very important. Last step is simply deleting the temporary file and directory.

See also

- Game of Thrones fans, feast on these shapefiles: `https://www.cartographersguild.com/showthread.php?t=30472`
- MapCruzin website: `http://www.mapcruzin.com`

Crafting an interactive globe using plotly

Until now, this chapter explored several core points related to mapping. We saw how maps can deliver important information, how paths, polygons, and points can be used to draw maps, how to read shapefiles using nothing but R, and how to set projection types and scales.

Now we will explore the advantages of having interactive maps. Even more than that, the advantages of having interactive globes. This recipe will make a globe that you can spin at will, and it does not request shapefiles at all, though they can be used if needed.

For this particular recipe, we'll be using the `plotly` package to map countries affected by the 2009 banking crisis. On this course, the recipe will introduce you to a whole new way of mapping using `plotly`. Data here is a little different; we will be looking for some columns names instead of actually data frame observations. Now for the requirements.

Getting ready

Data comes from the `Ecdat` package--you know the drill:

```
> if( !require(Ecdat)){ install.packages('Ecdat')}
```

After making sure that data will be available, it's time to plot. Once again, we have a lengthy code but most of it is only properties being set, very standard calls.

How to do it...

Let us craft an interactive globe:

1. Load the `Ecdat` package and the `bakingCrises` data frame, then do a little data manipulating:

```
> library(Ecdat)
> data(bankingCrises)
> row_year <- match(2009,bankingCrises$year)
> countries <- colnames(bankingCrises[,bankingCrises[row_year,] ==
1])
```

2. Preset some properties in the form of lists for later use:

```
> axis_props <- list(
  showgrid = T, gridcolor = toRGB("gray40"), gridwidth = 0.5
 )
> globe <- list(
  showland = T, showlakes = T, showcountries = T, showocean = T,
  countrywidth = 0.5,
  landcolor = toRGB("grey90"),
  lakecolor = toRGB("white"),
  oceancolor = toRGB("white"),
  projection = list(
    type = 'orthographic',
    rotation = list(
      lon = -100, lat = 40, roll = 0
  ),
  lonaxis = axis_props,
  lataxis = axis_props
  )
 )
```

3. Use the `plot_geo()` function to plot the geography:

```
> library(plotly)
> plot_geo(width = 528, height = 528, locationmode = 'country
names') %>%
    add_trace(locations = ~countries, showscale = F, z = 1,
    hoverinfo = 'text', text = ~countries) %>%
    layout(geo = globe)
```

If you are using the GUI, the result will be displayed as an HTML page; for RStudio users, click on the **Show in the new window** icon by the **Viewer** tab to see it. A static representation is as follows:

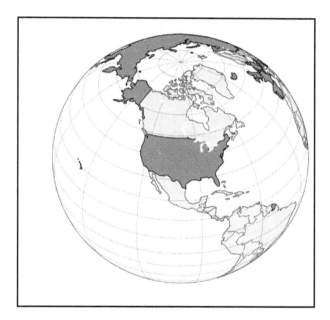

Figure 6.9: Globe with countries affected by 2009 banking crises

The actual plot is much cooler. You can drag the mouse to spin the globe, do a barrel roll, and stuff like that. By hovering the mouse, it shows the country name. Head to the explanations.

How it works...

Data manipulation is done in Step 1. It begins by loading the `Ecdat` package, from which the `bankingCrises` data frame comes. The `data()` function loads the frame. This data frame holds a column for years, ranging from 1985 to 2010, other columns are named after countries; for each one, the number 0 is displayed if it wasn't affected by the crises that year and 1 otherwise.

In order to find out what is the row for year 2009, the `match()` function was used and the value found stored in the `row_year` object. Following line uses `colname()` function to get columns' name that hold the number 1 for the row 210, in other words, countries affected by the banking crises of 2009. These names were stored into a vector called `countries`. Dot not miss all the operations under the brackets, they are very important.

Step 2 sets up a series of properties that will culminate on the globe projection type. These are pretty standard calls, fitting the `list()` format always; if there are any doubts, follow plot.ly/r/reference to the reference manual. The third step draws the globe.

In step 3, the first function called after `library()` is `plot_geo()`, which is very similar to `plot_ly()`. This recipe trusts a vector as data and not an actual data frame, so the `data` argument is not called. Instead, it called `width` and `height` arguments. These were picked for the book's requirement; you can set another one or even erase those and wait for the default sizes to come.

Notice the `locationmode` argument, inputted with `'country names'`. This is analogous to the `plot_ly()` mode argument and allows you to plot countries based on names, exempting the need for shapefiles and/or coordinates. The same argument could be called in the next function (`add_traces()`) instead.

The first argument named in `add_traces()` was `locations`, input with the vector `countries`. Scales were hidden by setting `showscale` to false (`F`). In order to color these countries, the number one was picked after the `z` argument; any constant would do it--it's a choropleth with a single value, hence a single color.

Afterward, `hoverinfo = 'text'` demands that only text is displayed when the mouse is hovered over those countries, text is signalized by the `text` argument.
Finally, `layout()` functions describes just the globe that we want, using the presets designed in Step 2.

Creating high quality maps

The previous chapters drew a series of aspects that should be taken care of in the way of making publishable plots and all these aspects felt very similar to one another. This won't be true for maps. Maps require a set of different aspects to be taken care of. For example, scatter, bar, and point plots might require bigger axes to make them publishable. Maps usually requires axes to be erased! Let's walk through the most important points before actually making it happen:

- Set a pretty color scale with intuitive breaks
- Relocate and customize legends
- Occupy the margins by selecting a projection type

This recipe's goal is to draw a publication quality choropleth carrying the same idea from the map made by recipe *Creating choropleth maps using ggplot2*. To the job!

Getting ready

This recipe takes off from the `merged_data` data frame made by recipe *Creating choropleth maps using ggplot2*:

```
> library(ggplot2)
> us_map <- map_data('state')
> library(Ecdat)
> us_prod <- Produc[Produc$year == 1985,]
> us_prod$region <- gsub('_',' ',tolower(us_prod$state))
> merged_data <- dplyr::left_join(us_map,us_prod[,c('region','gsp')],by =
'region')
```

Make sure that the `viridis` package is installed:

```
> if( !require(viridis)){ install.packages('viridis')}
```

Time to turn data into a map.

How to do it...

Let us get on with high quality maps:

1. Draw the basic map:

```
> library(ggplot2)
> h1 <- ggplot(data = merged_data) +
    geom_polygon(aes(x = long, y = lat, group = group, fill = gsp),
                 color = 'black') + theme_void()
```

2. Prepare objects to set legends' colors, breaks, labels, and bar size:

```
> clrs <- rev(viridis::magma(8))
> brks <- c(0,10000,seq(100000,500000,100000))
> lbls <- format(brks, nsmall = 2, big.mark = ',', scientific = F)
> bar <- guide_colorbar(barheight = unit(4,units = 'cm'),
                        barwidth = unit(2,units = 'mm'))
```

3. Use these objects to define a new gradient scale and resize the legend bar:

```
> h2 <- h1 + scale_fill_gradientn(colors = clrs, breaks = brks,
labels = lbls,
                                  guide = bar, name = 'GSP (US$)')
```

4. Pick a projection type, add an informative title, and move the legends inside the map:

```
> h3 <- h2 + coord_map() +
    labs(title = 'Gross State Product (GSP) - 1985',
         subtitle = 'United States of America') +
    theme(legend.position = c(.9,.1),
          text = element_text(face = 'bold'),
          plot.title = element_text(hjust = .5),
          plot.subtitle = element_text(hjust = .5))
> h3
```

The final result looks like the following illustration:

Figure 6.10: Improved quality map

Let's see how it was done.

How it works...

The first step draws a very simple map. You can glance at it by typing h1. The only bit of good practice comes from theme_void(), responsible for hiding axes. Afterwards, step 2 creates a series of new objects, each one taking care of one aspect of the about-to-come new gradient scale. The viridis package is called to draw the colors following the magma preset;rev() is used to make sure that darker colors represent greater GSP.

Step 3 actually implements the gradient scale change using `scale_fill_gradientn()`. It uses the magma set of colors coming from the `viridis` package but there are a bunch of others available, plus you can make your own scale by growing a vector of your choice and inputting it in the `colors` argument.

Another important change is done by the guide argument. It uses a `bar` object, which was created using `guide_colorbar()`, and sets the measures displayed by the legend color bar. Height was set for four centimeters while width was for two mm. The subsequent step has lots of changes.

It begins by picking mercator projection (`coord_map()`). The title and subtitle are added by the `labs()` function. Afterward, `theme()` conducts a bunch of changes. It relocates the legends to the inside of the map, sets all text to bold, and center-aligns both title and subtitle.

Important to highlight that these are very minimum to give away a publishable map. These minimum might widely vary depending on your necessity--there may be the need for other settings, other projection types, other color scale--it's not a recipe for bulletproof publishable map but more like a guide to what can be done.

See also

- To make even better maps, consult `https://timogrossenbacher.ch/2016/12/beautiful-thematic-maps-with-ggplot2-only`

- Learn more about making maps with R at `https://github.com/Robinlovelace/Creating-maps-in-R`

- There is also this good site for references: `http://spatial.ly/`

- Recipe *Creating choropleth maps using ggplot2*

This section carried the ways of maps. A very cool and good way to display spatial-related data. Next, we have a meeting with facets. This is a very powerful tool and can be combined with all that we've seen until now.

7
Faceting

This chapter will cover the following recipes:

- Creating a faceted bar graph
- Crafting faceted histograms
- Creating a facet box plot
- Crafting a faceted line plot
- Making faceted scatterplots
- Creating faceted maps
- Drawing facets using plotly
- Plotting a high quality faceted bar graph

Introduction

For the ones that already know faceting, there is no need to explain why they are important or what they do. For those not yet acknowledged, faceting is separating complex relations into more simple and visible ones. Think of it like the Christopher Columbus of data exploration, launching you to places (insights) you never wondered about.

A faceting grid splits a single bivariate relation into several ones displayed with respect to the interactions of some others categories. That's incredible because as the early chapters mentioned, the bivariate relations area much easier to understand. This way insights usually comes more frequently when complex problems are tackled with facets.

It's essential to outline that though facets help understand more complex relations, they aren't a device to deploy every single time. Still, if facets are required, ggplot2 supports it in a way that is very easy to understand and create those. Although by the end of 2017, there was no sight of ggvis doing something similar, for most cases, it's possible to convert a ggplot facet into plotly, hence achieving interactivity.

Creating a faceted bar graph

This recipe will create a faceted bar graph using the Titanic dataset. This particular set comes from base R packages, but it's not a data frame. To plot this data using ggplot2, we first need to to coerce this object to a data frame. Recipe will introduce the faceting function.

The goal here is to make a plot showing how many people survived and how many died in the Titanic tragedy. Facets are used to split this analysis both by gender (male and female) and age range (child or adult). There are no prior requirements other than ggplot2 and plotly packages installed.

How to do it...

This section shows you how to create a faceted bar graph:

1. Coerce the Titanic table to the data frame type:

    ```
    > data_titanic <- as.data.frame(Titanic)
    ```

2. Load ggplot2, design a bar graph, and add the facets using face_grid() function:

    ```
    > library(ggplot2)
    > bar <- ggplot(data_titanic, aes(x = Survived)) +
      geom_bar(aes(fill = Survived, weight = Freq)) +
      facet_grid(Sex ~ Age)
    ```

3. Check the result by calling the object storing the plot:

    ```
    > bar
    ```

Output might look much like the following illustration (Figure 7.1):

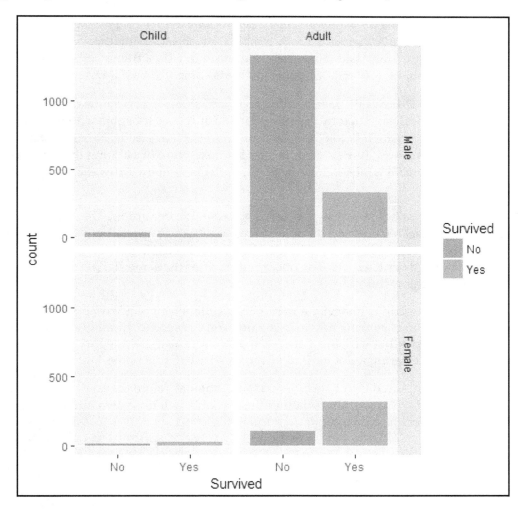

Figure 7.1 - Faceted bar graph, Titanic survivals based on age range and gender.

4. Also, the `plotly` package could be called to achieve an interactive version of it:

```
> plotly::ggplotly(bar)
```

Carry on to the explanations.

How it works...

The first step is conducting a simple data coercion. If one does try `class(Titanic)`, it will come out that this particular data is actually a table type object. Using the `as.data.frame()` function, the table was then coerced to a data frame and stored into the `data_titanic` object. ggplot2 requires that data come from a data frame.

In the sequence, step 2 draws the faceted bar graph and stores it into a new object called `bar`. The plot is designated by several chained functions. It begins with `ggplot()` initializing the `ggplot` which holds the data frame and the x aesthetic. Next, the bar geometry is added by `geom_bar()`. Argument `fill` takes care of painting the bars based on the `Survival` variable while `weight` argument tells how many cases each bin must carry.

These would be the basics of brewing a colored side-by-side bar graph. The `facet_grid()` function was then stacked, creating the facets. This function is supplied with the variables ruling the facets. The variable inputted before the ~ signal is used to determine the categories displayed as grid's rows. The one inputted after the same signal sets the category displayed as grid's columns.

As the final result, the grid is given by a matrix that, unless we specify otherwise, has the same number of columns as there are unique values on the second variable and many rows as unique values on the first variable. Facets can also show a single category, which can be handled by simply declaring a dot instead of some other variable name.

Taking the ~ signal inputted into `facet_grid()` function as reference point, the side which a variable is inputted will determine whether this variable will be shown as a facet row or a facet column.To understand it better, try the following code:

```
> ggplot(data_titanic, aes(x = Survived)) +
        geom_bar(aes(fill = Survived, weight = Freq)) +
        facet_grid( . ~ Age )
```

Above code will display a faceted bar graph with the age range values splitting the plot into columns and no variable splitting the plot rows, just like the following figure (Figure 7.2):

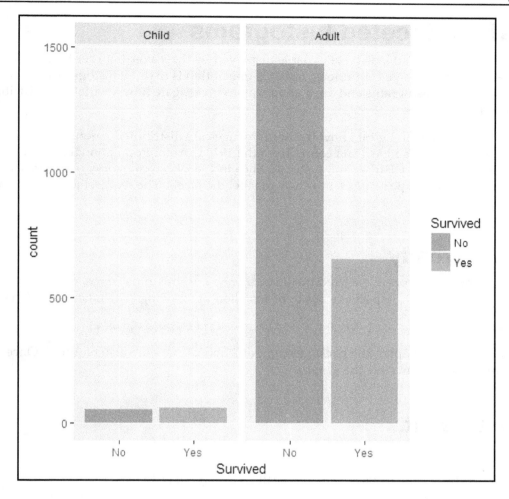

Figure 7.2 - Titanic survivals based on age range.

Finally, the last step draws an interactive faceted bar graph by simply inputting the previously created object (`bar`) into `plotly`'s `ggplotly()` function. Notice how the recipe choose to call the single function without loading the whole package using the `<package>::<function()>` syntax. The next recipe delivers facets to histograms.

Crafting faceted histograms

The previous recipe had a discrete variable displayed by the x axis. In order to turn ourselves toward a single continuous variable, one option is to draw histograms. Facets are also available for histograms and are a good way to investigate how a variable is distributed across some categories.

For this recipe, we will dig into how the hourly wages are distributed among men and women, married and single. Data comes from the 1976 Current Population Survey. Data was collected by Henry Farber and Justin M. Shea in 1988. Both categories are represented by binaries so this recipe brings a new way to label the facets. The requirements department lies ahead.

Getting ready

In order to make it happen, we need the `wooldridge::wage1` data frame, which is another way to say, "`wooldridge` package has to be installed". Following code takes care of that:

```
> if( !require(wooldridge)){ install.packages('wooldridge') }
```

As is usual for this chapter, the packages `ggplot2` and `plotly` are also required. Once these are ready, we can code the graphs.

How to do it...

We proceed as follows:

1. Draw a regular histogram, then call `facet_grid()` to facet it:

```
> library(ggplot2)
> hist <- ggplot(data = wooldridge::wage1) +
    geom_histogram(aes(x = wage), binwidth = 2) +
    facet_grid( married ~ female, labeller = label_both)
> hist
```

Once the `hist` object is called, the result may look like the following one:

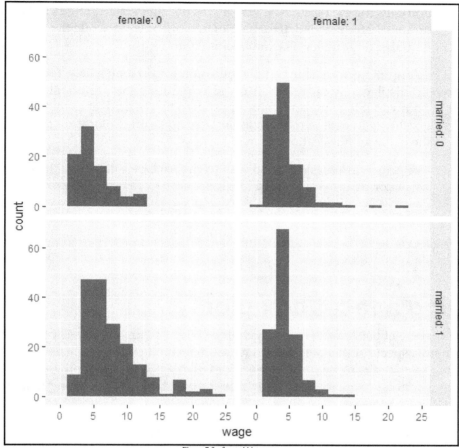

Figure 7.3 - faceted histogram.

2. Use `ggplotly()` to coerce it to a `plotly` interactive graph:

```
> plotly::ggplotly(hist)
```

Next section explains how `labeller` argument works.

How it works...

Step number 1 draws the faceted histogram and stores it on an object called `hist`. The `geom_histogram()` function was called in order to make a histogram out from the data set. As our faceted figure is also a histogram, the same principles discussed previously do apply--picking the proper `binwidth` (or `bins`)is essential to achieve a good result.

The next function calls for the facets. The way it was designated, `facet_grid()` made the `married` variable (1 for married, 0 for single) to work as rows while the `female` variable (1 for females, 0 for males) is exhibited as columns.

If the `labeller` argument were skipped, the outcome would look a little bit confusing as grid rows would display only the numbers 0 and 1. By filling this argument with `label_both`, both variable name and value are shown by the grid labels at the same time. This is a very good way to deal with them in order to make an exploratory figure; however, it does not fit the needs of publication figures.

 Factoring variables is a good way to choose labels displayed by the grid. By factoring categories, grid labels are set before factor labels.

Step 2 simply conducts the `plotly` conversion. The `ggplot` object named `hist` is coerced into a `plotly` figure.

Creating a facet box plot

With faceting tools at hand, we will now give the `car::Salaries` data frame a better look. There are many aspects of this particular data set that stood out in the analysis made at previous chapters. In this recipe, a facet box plot will be crafted. We shall use `ranks` and `discipline` variables to create facets. Variables `sex` and `salary` are going to fit respectively the *x* and *y* axes.

Variable `discipline` is assigned with A for theoretical departments and B for applied ones, so this recipe will also teach how to relabel these in order to make it intuitive.

How to do it...

Let us now create a facet box plot:

1. Store data into a new object and factor `discipline` properly:

```
> library(car)
> data_box <- Salaries
> data_box$discipline <- factor(data_box$discipline, labels =
c('theoretical','applied'))
```

2. Craft a box plot and call `facet_grid()`:

```
> library(ggplot2)
> boxplot <- ggplot(data = data_box) +
    geom_boxplot(aes( x = sex, y = salary), position = 'identity') +
    facet_grid(rank ~ discipline)
> boxplot
```

The resulting plot is similar to the following one (Figure 7.4):

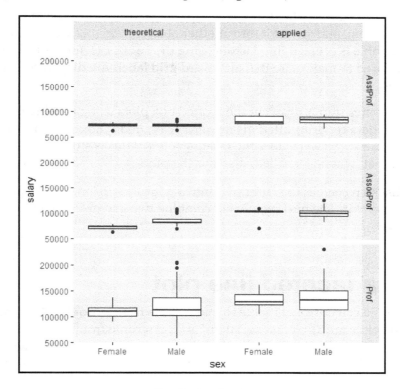

Figure 7.4 - Faceted boxplot.

3. Coerce it using `ggplotly()` if there is the need for interactivity:

```
> plotly::ggplotly(boxplot)
```

Let's see how this played out.

How it works...

To begin with, Step 1 starts by loading the `car` package, from which the data frame `Salaries` comes from, and stored it into another object (`data_boxplot`). Then the `discipline` variable is coerced into factors using the `factor()` function. The `labels` argument is declared to make sure that afterward grid labels are displayed in a more intuitive manner.

In the sequence comes step 2, drawing the faceted box plots using nothing but `ggplot2`. The manipulated data set is inputted inside `ggplot()`, `geom_boxplot()` calls for box geometry while `facet_grid()` does the faceting job. All this is stored into a `ggplot` object called `boxplot` that, whenever called, displays the plot.

As usual, the last step coerces the latter plot into a `plotly` version, thus making an interactive one out of it. The next recipe will combine two geometry functions to create a faceted line figure.

Crafting a faceted line plot

As long as there is a categorical variable to make facets from it, `ggplot2` might able to pull it. That said, line plots are also contemplated. Lines can come from `geom_lines()`, `geom_path()`, and also `geom_smooth()`. For this particular example, we will use the last one to craft a faceted line plot.

This recipe digs the relation between education (expressed in years) and wages (represented by hourly earnings). To enhance analysis, facets are deployed to contrast these aspects across single and married males and females. This result is achieved by combining our beloved `ggplot2` along with data coming from the `wooldridge` package.

Getting ready

Make sure to have the `wooldridge` package installed:

```
> if( !require(wooldridge)){ install.packages('wooldridge')}
```

Data frame is named `wage1`; a good way to get to know it is by typing `?wage1` in the console once the package is properly loaded. Now you're ready to plot.

How to do it...

Let us now start with crafting a faceted line plot:

1. Load the package and set `geom_point()` and `geom_smooth()` to describe a tendency:

```
> library(ggplot2)
> lines <- ggplot(data = wooldridge::wage1,
                  aes(x = educ, y = wage)) +
  geom_point(alpha = .2) +
  geom_smooth(se = F, size = 2) +
  facet_grid(female ~ married, labeller = label_both)
> lines
```

Here is the output of the preceding code:

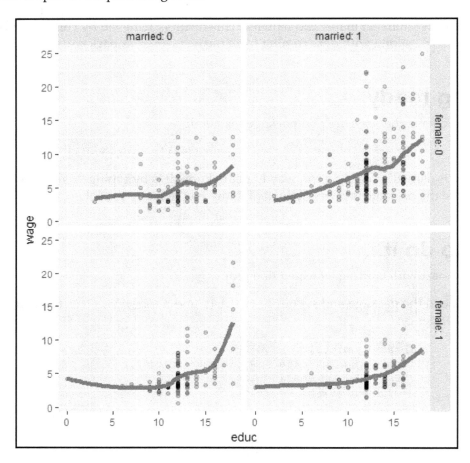

Figure 7.5 - faceted lines graph.

2. The `plotly` coercion is available:

```
> plotly::ggplotly(lines)
```

How it works...

Data frame `wage1` holds 526 observations on 24 variables. One will agree that a simple plot hardly grasps important aspects; facets device deepens the analysis. Step 1 draws the whole plot and stores it in an object called `lines`. As usual, it begins with the use of `ggplot()`, holding data and aesthetics to pass on to adjacent layers.

Immediately, the next step shows the `geom_point()` function with `alpha` set to 0.2. Whenever plotting any kind of trend it's usually well advised to show the points from which the trend originate from. Next, `geom_smooth()` draws the tendency using the loess method. The `se = F` argument removes the confidence interval while `size` makes lines thicker.

Finally, `facet_grid()` makes the facets. By declaring `label_both` as `labeller`, both value and variable are displayed by the grid label. The `female` variable holds the number 1 to female observations and 0 to male. The `married` variable shows 1 to married ones and 0 to non-married. Afterward, `lines` is called into the console to exhibit the result.

 To create your own `labeller` function and input it as `labeller` is also a possibility. Do not forget to not include parenthesis when naming your function into the `labeller` argument by `facet_grid()` function.

The last step simply coerces the `static` illustration into a `plotly` interactive figure. The `ggplotly()` function pulls the tricks very well here.

There is more

There are several types of lines available and it's always good to know them and how data will behave whenever presented to one of them. This recipe intended to draw a tendency line that suited the data presented--a point dispersion. The `geom_line()` function will draw lines between the coordinates but only after ordering it by the x variable. `geom_path()` does about the same but obeys the order given by data without ordering it, which makes it perfect to draw maps (coasts, boundaries, and so on).

Important to outline that faceting lines is always an alternative to plotting a whole bunch of lines all together. Sometimes, too many of them creates an incredible fuzz. Next, we will see how to make a faceted scatterplot.

Making faceted scatterplots

It's not hard to figure out how a faceted scatterplot can be drawn using the previous recipe just by skipping one single function (geom_smooth()). Nonetheless, this recipe is sailing outer seas while investigating heights (centimeters) and weights (kilos) coming from Australian athletes of different sports and categories.

In order to accomplish this, we're relying on the DAAG::ais data set. To avoid the excess of information, the analysis is narrowed, contemplating a few sports only, not all the ones present in this data frame.

Getting ready

Look out for the DAAG package:

```
> if( !require(DAAG) ){ install.packages('DAAG') }
```

Once it's installed, the recipe can go on.

How to do it...

Let us start with making faceted scatterplot:

1. Store the data frame in a new variable and narrow it down:

   ```
   > data_sport <- DAAG::ais
   > sports <- c('B_Ball','Field','Row','T_400m')
   > data_sport <- data_sport[data_sport$sport %in% sports,]
   ```

2. Draw a scatterplot as usual and sum the facet_grid() layer:

   ```
   > library(ggplot2)
    scatter <- ggplot(data_sport) +
      geom_point(aes(x = ht, y = wt), alpha = .4) +
      facet_grid(sex ~ sport)
    scatter
   ```

This is the resulting figure:

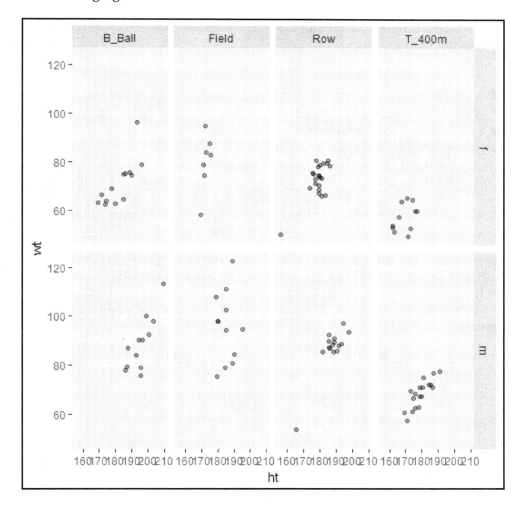

Figure 7.6 - Australian athletes height versus weight.

3. Coerce to `plotly`:

```
> plotly::ggplotly(scatter)
```

How it works...

The very first step addresses data manipulation. The data frame `ais` coming from the DAAG package is stored into this new variable, `data_sport`. Variables later called by this recipe are as follows:

- `ht`: Athlete height in centimeters
- `wt`: Athlete weight in kilos
- `sex`: A factor holding two levels, f for female and m for male
- `sport`: 10 level-factor representing 10 different sports

After storing data into a different object, a vector (`sports`) is created. It holds strings only for the sports that we are going to focus on this recipe -- 10 sports is too much, only 4 were picked. The line after that is actually filtering `data_sports`; only rows having these sports are included into the data frame after running this line.

The next step makes the drawing. The whole plot is stored into an object called `scatter`. Three functions are stacked to form the faceted scatterplot. The first one brings data and initializes the `ggplot`, then `geom_point()` defines the basic aesthetics and adds alpha blending to the points. Finally , `facet_grid()` orders the facets. Calling `scatter` will output the resulting figure.

The *x* axis may look somewhat strange. To solve this, try calling the following:

```
> scatter +
  scale_x_continuous(labels = seq(1.6,2,.2),
                     breaks = seq(160,200,20)) +
  xlab('heigth (meters)')
```

This code block will result in a more neat *x* axis, now representing meters and with a proper label. One could try to deliver some modifications to the *y* axis. A good modification would be to grow more breaks. The final step simply conducts the coercion from the static `ggplot` to the interactivity given by `plotly`. This closes the actual recipe. The next one will draw facets on maps.

Creating faceted maps

Bringing facets to maps will require a little more work with respect to the data manipulation. Departing from the experience handed down by Chapter 6, *Crafting choropleth maps using ggplot2* recipe, this recipe will draw a faceted choropleth containing two years, 1970 and 1986, of US gross states production (gsp).

Basically, what we will need is to have the whole coordinates data frame duplicated, one for each combination given by the facets, in this case only two. This recipe will teach how to manipulate data in order to make faceted maps.

Getting ready

Data is coming from the Ecdat package and dplyr is used to deploy some data manipulation; check whether both are already installed:

```
> if( !require(Ecdat)){ install.packages('Ecdat')}
> if( !require(dplyr)){ install.packages('dplyr')}
```

With these ready, we can manipulate data to create a faceted choropleth.

How to do it...

Creating faceted maps is done as follows:

1. Load ggplot2 and the US map:

```
> library(ggplot2)
> us_map <- map_data('state')
```

2. Load Ecdat and split Produc data by year:

```
> library(Ecdat)
> us_prod1 <- Produc[Produc$year == 1970,]
> us_prod2 <- Produc[Produc$year == 1986,]
```

3. Create matching columns, coerce a naming convention, and merge datasets:

```
> us_prod1$region <- gsub('_',' ',tolower(us_prod1$state))
> us_prod2$region <- gsub('_',' ',tolower(us_prod2$state))
> merged_data1 <- dplyr::left_join(
    us_map,us_prod1[,c('region','gsp','year')],by = 'region')
> merged_data2 <- dplyr::left_join(
    us_map,us_prod2[,c('region','gsp','year')],by = 'region')
```

4. Bind the rows within the merged datasets:

```
> merged_data <- rbind(merged_data1,merged_data2)
```

5. Using the recently merged data, craft and plot the faceted map:

```
> choropleth <- ggplot(data = merged_data[!is.na(merged_data$year),]) +
    geom_polygon(aes(x = long, y = lat, group = group, fill = gsp),
                color = 'grey') +
    facet_wrap(~ year, ncol = 1) + coord_map() + theme_void()
> choropleth
```

Calling `choropleth` will display the final result:

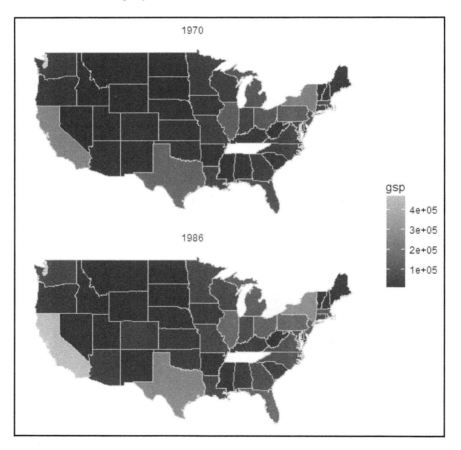

Figure 7.7 - Faceted choropleth.

Let's see how the map is coming out.

How it works...

The recipe begins by loading `ggplot2` and using its `map_data()` function to give birth to a data frame with US states coordinates separated by states (`region`). Step 2 manipulates the `Ecdat::Produc` dataset; after `Ecdat` is loaded, data for the year that equals 1970 is stored into `us_prod1` while `us_prod2` receives data for the year 1986.

Step 3 starts by creating a column named `region` by each of those datasets. The column is named `region` in order to match the `us_map` column name. This column coerces its own `state` column to follow the naming convention displayed by `us_map$region`, all lowercase and space-separated values.

Next, two new data frames are created, `merged_data1` and `merged_data2`. These are created by merging respectively `us_prod1` and `us_prod2` sets with coordinates (`us_map`); merging was done by `dplyr`'s `left_join()` function. This data held together the gsp and states coordinates.

These datasets hold all the information needed to draw the maps and fill them accordingly to the gsp of each state, but still we have two datasets while only one can be inputted per layer. The solution is to combine the rows to create a new dataset; step 4 does binds them using `rbind()`.

Last step is drawing the faceted choropleth. `ggplot()` is inputted with a selective call for data; rows for which NAs are displayed by the column year are removed. The `geom_polygon()` layer draws the choropleth while `facet_wrap()` asks for facets, `coord_map()` picks the projection type and `theme_void()` has the axes erased.

Using `facet_wrap()`, the first argument still accounts for an expression calling the facets, but there is no variable on the expression's left side. Nothing should be named in the left side. Instead, the right side receives the variable ruling the facet while argument `ncol` allocates each subplot into the gird.

Notice how the state of Tennessee is blank. The `Ecdat::Produc` data frame does not bring gsp for this particular state causing it to be blank. Filling it with grey would require only a single function to be added:

```
> choropleth + geom_polygon(data = us_map[us_map$region == 'tennessee' ,],
                            aes(x = long, y = lat, group = group),
                            fill = 'grey')
```

Now the Tennessee state fill color meets the border color:

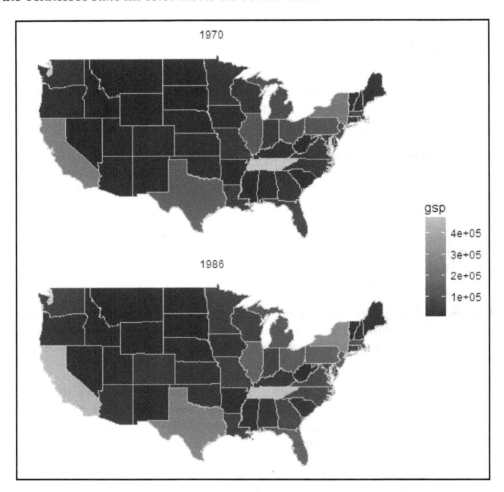

Figure 7.8 - Coloring Tennessee.

The `us_map` data frame alone handled this task. Do not forget to make a selective call for the `'tennessee'` region inside the brackets. This recipe took good care of plotting faceted choropleths using `ggplot2`; the next one will discuss how to brew faceted plots using only `plotly`.

See also

- Check Rudis's faceted map: `https://rud.is/b/2015/07/09/faceted-world-population-by-income-choropleths-in-ggplot/`
- `Chapter 6`, *Crafting choropleth maps using ggplot2* recipe

Drawing facets using plotly

By its version 0.4.3, `ggvis` did not support facets, but at the same time, `plotly` kind did. As the current chapter had stressed, `plotly` is able to coerce several `ggplot` facets properly. This recipe will show you how `plotly` can be used to brew facets from scratch using `subplot()` function.

Drawing nice facets from scratch using `plotly` is not an easy task. Also, facets breed this way can be seem more as embed graphs though. It's very code-demanding and lots of data manipulation may be required. Yet there is this possibility and some nuts and bolts to go through. Plotting separated titles is very tricky as this example shows.

This recipe will adopt the Titanic context and handle a simple comparison between child and adult survivals, similar to the plot displayed by the recipe, Creating a faceted bar graph. Even if a very simple facet is being created here, this example can be extended and generalized to create more complicated ones. Also think carefully about creating a `plotly` from scratch or alternatively creating a `ggplot2` facet and coercing it into `plotly`.

How to do it...

Let us get started with the recipe:

1. Manipulate data to compute how many children and adults had survived or not:

```
> titanic <- as.data.frame(Titanic)
> survived <- c('Yes','No')
> count1 <- c(sum(titanic$Freq[ titanic$Survived == 'Yes' &
                                 titanic$Age == 'Child']),
```

```
                    sum(titanic$Freq[ titanic$Survived == 'No' &
                                      titanic$Age == 'Child']))
> count2 <- c(sum(titanic$Freq[ titanic$Survived == 'Yes' &
                                titanic$Age == 'Adult']),
             sum(titanic$Freq[ titanic$Survived == 'No' &
                               titanic$Age == 'Adult']))
```

2. Create a list to work as title properties:

```
> title <- list(
    font = list(size = 18),
    xref = 'paper',
    yref = 'paper',
    yanchor = 'bottom',
    xanchor = 'center',
    align = 'center',
    x = .5,
    y = 1,
    showarrow = FALSE)
```

3. Append an element named text to the first position to fit the actual title:

```
> title1 <- append(title,list(text = 'Child'), 0)
> title2 <- append(title,list(text = 'Adult'), 0)
```

4. Create two separate plots:

```
> library(plotly)
> b1 <- plot_ly(x = survived, y = count1, type = 'bar',
                color = survived, showlegend = F) %>%
    layout(annotations = title1)
 b2 <- plot_ly(x = survived, y = count2, type = 'bar',
                color = survived) %>%
    layout(annotations = title2)
```

5. Join these two to create a facet:

```
> subplot(b1,b2, shareY = T, titleX = T, titleY = T,
          nrows = 1)
```

Check a snapshot from the resulting plot at the following illustration (Figure 7.9):

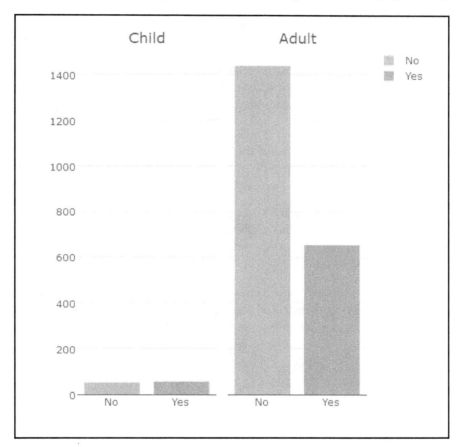

Figure 7.9 - Simple faceted bar graph by plotly.

Now for the explanations.

How it works...

To create facets using `plotly::subplot()` may be code-demanding but not that difficult. As we go through every step, we may reinforce how it can be easily adapted to meet other needs. Step 1 manipulates the data. It begins by coercing the `Titanic` table into a data frame and storing it into an object called `titanic`; coercing is done by `as.data.frame()`.

Next, a vector called `survived` is created with values `'Yes'` and `'No'`. Later, it will fit the *x* axis. Following this line, vectors `count1` and `count2` are being created. The first one contains the number of survival and non-survival children; the second holds analogous numbers for adults.

Step 2 draws a list holding standard properties used to create titles for each one of the subplots. This list is named `title` and most of its elements names are very intuitive, but some deserve more attention. Elements `xref` and `yref` rule the referencing type that the coordinates x and y will rely on.

These were set after `'paper'`, so imagine an invisible rule ranging from 0 to 1 working to reference each axis. Thus x = .5 and y = 1 means that text will be centered at plot's top. This list will fit `annotations` inside `layout()` later to set subplot titles.

Still the `text` element is missing. Step 3 adds it to the `title` list in the first position using the `append()` function. The first position is important, any other won't make it happen. This new element carries the titles text. Two new lists were created here, `title1` and `title2`, one for each subtitle.

Step 4 finally draws the bar charts. Notice how `b1` has its legends hidden and `b2` doesn't. This was done to avoid having duplicated legends. The `layout()` function receives titles into the `annotations` argument. The last step joins the two plots using the `subplot()` function.

See also

- See Branden's (bcd) subplots title solution: `https://rpubs.com/bcd/subplot-titles`

- The Creating a faceted bar graph recipe

Plotting a high quality faceted bar graph

To create publish-quality faceted bar graphs is not that different from creating publish-quality regular bar plots. This recipe will follow the usual steps we had been following until now: grow axes, make labels account full names, and resize texts. Besides, this changes, recipe will also adjust facet labels and colors in general.

Another cool thing is to do whenever your x and `fill` aesthetics are matching is to set legends to replace the x axis title. This recipe will also demonstrate this.

How to do it...

We proceed with plotting a high quality faceted bar graph:

1. Draw a basic faceted bar graph to work as the departure point:

```
> library(ggplot2)
> base <- ggplot(data = as.data.frame(Titanic),
                  aes(x = Survived)) +
    geom_bar(aes(fill = Survived, weight = Freq), colour = 'black',
width = 1) +
    facet_grid(Sex ~ Age) + theme_bw()
> h1
```

The `base` object looks like the following illustration (Figure 7.10):

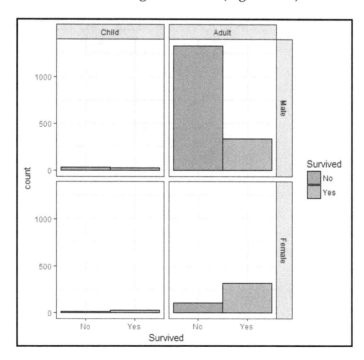

Figure 7.10 - Starting faceted bar graph.

The *y* axis title does not feel neat and the x axis will be replaced by legends.

2. Rename the y axis title and remove the x axis title:

```
> h1 <- base + ylab('persons') +
    xlab('')
```

3. Pick new colors for each bin, rework the legend's title, and make the y axis bigger:

```
> h2 <- h1 +
    scale_y_continuous(labels = seq(0,16000,200),
                       breaks = seq(0,16000,200),
                       minor_breaks = 0) +
    scale_fill_manual(values = c('No' = 'red',
                                 'Yes' = 'seagreen'),
                      name = 'survived :')
```

4. Use `theme()` to resize texts, relocate legends, and pick a different color for the strip background:

```
> h3 <- h2 + theme(text = element_text(size = 14),
                   axis.text = element_text(size = 14),
                   legend.text = element_text(size = 13),
                   strip.text = element_text(size = 13),
                   legend.position = c(.5,-.1), legend.direction =
'horizontal',
                   strip.background = element_rect(fill =
'lightyellow'),
                   plot.margin = unit(c(.2,.2,1,.2),'cm'))
> h3
```

The final result is much more publishable, as following figure demonstrates:

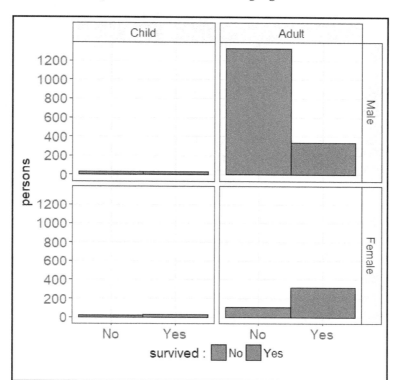

Figure 7.11 - Publication quality faceted bar graphs.

How it works...

Step 1 simply draws the faceted bar graph that will work as the departure point to achieve publication quality. Highlights will be given to the argument, width = 1, growing bins larger and the theme_minimal() layer that is setting up a new default theme, neater and cleaner.

Step 2 fits more adequate title to the *y* axis while removing the *x* axis one, so that legends can occupy this space. It uses the xlab() and ylab() functions to accomplish such a mission. Yet the *x* axis must be grown. Step 3 grows the axes bigger and manually picks the fill colors. Also, by setting the name argument, the legend's title is reworked, making it more adequate to fit as the axis title.

The last step uses `theme()` to change a series of theme aspects. First, it starts by resizing texts coming from axes labels, titles, and even from strips (Child/Adult and Male/Female). Next, legends are relocated to fit the bottom of the figure using the `legend.position` argument; orientation is also tweaked with `legend.direction`--horizontal feels much better.

Another important argument called was `plot.margin`, making sure there is enough room for legends to fit the *x* axis space. To end with, `strip.argument` is being set to fill the strip with another color. Luckily, there was no need to change facets labels, they were already fine but if there is a need, just use `factor()` to promote such a change.

8
Designing Three-Dimensional Plots

This chapter covers the following recipes:

- Drawing a simple contour plot using `ggplot2`
- Picking a custom number of contour lines
- Using the `directlabels` package to label contours
- Crafting a simple tile plot with `ggplot2`
- Creating a simple raster plot with `ggplot2`
- Designing a three-dimensional plot with plotly
- Crafting a publication quality contour plot

Introduction

This chapter is dedicated to three-dimensional plots. As its own documentation stresses, `ggplot2` is not able to draw true 3D surfaces, yet in a certain way, the package is up to the task. Some geometries can be used to visualize 3D surfaces in 2D. This chapter introduces them, the prerequisites, how to produce each of them, and which to use.

We will use geometries to imply the commented visuals, which are contour, tile, and raster plots. All those 3D representations on 2D planes coming from `ggplot2` can be coerced into `plotly`. Besides, `plotly` is able to draw true 3D surfaces and this chapter also points out how.

Drawing a simple contour plot using ggplot2

Contour plots draw lines to represent levels between surfaces. As with other 3D representations, we now need three variables, x, y, and z, and speaking for `ggplot2`, data frame must display a single row for each unique combination of x and y. That is why it's easier to bring these visuals by applying 2D kernel density estimations -- there is a single row for each unique combination of x and y.

This recipe will demonstrate a very easy way to create and plot those estimates by drawing contour plots with `ggplot2`. We will be using variables `speed` and `dist` from `car` data frame to draw this plot. Recipe highlights the very basics of making a contour plot understandable while it teaches how to improve this visual by drawing filled polygons instead of empty curves.

How to do it...

We proceed as follows for the recipe:

1. Call for `geom_density_2d()` in order to compute the 2D kernel density estimates and draw curves:

```
> library(ggplot2)
> ggplot(data = cars, aes(x = speed, y = dist)) +
    geom_density_2d(aes(colour = ..level..))
```

Resulting plot is showed by following illustration (Figure 8.1):

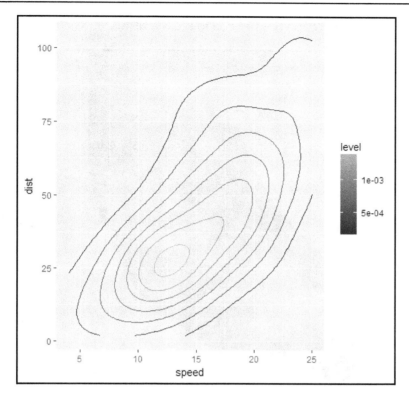

Figure 8.1 - Simple contour plot

2. To fill these curves, use `stat_density_2d()` instead while calling for `geom = 'polygon'`:

```
> ggplot(cars, aes(x = speed, y = dist)) +
    stat_density_2d(geom = 'polygon',
                    aes(fill = ..level..),
                    colour = 'yellow') +
    ylim(-10,110) + xlim(0,30) +
    coord_cartesian(xlim = c(5,25), ylim = c(0,100))
```

Look at the following illustration (Figure 8.2) to see the result:

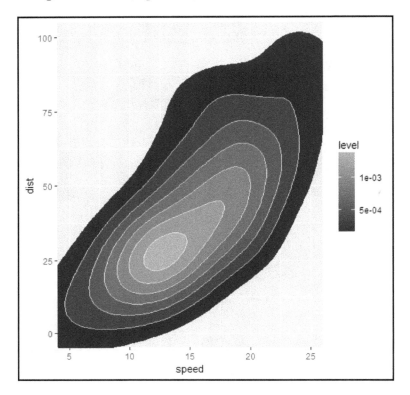

Figure 8.2 - Replacing empty curves with polygons

Now let's see what are the basics of drawing a very simple yet neat contour plot.

How it works...

The first step loads `ggplot2` and initializes a `ggplot` using the `cars` data frame while setting x and y aesthetics. You may be missing the z, but do not; the next layer, `geom_density_2d()`, is at the same time computing 2D kernel density estimates and fitting them as z.

> `geom_density_2d()` uses the `MASS` package's `kde2d()` function to compute 2D kernel density estimates. If running this code rolls a warning, try installing the mass package.

If you already had your z variable matching the previous told data conditions (must have a single row for each unique x and y combination), you should replace `geom_density_2d()` by `geom_contour()` while fitting the z variable into `aes()`.

> You already have your z variable in the data frame; input it in `aes()` and call for `geom_contour(aes(colour = ..level..)` instead.

There is `aes(colour = ..level..))` left to explain. If you happen to use `geom_countour()`, try not to miss it either. The `..level..` variable is computed by function `geom_density_2()`. The `colour` argument is not mandatory but skipping it may display a rather confusing illustration--lines will be all the same color, thus not giving a hint on whether insider lines means *higher* or *lower levels*. Check the following figure (Figure 8.3) for an example:

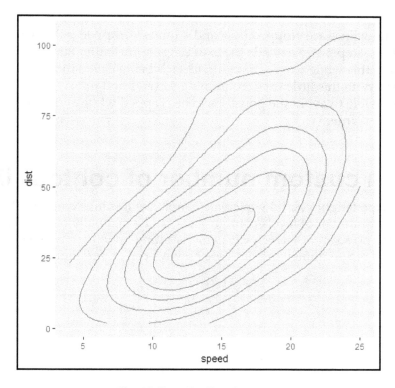

Figure 8.3 - Contour plot without colour argument

Figure 8.3 demonstrates how confusing the result can be. Next comes step 2--in several ways, it's working just like the previous one but there are a few tricks to explain. ggplot is initialized in the same way. The stat_density_2d() layer does about the same statistical transformation that the last step did, computing 2D kernel density estimates and inputting it as z.

The first trick is to use the stat_* family function instead of geom_*, this way geom argument is available. This argument is then used to override the default geometry and set polygons in place. With polygons, aes(fill = ..level..) works analogously as aes(colour = ..level..) did previously, contours are painted using the colour argument then.

> To reproduce a similar result when you already have a z variable, replace stat_density_2d() with stat_contour(). Do not forget to input aes(z = <your variable>) while keeping aes(fill = ..level..).

Did you notice how lines are cropped by x and y limits? Cropped polygons won't look that neat; to avoid this, step 2 also extends the axes range sufficiently. Functions xlim() and ylim() are doing this while coord_cartesian() is being called to zoom in with xlim and ylim arguments. With this little trick (combining *lim() and coord_cartesian() functions) it's possible to avoid the polygons to be cropped while avoiding graphical limits to be unnecessarily large.

Picking a custom number of contour lines

The previous recipe taught you how to create simple yet intuitive contour plots. This one will show how the number of levels/contour lines can be manually picked. There are mainly two arguments to do so and this recipe is demonstrating how these two works. Taking off from the previous recipe framework, let's see how we can go for another amount of lines/polygons.

How to do it...

Let us start with picking a custom number of contour lines:

1. Directly call `bins` to set the number of levels that the plot will display:

```
> library(ggplot2)
> ggplot(data = cars, aes(x = speed, y = dist)) +
    geom_density_2d(aes(colour = ..level..), bins = 15)
```

A great number of bins may be difficult to visualize as the following image (Figure 8.4) shows:

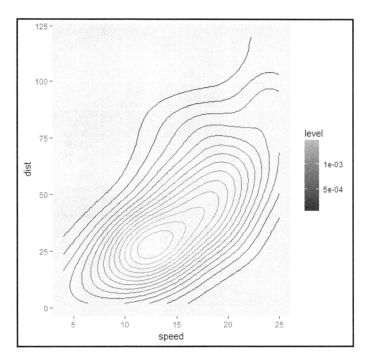

Figure 8.4 - Using bins to set the number of contours

2. The `binwidth` argument is an alternative:

```
> ggplot(data = cars, aes(x = speed, y = dist)) +
    geom_density_2d(aes(colour = ..level..), binwidth = .0005)
```

Too few contours may not display enough information, check following image (Figure 8.5):

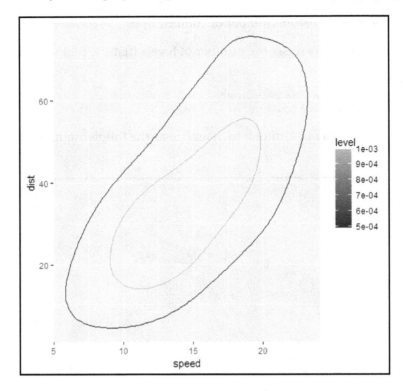

Figure 8.5 - Using binwidth to set the number of contours

To parametrize the number of contours using `bins` or `binwidth` is a situational choice, let's understand both parameters.

How it works...

Before rolling to the explanations, a little disclaimer.These two ways of selecting the number of contours also work whether you use `geom_density_2d()`, `geom_contour()`, `stat_density_2d()`, or `stat_contour()`. Step 1 shows you how to select the number of contours using the `bins` argument.

Argument `bins` accounts for the number of levels, hence by setting *n* as `bins`, you get *n-1* contours lines--a larger number means a greater number of contour lines. The next step uses `binwidth`, which stands for the distance among contours. Inputting a larger number leads to fewer contours.

A large enough number makes it impossible to generate contour data and a warning is returned. This number may differ across data. It's important to outline that picking the right number of contours will make graphics easier to understand as picking wrong ones might make it harder.

Another important thing to keep in mind is to use the `size` in order to enlarge lines. Do not forget that this code could receive more layers, it's not unusual to display points (`geom_point()`) along with contours. Following recipe is teaching how contour lines can be improved by displaying labels inside the contours.

Using the directlabels package to label the contours

If you ever try to display each contour value by the line itself using `stat_density_2d(geom = 'text', aes(label = ..level..))` (or `stat_contour(*)`), you shall get yourself a hard time. The resulting visual might be very confusing, numbers will take over the plot like a messy zombie horde. However, there is an easy alternative achieved with `directlabels` package. This one package will do all the hard work for you plus your family and friends shall think of you as a great R *shinobi*.

Getting ready

Let's see how `directlabels` can be used to label contour lines. Only make sure to install `directlabels` package first:

```
> if( !require(directlabels)){ install.packages('directlabels')}
```

Internet connection has to be on if the package is not installed yet.

How to do it...

Let us now get started on recipe:

1. Design the desired contour plot:

```
> library(ggplot2)
> plot <- ggplot(data = cars, aes(x = speed, y = dist)) +
    geom_density_2d(aes(colour = ..level..))
```

2. Input the plot into `direct.label()` function:

```
> library(directlabels)
> direct.label(plot, list(top.pieces, colour = 'black'))
```

Result is given by the following illustration (Figure 8.6):

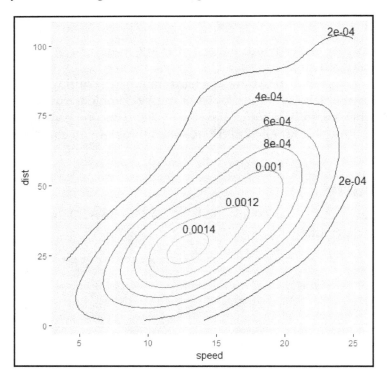

Figure 8.6 - contour plot with direct labels

How it works...

The primary step is designing a simple contour plot and storing it in an object called `plot`. Step 2 inputs this object into `direct.label()` function. This function has to be inputted at least with the plot to be changed and a positioning `method`. This second argument can have a single string (like `'top.pieces'` or `'bottom.pieces'`) or a list.

If you choose to input a single string you will be only customizing the position which the labels appear. If you use a list otherwise, there are several aspects available to customize. By naming `colour = 'black'` for an example, all labels' colors were set to black. Skipping this element shall result in colored labels. There several things you can do, for example, draw rectangles around the labels.

See also

- Check out the reference manual to see what changes could be made at `https://cran.r-project.org/web/packages/directlabels/directlabels.pdf`

Crafting a simple tile plot with ggplot2

Tiles are essentially rectangles. Actually, the documentation of `ggplot2` stresses that both `geom_rect()` and `geom_tile()` "do the same thing but are parameterized differently". Imagine seeing a roof from the top and each color of tile stands for a different value of `z`, this is tile plots.

Function `geom_tile()` draws rectangles, often the filling colors stands for some continuous variables. The usual purpose they are used with is to represent 3D surfaces in the two dimensions plane. Using `cars` data set, let's see how `ggplot2` can pull out a tile plot from it.

How to do it...

Use `stat_bin_2d()` to compute a third variable and output a tile plot:

```
> library(ggplot2)
> ggplot(data = cars, aes(x = speed, y = dist)) +
    stat_bin_2d(aes(fill = ..count..),
               binwidth = c(5,15),
```

```
colour = 'green',
size = 1.05)
```

A tile plot can be seen at the following illustration (Figure 8.7):

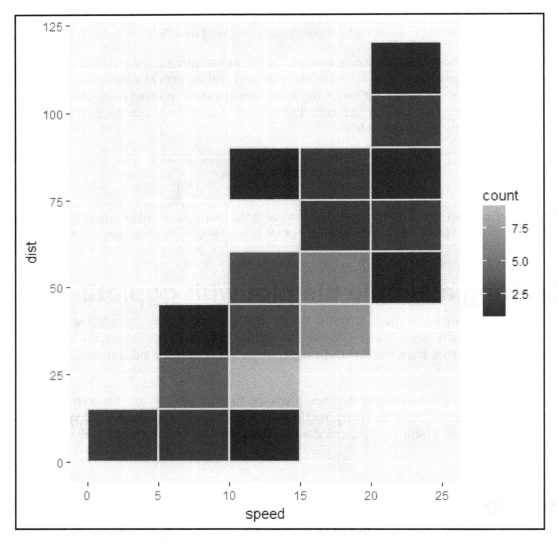

Figure 8.7 - Tile plot draw using ggplot2

Now for the explanations.

How it works...

In order to output a proper tile plot using `ggplot2`, start by initializing a `ggplot`, declaring your x and y variables. If you already have your z variable, you might rather use `geom_tile()` instead of `stat_bin_2d()`. The thing with this last function is that it computes a variable named `..count..`, accounting for the number of points fitting inside each tile.

Instead of naming a third variable as z, name it as `fill`, this is the way tiles work. This recipe inputs the `..count..` variable as fill. In the sequence comes the `binwidth` argument, it has a core role. This argument must have a vector with two elements, it tells `ggplot2` the tile size measured in x and y units.

 Parameter z is not understood by `geom_tile()` nor by `stat_bin_2d()`. The `fill` parameter is the one really working as the "third (z) axis".

Arguments coming next only set up the lines around tiles--`colour` makes a stand for which color the lines would be while the `size` argument makes them a little bit thicker. This plot could also have more functions combined; think for an instance of what could be done using `stat_bin_2d(geom = 'text')`:

```
> library(ggplot2)
> ggplot(data = cars, aes(x = speed, y = dist)) +
    stat_bin_2d(aes(fill = ..count..),
                binwidth = c(5,15),
                colour = 'green',
                size = 1.05) +
    stat_bin_2d(geom = 'text', aes(label = ..count..),
                binwidth = c(5,15), colour = 'white',
                size = 16)
```

Above code would result in the following illustration (Figure 8.8):

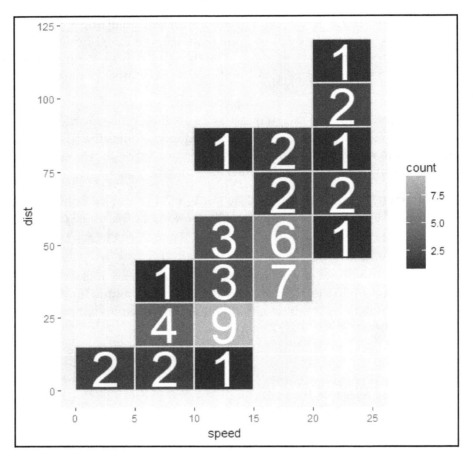

Figure 8.8 - texted tiles

Figure 8.8 could dismiss legends as the number of observations found inside each tile is already displayed by them. The `stat_bin_2d()` function's default geometry is tile, the previous code block changes it to text by explicitly calling the `geom` argument. Notice how this combination could also deal with over plotting.

To end with, it's important to outline that tiles can fit different sizes. Usually, different sizes for each tile are achieved by setting the `width` argument.

Creating simple raster plots with ggplot2

Raster plots can be seen as optimized tile plots. By adopting this geometry, there is no need to pick the `binwidth` argument. This makes the plot brewing process easier sometimes. It may be faster than brewing tiles while it also produces a smaller output when saved to PDF.

The `ggplot2` documentation considers raster geometry as a high performance special case when all tiles are the same size. This recipe demonstrates how to craft a simple raster plot with ggplot2. Using the `car` data set, a third variable will be computed by the `stat_density_2d()` function and then used to fill the raster. Explanations are highlighting alternative functions.

How to do it...

Here is how we proceed with the recipe:

1. To simultaneously compute `..density..` and plot a raster, use `stat_density_2d()`:

```
> library(ggplot2)
> ggplot(data = cars, aes(x = speed, y = dist)) +
  stat_density_2d(aes(fill = ..density..),
                  geom = 'raster', contour = F)
```

Result looks like the following image (Figure 8.9):

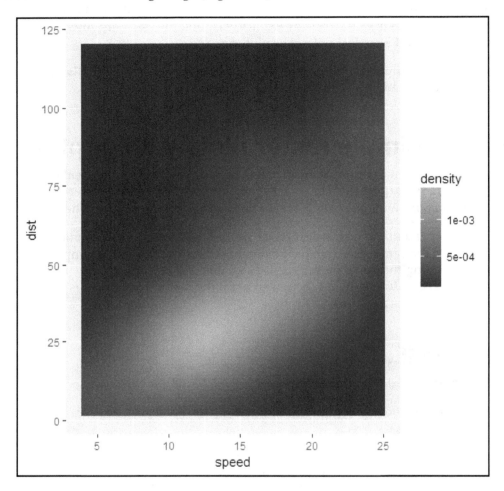

Figure 8.9 - simple raster plot

2. The `trans` argument coming from the `scale_fill_*` function can change the colors' order:

```
> ggplot(data = cars, aes(x = speed, y = dist)) +
  stat_density_2d(aes(fill = ..density..),
                  geom = 'raster', contour = F) +
  scale_fill_distiller(trans = 'reverse')
```

Now darker colors are up to greater densities, check the following image (Figure 8.10):

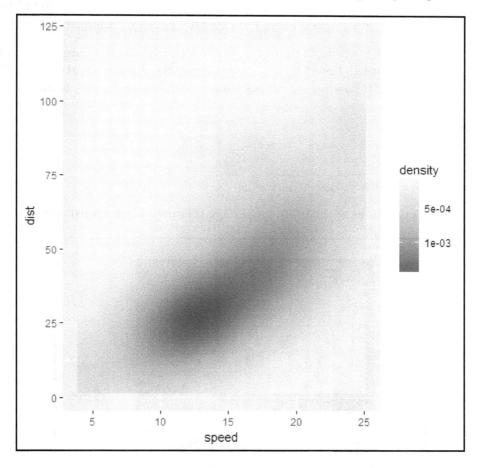

Figure 8.10 - reversing the color scale

Next section has the explanations.

How it works...

As usual, the recipe starts by loading the package. After initializing `ggplot`, the first step calls for `stat_density_2d()` function in order to do some computation and seek the desired geometry. This function computed `..density..` variable, a 2D kernel density estimate. Fill argument (`aes(fill)`) is chosen after `..density..` variable at this same function.

Such an argument is essential to raster geometry. Just like tiles, the third variable has to be input as `fill` and not `z`. Afterward, `geom = 'raster'` is named to call for the raster geometry. The `contour` argument is set to FALSE so tile geometry can take place properly.

If there is no need to ask for computations coming from `ggplot2`, the `geom_raster()` function can be used instead; however, `fill` is still essential. Raster can also be combined with a contour plot. The following code block uses `geom_density_2d()` to add contours to the raster:

```
> library(ggplot2)
> ggplot(data = cars, aes(x = speed, y = dist)) +
  stat_density_2d(aes(fill = ..density..),
                   geom = 'raster', contour = F) +
  geom_density_2d(colour = 'white')
```

Contours act like guidelines as the following image (Figure 8.11) demonstrates:

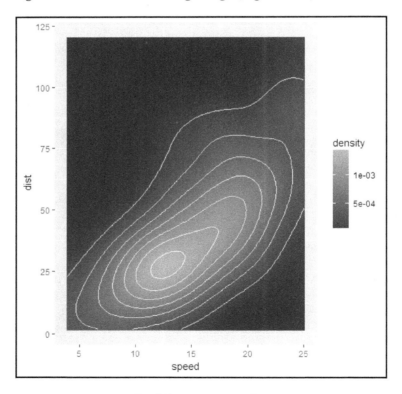

Figure 8.11 - raster and contour combined

There is more

There is no easy/right answer to what plot (contour/tile or raster) to choose. Let's begin with the necessity. Once you are settling for one of the three--contour, tile, or raster plots--I'm assuming that you need to represent a 3D surface in a two-dimensional plane. That's not always true; one of the reasons that crafting visuals is fun, is because creativity pays off.

One way to go would be to try them all and pick the one that feels better. A shortcut to do it would be to combine raster and contours. Trying the three geometries will not be that hard but if you need to do it many times, you got yourself a lot of extra work that maybe could be avoided, which leads us to alternative number two: data knowledge.

Contours tend to work better when x and y forms an evenly spaced grid. Tiles can be of great use with smaller and simpler sets of data. Raster plots are up to more complex data formations. It's also important to outline that raster also plays along with granularity.

Once you pick a geometry, there is more work ahead. You can tweak some arguments to see if some insight comes easier. If the figure aims for publication, it might call at least for more complete and bigger axes, resized texts, and legends might need to be reworked.

Designing a three-dimensional plot with plotly

True three-dimensional plots can be drawn using `plotly`. There are a wide range of types available, from 3D scatter plots, to 3D lines, 3D surfaces, and 3D meshes. There is a great thing about 3D plots made with `plotly`--the user is able to drag the illustration, see it from different angles, and zoom in and out.

Getting ready

Make sure that the MASS package is already downloaded and installed:

```
> if( !require(MASS)){ install.packages('MASS')}
```

If it's missing and internet connection is fine, above code will do the job for you.

How to do it...

Here is how we design a 3 dimensional plot with `plotly`:

1. To begin with, have your data created using `MASS::kde2d()`:

```
> cars_d <- MASS::kde2d(cars$speed, cars$dist, n =50)
```

2. Call `plot_ly()` and use `add_surface()` to create a 3D surface:

```
> library(plotly)
> plot_ly(x = cars_d$x,
          y = cars_d$y,
          z = cars_d$z) %>%
    add_surface()
```

A snapshot from the original output can be seen at the following image (Figure 8.12):

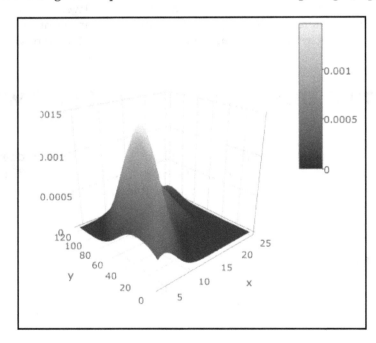

Figure 8.12 - plotly 3D surface

Let's see how the cards are playing.

How it works...

The first step creates a list called `cars_d` (cars density). This list was created using the `MASS::kde2d()` function. It creates a two-dimensional kernel distribution estimates based on the `car` data frame variables, `speed` and `distance`. This list carries the data that we need in order to represent the surface.

Step 2 draws the 3D surface. Coordinates x, y, and z come from the `card_d` list, all of them inputted in `plot_ly()`. Using a pipe operator (`%>%`) along with `add_surface()`, the 3D surface is finally drawn. A cool thing about the actual plot is the possibility to change angles and zoom in and out.

The tools to move around the figure can be found whenever you hover the mouse by the **viewer tab** or the HTML page holding the image. Options available are **Zoom**, **Pan**, **orbital rotation**, and **turntable rotation**. All of them work through mouse drags (or scroll rolling), but it's imperative to activate one before using it.

Used data followed the same logic as the recipes before this one, same kernel estimates as well. Sometimes, RStudio may display empty images by the **vierwer tab**, usually clicking on **Show in new window** might solve it. To draw 3D scatter plots and 3D lines is about the same as drawing 2D ones--only that 3D requires naming the z variable (rarely few more adjustments are needed). Now let's see what we can do to craft a publication quality contour plot using `ggplot2`.

Crafting a publication quality contour plot

Several steps might be required in order to achieve publication quality. The very least ones would be reworking text sizes (legends, labels, titles) and growing axes. Besides covering these changes, this recipe also makes the contours thicker, selects another default theme, picks another color scale, and move legends to the inside.

How to do it...

Let us now start with crafting a publication quality contour plot:

1. Create a contour plot to work as a departure point using `stat_density_2d()`:

```
> library(ggplot2)
> h1 <- ggplot(cars, aes(x = speed, y = dist)) +
  stat_density_2d(aes(colour = ..level..), size = 1.2) +
  theme_minimal()
```

2. Change the color scale by calling `scale_colour_distiller()`:

```
> h2 <- h1 +
  scale_colour_distiller(direction = 1, name = 'density',
                         breaks = seq(0.0002,0.0014,0.0002),
                         labels = format(seq(0.0002,0.0014,0.0002),
                                         scientific = F))
```

3. Make axes to hold the variables' complete name and measure unit:

```
> h3 <- h2 + xlab('speed (mph)') + ylab('distance (ft)')
```

4. Use `scale_*_continuous()` to grow axes:

```
> h4 <- h3 + scale_y_continuous(breaks = seq(0,130,10),
                                labels = seq(0,130,10),
                                minor_breaks = 0) +
    scale_x_continuous(breaks = seq(4,26,2),
                       labels = seq(4,26,2),
                       minor_breaks = 0)
```

5. Move the legend, draw its background, and rework text sizes:

```
h5 <- h4 + theme(legend.position = c(.2,.75),
    legend.background = element_rect(color = "black",
                                     size = .2,
                                     linetype = "solid"),
          legend.text = element_text(size = 13),
          legend.title = element_text(size = 14),
          axis.text = element_text(size = 15),
          axis.title = element_text(size = 18))
```

6. Use `guides()` so that the legend's titles and labels do not overlay one another:

```
h5 + guides(colour = guide_legend(title.vjust = .1))
```

Following image (Figure 8.13) shows the final result:

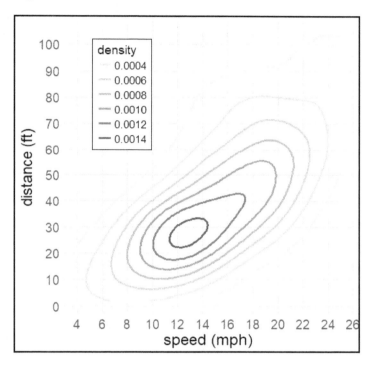

Figure 8.13 - High quality contour plot

Let's see how each of these steps unfold.

How it works...

Step 1 draws the base contour plot. To do so, the `stat_density_2d()` function is used. Notice the `colour` and `size` arguments. The first one is declared inside `aes()` to attach colors to each contour. The second one is declared to make contours thicker. This step also called `theme_minimal()` to set up several theme aspects at once.

The next step calls `scale_colour_distiller()` for several changes. Mainly to easily tweak the color scheme. Declaring `direction = 1` makes the darker colors account for larger values (it may feel more intuitive this way); `name` changes the legends' title; `breaks` picks the breaks to be displayed by legends and `labels` is labeling them.

Step 3 does a very basic change. By calling `xlab()` and `ylab()`, axes labels are replaced by the complete names along with measure units. The next step simply grows the axes bigger using `scale_*_continuous()` functions. Step 5 asks for `theme()` in order to replace legends and resize texts in general.

Finally, the plot is called by step 6 but not without some adjustments. The `guide()` function was then called to avoid the legends' title and labels to overlay one another. You can call the plots `h1` to `h5` to see the changes that took place at each step.

9
Using Theming Packages

This chapter covers the following recipes:

- Drawing a bubble plot
- Popular themes with `ggthemes`
- Applying sci themes with `ggsci`
- Importing new fonts with the `extrafont` package
- Using `ggtech` to mimic tech companies' themes
- Wrapping a custom theme function
- Applying awesome themes and checking misspells with `hrbrthemes`

Introduction

Themes are capable of making a plot more attractive and/or suitable. When we speak about `ggplot2`, the default themes are actually very good as data exploration material, but not so suitable for publication and a wide variety of tweaks must go on in order to improve quality.

Much of this is done under the `theme()` function. An alternative way to go is to use theming packages instead. There are tons of these available; consider using them for exploratory purposes as they don't require a lot of extra work. With a single function, you can set the same theme from The Economist, for example. This chapter will demonstrate how to use a bunch of theming packages.

You can also make the plot funnier with themes like Twitter or Google. Consider setting an Easter egg into your plot by using a color scale based on The Simpsons or Rick and Morty TV show. Last but not least, use wonderful fonts that improve your plot in a very detailed yet important way; do this with the Master Rudis' package (`hrbrthemes`).

A very good reason to pay meticulous attention to theme issues is that no matter how good your work was in between axes, theming choices matter a lot. Picking a good theme over a bad one means that you're enhancing and validating your good work over depreciating it.

All this will be discussed in this chapter. Oh yes, we did not see a code for bubble plots yet, am I right? Here, we will also check a recipe to draw those babies. This bubble plot is going to be our testing subject for most of this chapter.

Drawing a bubble plot

Until now, we saw how we can work points' shapes and colors to display more information, but what about sizes? Sizes are also a feasible option. Plots that combine circles with sizes to transmit information are known as bubble plots. This recipe's intention is to brew the working material for the following recipes; to do this, we will craft and store a bubble plot.

For now, a little context. By the end of the 16th century, Spain had this navy that was called *"La Feliscima Armada"*. Here, we are analyzing the relation between soldiers, sailors, and ships held by each navy fleet. What are you expecting? Will the fleet with more sailors be the fleet with more ships? Let's call `ggplot2` to solve this question by drawing a bubble plot on this query.

Getting ready

The dataset we are about to use is called `Armada` and comes from the `HistData` package, so we better check the last one:

```
> if( !require(HistData)){ install.packages('HistData')}
```

The `Armada` data frame has 10 observations on 11 variables. The ones we look for are `sailors`, `soldiers`, `Armada` (fleet reference), and `ships`.

How to do it...

Let us now start with drawing a bubble plot:

1. Load the `HistData` and `ggplot2` packages:

```
> library(ggplot2)
> library(HistData)
```

2. Using the `HistData::Armada` data frame, build and store a bubble plot:

```
> bubble <- ggplot(Armada, aes(x = sailors, y = soldiers)) +
    geom_point(aes(colour = Armada, size = ships), alpha = .6) +
    scale_color_brewer(palette = 'Set3' ,guide = F) +
    scale_size_continuous(range = c(5,25)) +
    geom_text(aes(label = Armada), size = 3) +
    xlim(100,2000) + ggtitle('La Felicisima Armada')
```

After this last code block, calling bubble will output something like the following illustration (Figure 9.1):

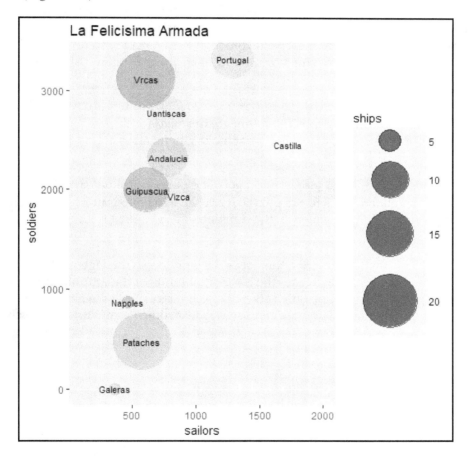

Figure 9.1 - Sailors x Soldiers x Ships bubble plot.

Before getting to theme packages, let's understand how this bubble plot had rolled.

How it works...

The recipe begins by loading the `HistData` package, from which the `Armada` data frame is coming from, and `ggplot2`. All the hard work can be now handled by Step 2. Several functions are chained in order to craft the bubble plot, all under a new object, `bubble`.

The second step starts with `ggplot()` initializing the plot. The `geom_point()` function is called next. The main features that define the bubble plot are drawn here. The `colour` argument is set to paint points with respect to the fleet name; `Armada` is also the name of the variable holding each of these names. Next comes `size = ships`, so relative points size make reference to the number of ships coming from each observation. Alpha blending is also added here.

Proximate function called is `scale_color_brewer()`. Two things are tweaked here--the color palette is changed and legends for colors are disabled (`guide = F`). Colors are often a good feature for bubble plots but are not what makes them; sizes are, so it's often well advised to stack `scale_size_*`.

The next line calls `scale_size_continuous()`. The `range` parameter makes sure that we find more suitable relative sizes to the points. It specifies the maximum and minimum size of the plotting symbol. In the sequence, the functions `geom_text()`, `xlim()`, and `ggtitle()` are stacked.

The first one asks for texts to describe the fleet's designation so the legends for colors are not needed anymore. The second increases the horizontal limits of the graphic thus avoiding points to be cropped. The last one only sets a title to the plot. Now we have our subject stored into the `bubble` object. Now we can use it to test some themes and color schemes.

Popular themes with ggthemes

What if you could set themes similar to the ones coming from FiveThirtyEight, The Economist, or the Wall Street Journal? Using the ggthemes package, this is easy to achieve. There are a bunch of other themes available such as Stata, Excel, and Pander. This recipe's goal is to demonstrate how to generally assign some themes from this package.

Getting Ready

There are two requirements. In the first place, we need a ggplot object to draw on; this recipe uses the bubble object created in the previous recipe. You can either make sure it's available on your environment by running that recipe or adapt this recipe by replacing bubble with a ggplot of your own. You also need to make sure that ggthemes is properly installed:

```
> if(!require(ggthemes)){ install.packages('ggthemes')}
```

To the playground!

How to do it...

The following steps delineate how to proceed with the recipe:

1. Load ggthemes and stack theme_fivethirtyeight() to reach for the FiveThirtyEight theme:

```
> library(ggthemes)
> bubble +
  theme_fivethirtyeight()
```

Summing `bubble` with `theme_fivethirtyeight()` results in the following plot (Figure 9.2):

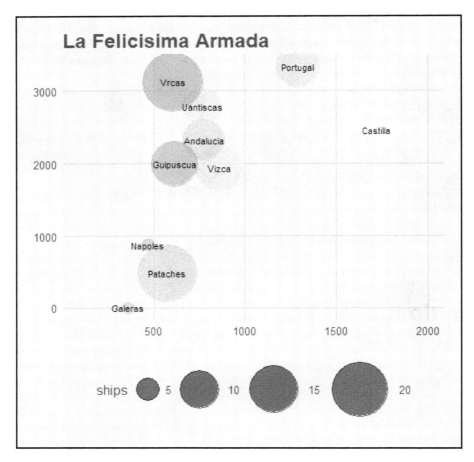

Figure 9.2 - bubble plot with FiveThirtyEight theme.

2. Combine `theme_stata()` and `scale_colour_stata()` to reach for the Stata theme:

```
> bubble + theme_stata() +
    scale_colour_stata(guide = F)
```

As a result, we get the following image (Figure 9.3):

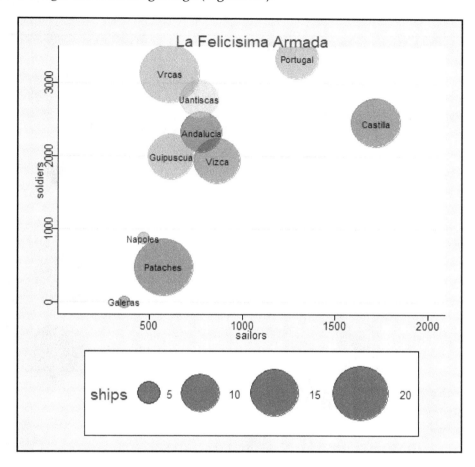

Figure 9.3 - Stata theme.

3. The pander theme can be achieved by combining `theme_pander()` with `scale_color_pander()`:

```
> bubble + theme_pander() +
    scale_color_pander(guide = F)
```

This is the one I like better when it comes to bubble plots in general. Check the following image (Figure 9.4):

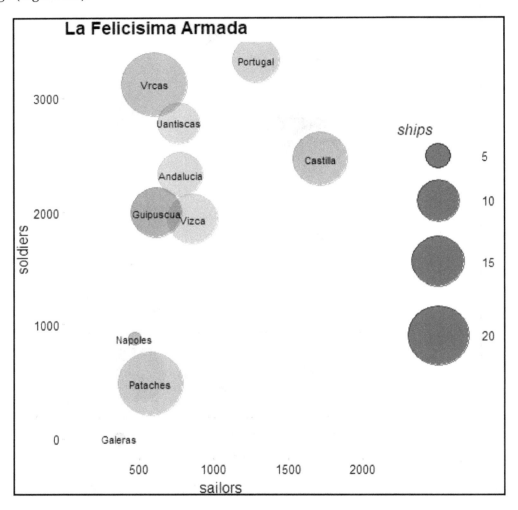

Figure 9.4 - pander theme.

We have some explanations to go through.

How it works...

All three steps are analogous. The first one sums the `bubble` object with `theme_fivethirtyeight()` to ensure that we reach the FiveThrityEight theme. We are not completely reaching this theme because color is not right; the recipe purposely skipped `scale_color_fivethirtyeight()` because this color palette can handle only three different values--`bubble` requires 10 different ones.

Step 2 reaches for the Stata theme with `theme_stata()`. The `scale_colour_stata()` function is used to replace the existing color scale. Legends for colors are hidden by setting `guide = F`. You can totally fool your friends by making them believe your incredible graph was made using Stata, this is a ninja advanced deceiving technique indeed.

When it comes to `ggthemes`, both `scale_color_*()` and `scale_colour_*()` works the same.

The last step demands the pander theme. Color scale also supports 10 different colors so it was called. I personally think that, from all the themes available at `ggthemes`, pander is the one that better goes with our bubble plot. Generally, themes are called by functions like `theme_*()`, while color scales can be demanded by `scale_fill_*()` or/and `scale_color_*()`.

There's more...

These are not the only themes available. You might want to check a package overview at GitHub--there is a series of examples on how to mimic The Economist or The Wall Street Journal figures. The package also disposes of a geometry of its own and a special color scale for the color-blind people.

This color palette is very useful and can be called by stacking `scale_*_colorblind()`. A "con" is that it can handle only eight colors at a time, the only reason that I did not used here. Yet it's very useful, consider using it every time.

See also

- The Drawing a bubble plot recipe
- Check `ggthemes` overview at `https://github.com/jrnold/ggthemes`

Applying sci themes with ggsci

If you are looking for popular journals' color scales or TV show-based ones, you're looking for the `ggsci` package. Within it, you find scales based on the **Journal of Clinical Oncology** (**JCO**) and The University of Chicago. There are also scales based on Tron Legacy, Star Trek, The Simpsons and Rick and Morty.

This package is different from `ggthemes` because it carries only color scales and zero themes. Still, there are a lot of palettes available and theming functions coming from anywhere can be combined to achieve very cool results. Let's stick with the `bubble` object to demonstrate a couple.

Getting Ready

We're about to call the `bubble` object created in the *Drawing a bubble plot* recipe; if you can't see it in your environment, make sure to run that recipe before going on. We also need to make sure that the `ggsci` package is properly downloaded and installed:

```
> if(!require(ggsci)){ install.packages('ggsci')}
```

Now let's test a couple color scales.

How to do it...

The following steps are demonstrating a few color scales coming from `ggsci` package:

1. Stack `scale_*_ucscgb()` to ask for the UCSC Genome browser:

```
> library(ggsci)
 bubble +
   theme_bw() +
   scale_color_ucscgb(guide = F)
```

Result is exhibited by the following image (Figure 9.5):

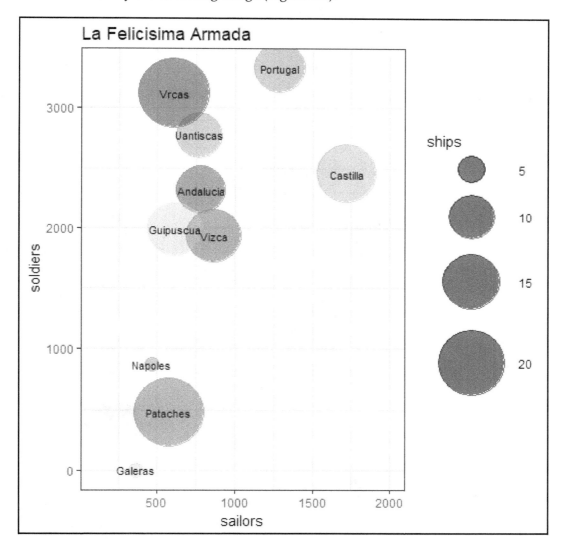

Figure 9.5 - UCSC Genome Browser color scale.

2. Add `scale_*_rickandmorty()` to summon a color scale based on the TV show, Rick and Morty:

```
> bubble +
    theme_bw() +
    scale_color_rickandmorty(guide = F)
```

This color scale is demonstrated by the following image (Figure 9.6):

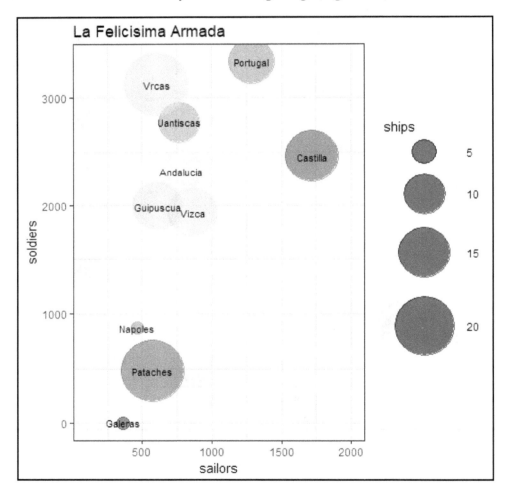

Figure 9.6 - Rick and Morty color scale.

How it works...

The `ggsci` package is able to assign color scales to your `ggplot`. Steps 1 and 2 are analogous. Both start by calling the `bubble` object and stacking `theme_bw()`, only then the color scale is called. This color palette can either be assigned to `fill` and `colour` parameters, depending on which one you had named before. This is also true for `ggtheme` schemes.

The bubble plot had only the `colour` parameter assigned, so the recipe only called for `scale_color_*`. Legends for colors were turned off by setting `guide = F` inside these functions. Some scales, like `uchicago` has more than one palette type available by the same function. Entering `scale_color_uchicago(palette = 'light')` is different from entering `scale_color_uchicago(palette = 'dark')`.

Another thing about this package is that calling `scale_color_*` and `scale_colour_*` draws the same result. Always be sure that the scale used does support the number of colors do you need, warnings may tell you if don't. The See also section provides a link to a wide variety of examples and references.

See also

- The Drawing a bubble plot recipe
- Check a more complete guide to `ggsci` at `https://cran.r-project.org/web/packages/ggsci/vignettes/ggsci.html`

Importing new fonts with the extrafont package

This recipe teaches you how to use the `ggtech` package to coerce themes to resemble some tech companies (like Google, Facebook and Twitter) styles. To do this, we first need to have some fonts installed into our system and only then we can have them imported into R to later be used.

This recipe demonstrates how fonts required by ggtech can be installed and imported into your R Session. By learning it, you will also be able to import and use any font installed into your system. The main package used to this intent is extrafont.

Getting Ready

For this recipe, two packages are going to be called, downloader and extrafont; make sure that both are installed by running the following code:

```
> if(!require(downloader)){install.packages('downloader')}
> if(!require(extrafont)){ install.packages('extrafont')}
```

Now that we have both packages installed, proceed to font downloading, installation, and importation processes.

How to do it...

Importing new fonts with the extrafont package proceed as follows:

1. Use downloader::download() in order to download the fonts:

```
> library(downloader)
> download('http://bit.do/fbfont', 'facebook-letter-faces.ttf', mode =
'wb')
> download('http://bit.do/google_font', 'product-sans.ttf', mode = 'wb')
> download('http://bit.do/circularfont1', 'Circular Air-Medium 3.46.45
PM.ttf', mode = 'wb')
> download('http://bit.do/circularfont2', 'Circular Air-Bold 3.46.45
PM.ttf', mode = 'wb')
> download('http://bit.do/picofont', 'pico-black.ttf', mode = 'wb')
> download('http://bit.do/arisafont', 'arista-light.ttf', mode = 'wb')
```

2. Go into your working directory, search for the downloaded fonts (.ttf extension), and install them.

3. Import them to your R Session using the `extrafont` package:

```
> library(extrafont)
> font_import(pattern = 'facebook-letter-faces.ttf', prompt = F)
> font_import(pattern = 'Circular', prompt = F)
> font_import(pattern = 'Circular', prompt = F)
> font_import(pattern = 'product-sans.ttf', prompt = F)
> font_import(pattern = 'pico-black.ttf', prompt = F)
> font_import(pattern = 'arista-light.ttf', prompt = F)
```

4. Call `fonts()` to see which external fonts are imported.

Now let's see how these steps unfolded.

How it works...

The first step trusts the `download()` function from the `downloader` package to download the font files. This function's arguments account respectively for the download link (URL), a string naming the file (this can optionally carry a path), and the download mode, here set to binary (`'wb'`).

 `downloader::download()` is actually a function wrap on `download.file()` with settings automatically adjusted based on user's platform; think of it as a cross-platform user-friendly version of `download.file()`.

This recipe used shortened URLs so that the code does not get too lengthy. If any of those are broken, you can reach for new ones by doing a little web search. The `mode = 'wb'` parameter asks the file to be downloaded in binary mode.

For step 2, you need to go all the way to the working directory and install the fonts. Windows users can do this either by double-clicking on the font file and then hitting install or by moving them to C:Windows/Fonts/. This step could be spared by downloading the file directly to the system font library folder. For some OS, that would require changing folder permissions and other things.

 Call `download('<download URL>','<font library path>/<font file name.tff>', mode = 'wb')` to download and install the font right away. It may not work for some systems.

Once we are sure that the fonts are installed, the next step is to import/register them into the R session using `extrafont`. This step may be repeated whenever the session is (re)started and you desire to use some non R native fonts. The function responsible for the importation process is called `font_import()`.

The `pattern` argument searches for the font in your system library while `prompt = FALSE` turns off a prompt authorization to proceed with importation. Step 4 checks whether those fonts are available by entering `extrafont::fonts()`; another option is `extrafont::fonttable()`.

There's more...

Whenever you need another font from those R native, reach the `extrafont` package to import them from your system library. An easy way to do this is calling `extrafont::loadfonts()`. They can later be referred by the names that the `fonts()` function shows. Knowing this, you can customize your `ggplot2` even more with brand new fonts.

Using ggtech to mimic tech companies themes

The `ggtech` package is useful to mimic themes from tech companies like Facebook, Google, Airbnb, Etsy, and Twitter. I find the last one pretty amazing to do some Twitter analysis, like word frequency or even to design a plot I wish to tweet. Once we get all the required fonts properly installed and imported, using `ggtech` is actually very easy; there are also geometries available. This recipe aims for a Twitter thematic plot.

Getting Ready

First things first, make sure to have `ggtech` installed; we need the `devtools` package for this. Also make sure that the fonts installed in the previous recipe are loaded into your R session using the `extrafont` package:

```
> if(!require(extrafont)){ install.packages('extrafont')}
> extrafont::loadfonts()
> if(!require(devtools)){ install.packages('devtools')}
> if(!require(ggtech)){
    library(devtools)
    install_github("ricardo-bion/ggtech", dependencies=FALSE)}
```

Let's understand what this package can do.

How to do it...

Let us understand how to use ggtech to mimic tech companies themes:

1. Create a data frame object:

```
> dt <- data.frame(x_axis = rep(1:3,each = 3),
                   y_axis = rep(1:3,3))
```

2. Call `ggplot2` and draw the basic aesthetics on the `dt` data frame:

```
> library(ggplot2)
> p <- ggplot(data = dt, aes(x = x_axis,
                             y = y_axis)) +
    xlim(c(0,4)) + ylim(c(0,4))
```

3. Add a title and call `ggtech` to coerce a geometry and theme:

```
> library(ggtech)
> p + ggtitle('Twitter plot') +
    geom_tech(theme = 'twitter') +
    theme_tech(theme = 'twitter')
```

The following illustration (Figure 9.7) is outputted:

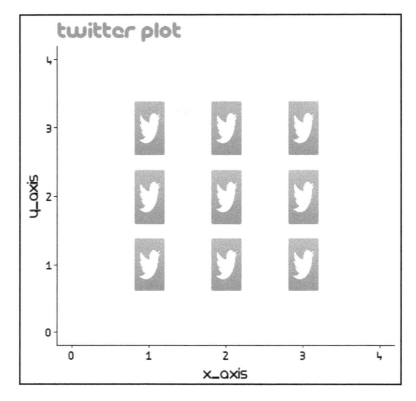

Figure 9.7 -Twitter plot.

Let's understand how each of these functions were used.

How it works...

The recipe starts by creating a data frame in step 1. The dataset is named dt, variables are x_axis and y_axis. To create the first one, the rep() function was used to repeat each element from the list three times; for the second variable, rep() repeated the entire list three times. Then we called dt for a demonstration.

The second step draws the basic aesthetic mappings of the `ggplot` while increasing plot limits using the `xlim()` and `ylim()` functions. Notice that the `ggplot2` package was loaded; it's not only necessary to initialize the `ggplot` object, but also to coerce themes using `ggtech`. All these calls were stored into an object named `p`.

 `ggtech::theme_tech()` is always calling for `ggplot2::theme_classic()` on the behind scenes; if we skip or detach `ggplot2`, `theme_tech()` may not work properly.

Step 3 is very useful to understand what `ggtech` is primarily capable of. It starts off by calling `p` and attaching a title. Title is not assigned by `ggtech` but by `ggplot2`. Next, `geom_tech()` is called to add Twitter icons; icons are picked by the argument, `theme`. It works just like `geom_points()` but displays icons instead.

 Many icons can be displayed by `geom_tech()`; they are all set by strings. `'google'`, `'airbnb'`, `'etsy'`, and `'twitter'` are available.

Afterward, `theme_tech()` is called to change default theming. It's responsible for changing grids, background color, and also font family and title color. It works in a very similar way to `geom_tech()`; the theme argument picks the theming-based style. Notice how different font families are used over axes and title.

There's more...

Now that you know `ggtech`, try to apply its themes in your tech companies plots or maybe make more customized plots to fit your tweets. Combining `geom_tech(theme = 'twitter')` with `geom_line()` is a great way to draw lollipop plots on Twitter data.

See also

- The installing and importing new fonts recipe
- Check several `ggtech` useful examples at `https://cran.r-project.org/web/packages/ggsci/vignettes/ggsci.html`

Wrapping a custom theme function

After using `ggplot2` and performing theme changes several times, there are always theme tweaks you find yourself going for too often. This recipe goal is to demonstrate how to wrap theme functions into tailormade ones. Wrapping your preferences in a single function makes the process of crafting publish quality plots so much easier.

Getting ready

This recipe will test the custom theme function in the `bubble` object created by previous recipe, *Drawing a bubble plot*. If you wish to keep this way, make sure to have this object on your environment by running the recipe if it's missing. Another option is to draw an `gg` object of your own to replace `bubble` into the recipe. Do as you please.

How to do it...

Let us start with wrapping a custom theme function:

1. Create a function that calls for `theme()`:

```
> theme_custom <- function(s.legend1 = 14,
                           s.legend2 = 14,
                           s.axes1 = 14,
                           s.axes2 = 15, ...){
    theme_classic() +
      theme(legend.text = element_text(size = s.legend1),
            legend.title = element_text(size = s.legend2),
            axis.text = element_text(size = s.axes1),
            axis.title = element_text(size = s.axes2),
            plot.title = element_text(size = 18), ...)}
```

2. We can test it on any `ggplot`; do not forget to have `ggplot2` loaded. Once it's loaded, we can apply it on a `gg` object:

```
> bubble + theme_custom()
```

Now our old friend bubble plot has resized texts and classic theme as following image (Figure 9.8) demonstrates:

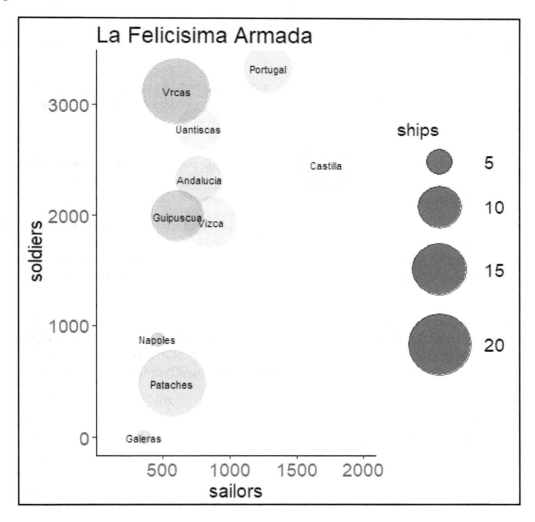

Figure 9.8 - using custom theme function.

Let's check on the nuts and bolts.

How it works...

Our custom theme function (`theme_custom()`) is designed in step 1. It begins by calling `theme_classic()` and then stacking the `theme()` function. The recipe did this by adding classic theme plus setting sizes for various texts, from axes labels and titles to legends titles and labels and also plot title.

 To design a theme function, it's not necessary to have `ggplot2` loaded. On the other hand, to run that same function, you might need the package to be properly loaded.

Any preset theme could be called or no `theme_*()` at all. Next comes the `theme()` function demanding additional changes. You can call any change that `theme()` allows; the way the recipe did, it's only resizing texts but the options are almost unlimited.

Using `theme()`, it's possible to change text sizes, colors, and fonts. Changing background colors, grids lines, drawing rectangles around the legends, and moving them around are examples of what this function is can do to `ggplot`. A person can also set arguments in an inaccessible way, just like `plot.title` was designated--title's text size is 18, no matter what.

Another way to name arguments is making them accessible just like `s.legend1` is. It accounts for legends' label size with a default value of 14, yet a user can perfectly change it by simply naming this argument with another value when calling for `theme_custom()`. There are no limits to ways a user could parametrize his own theme function; be creative.

The recipe also called for ellipsis (`. . .`) as a function input, so any other `theme()` argument is reachable by `theme_custom()`. Step 2 simply tests `theme_custom()` on the first plot designed in this chapter, `bubble`. As a result, we got texts coming from title, axes, and legends increased; classic theme was also applied then.

See also

- The Drawing a bubble plot recipe

Applying awesome themes and checking misspells with hrbrthemes

This package came directly from the genius mind of Bob Rudis (thank you Rudis, you're awesome). From checking misspells to accessing whole awesome theme and color scales, hrbrthemes is your "guy". Themes coming from this package are well-thought in an incredibly detailed level; I personally think that these are the best ones available. I highly recommend you to check this recipe's *See also* section to understand in how many ways hrbrthemes is well thought.

Getting Ready

To get hrbrthemes latest version, install it directly from GitHub and also make sure that the tidyverse and extrafont packages are available:

```
> if( !require(devtools)){ install.packages('devtools')}
> if( !require(hrbrthemes)){
devtools::install_github('hrbrmstr/hrbrthemes')}
> if( !require(tidyverse)){ install.packages('tidyverse')}
> if( !require(extrafont)){ install.packages('extrafont')}
```

Also make sure that the fonts, Arial Narrow and Roboto Condensed, are installed on your system. You can do this by running the recipe called *Importing new fonts with extrafont package*.

How to do it...

We proceed with the recipe as follows:

1. Load the hrbrthemes and tidyverse packages while reaching for Arial Narrow and Roboto Condesend fonts using extrafont:

```
> library(hrbrthemes)
> library(tidyverse)
> extrafont::loadfonts()
```

2. Draw a basic `ggplot2` scatterplot with a proper title and a misspelled subtitle:

```
> p <- ggplot(data = Puromycin,
             aes(x = conc,
                 y = rate,
                 colour = state)) +
    geom_point(size = 4) +
    labs(title = 'Reaction Velocity of\nan Enzymatic Reaction',
         subtitle = 'thiss ys missspelled')
```

When we enter p at the console, the following image (Figure 9.9) shall be outputted:

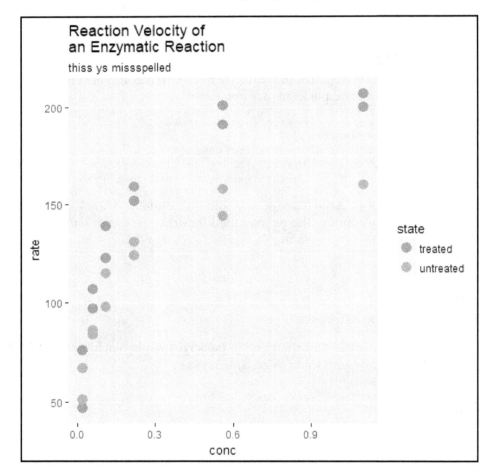

Figure 9.9 - Default themming ggplot2 scatterplot.

3. Call the `hrbrthemes` functions to change the previous theme and color scheme:

```
> p + theme_ipsum_rc() +
    scale_color_ipsum()
```

The output is represented by Figure 9.10:

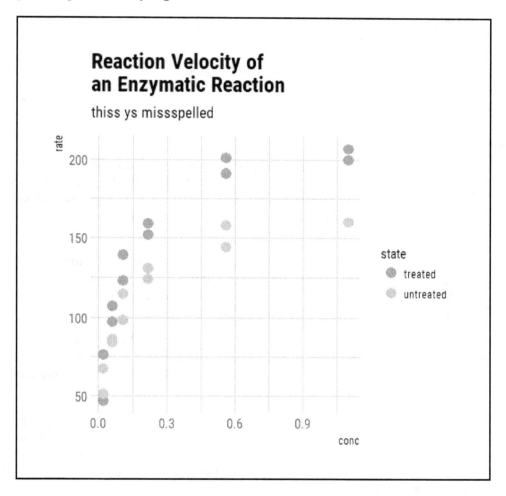

Figure 9.10 - hrbrthemes roboto condensed theme.

4. We can check words spelling with the `hrbrthemes::gg_check()` function; input it with plot p:

```
> gg_check(p)
```

As a result, we get messages telling where the misspelled words might be:

Possible misspelled words in [subtitle]: (thiss, ys, missspelled)
Possible misspelled words in [x]: (conc)

When inputted with plot p, `gg_check()` is telling us that the subtitle and *x* axis may have some misspelled words. It also points out which words may need to be rewritten.

How it works...

First of all, the recipe starts by loading all the packages that we need: `hrbrthemes`, `gcookbook`, and `tidyverse`. The last package also takes care of loading several other packages, like `ggplot2`. This first step used `extrafont::loadfonts()` to load fonts called by `hrbrthemes`; it's important to have fonts Arial Narrow and Roboto Condensed already installed.

 `extrafont::loadfonts()` registers fonts into your R session. All fonts available in the user's system library but not yet registered into the running session are loaded simultaneously. Run this function every time you start a new session and wish to use non-native fonts.

Step 2 draws a simple `ggplot2` scatterplot under an object named p. While `ggplot()` initializes the gg object and draws the basic aesthetic mappings, `geom_point()` is called to reach for point geometry and `labs()` writes the title and subtitle. Notice that the subtitle was misspelled on purpose.

Step 3 adds the Roboto Condensed-based theme to plot p by stacking `theme_ipsum_rc()`. A discrete color palette with nine colors is added by `scale_color_ipsum()`. The final step simply checks the misspelled words. The `gg_check()` function searches `ggplot`'s legends, title, subtitle, and axes for words that are possibly misspelled, telling the user where to find those and which ones may require attention.

There's more...

hrbrthemes does not stop there. There are a bunch of things it can do like easily change some scale to fit percent format with scale_*_percent(); other scale tweaks are also available. You might want to consult this recipe's *See also* section for some useful links on this amazing package.

See also

- A quick guide to hrbrthemes and package files can be found in the following GitHub repository https://github.com/hrbrmstr/hrbrthemes
- CRAN documentation is available at https://cran.r-project.org/web/packages/hrbrthemes/hrbrthemes.pdf
- A more complete explanation about typography importance and why to use hrbrthemes:
  https://cran.r-project.org/web/packages/hrbrthemes/hrbrthemes.pdf

10
Designing More Specialized Plots

This chapter covers the following recipes:

- Drawing wonderful facets zoom with the `ggforce` package
- Drawing sina plots with `ggforce`
- Using `ggrepel` to plot non-overlaying texts
- Visualizing relation data structures with `ggraph`
- Drawing alternative lollipop and density plots with `ggalt`

Introduction

This chapter will present some packages and functionalities that act as `ggplot2` supplements. I may start by disclaiming that if a specific geometry, stat, or position is not presented by `ggplot2`, there might be very good reasons. Every single new functionality is opinionated before getting on board in order to prevent users from making really bad decisions.

Hardly `ggplot2` had accidentally missed some kind of plot; it most probably choose to not incorporate some for user-safety purposes. That said, we are now sailing with no seat belts fastened. Think very carefully before applying any of the visuals that we're about to see. I shall confess though that these visuals are pretty amazing. You will learn how to craft zoom-facets, sina plots, and more cool stuff.

Drawing wonderful facets zoom with the ggforce package

Sometimes, you want to give a specific plot area more attention, but still grasp what is going on in the other sections. The answer rests in `ggforce`. Besides giving birth to new geometries, it also enables what is called facet zoom. While zooming a specific range, it also shows the entire figure by the side. Let's see a demonstration while using the `boot::motor` data frame.

Getting Ready

`ggforce` is relatively new. Downloading it from the GitHub repository might be a better option as we might encounter new features and less bugs. Also make sure to have the `boot` package downloaded; check how this can be done:

```
> if(!require(devtools)){install.packages('devtools')}
> if(!require(ggforce)){devtools::install_github('thomasp85/ggforce')}
> if(!require(boot)){install.packages('boot')}
```

To install from GitHub, we also require the package, `devtools`. Another required package is `boot`, which contains the `motor` data frame. This frame shows data on simulated motorcycle accidents; we are using `time` (measured in mile seconds since impact), `accel` (head acceleration in g), and `strata` (3 level factor).

How to do it...

Once we're prepared, proceed with the plotting as follows:

1. Load `ggforce` and `ggplot2` using the `library()` function:

```
> library(ggforce)
> library(ggplot2)
```

2. Draw a `ggplot` and stack a `facet_zoom()` function to create the zoom facet:

```
> ggplot(data = boot::motor,
         aes(x = times, y = accel)) +
    geom_point(aes(color = factor(strata))) +
    facet_zoom(xy = factor(strata) == 1,
               horizontal = F)
```

Resulting plot shall look similar to following image (Figure 10.1):

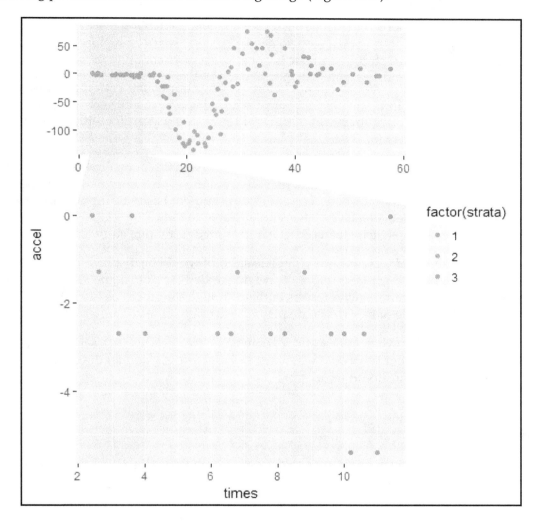

Figure 10.1 - ggforce zoom facet.

The full scatterplot is displayed at the top while the zoomed area can be seem at the bottom. Walk the plank (plank being the explanations)!

How it works...

Step 1 needs no explanations. We're loading `ggforce`; hence, enabling us to craft a facet zoom under a `ggplot`. To draw this, we also need `ggplot2`, so it's being loaded in the same step. A pretty simple usual step. The magic is done by the ones coming afterward.

Facet zoom is demanded by step 2, but not before we have our usual scatterplot drawn. The `ggplot()` function initializes it with the `boot::motor` data. Next, `geom_point()` is stacked while the `colour` argument set. This would give us a scatterplot with different colors pointing out to different strata.

The subsequent layer is `facet_zoom()`, which calls for the facet zoom. First, we must input it with arguments holding the axes' names that we want the zoom to occur--it could be only x, only y, xy at the same time, or both x and y. This argument has to be input with a logical expression to rule a subset, which can be any rule related to data. The recipe went to `xy = factor(strata) == 1`, which means only x and y ranges for strata equivalent to one.

As we worked both x and y zooms, the complete subplot would be displayed at the right side. Although, by setting `horizontal = F`, we demanded the not zoomed subplot to be displayed at the top. Naming only x results in the complete subplot to be displayed at the top no matter what, while only y would display it at the right side no matter what.

Another available option when both x and y zoom rules are declared is to set `split = T`. The `horizontal` argument is ignored when `split` is set to `TRUE` and all the corners get filled with subplots -- you should try it.

See also

- See some different ways of declaring facets zoom and more geometries associated with `ggforce` in this vignette:
  https://cran.r-project.org/web/packages/ggforce/vignettes/Visual_Guide.html

Drawing sina plots with ggforce

Do you remember `Chapter 3`, *Plotting a Discrete Predictor and a Continuous Response* when we tried jitter geometry to replace dot plots? A clear con was that it did not gave away any hint about the distribution format. Remember little difficulties with coloring some dot plots? Both could be contoured by `ggforce`'s sina geometry.

This recipe is designed to show an alternative way to visualize `car::Salaries` data frame and also to hand a little teaser about geometries coming from `ggforce`. We're about to explore a plot called sina, use it wisely.

Getting Ready

The `devtools` package is required to install `ggforce` from GitHub while `car` holds the data frame:

```
> if(!require(devtools)){install.packages('devtools')}
> if(!require(ggforce)){devtools::install_github('thomasp85/ggforce')}
> if(!require(car)){install.packages('car')}
```

The `car::Salaries` data frame is the one we will be using for now.

How to do it...

We can proceed with the recipe as follows:

1. Load both `ggforce` and `ggplot2` while also setting the seed pseudo random number generator:

```
> library(ggforce)
> library(ggplot2)
> set.seed(10)
```

2. Call for `geom_sina()` to stack the sina geometry:

```
> ggplot(data = car::Salaries,
         aes(x = rank,
             y = salary)) +
    geom_sina(aes(color = sex), alpha = .5)
```

As a result, the following image is outputted (Figure 10.2):

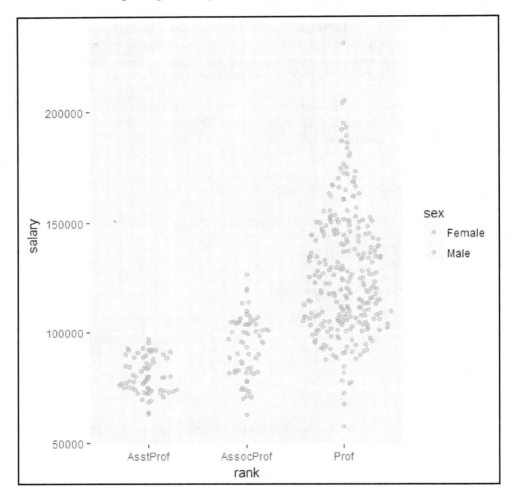

Figure 10.2 - sina geometry.

This points displacement gives a hint on what the distributions look like, almost a violin made of points.

How it works...

As it was not hard to draw it, understanding will not be hard too. Step 1 loads the packages and also sets a seed number to R's pseudo random generator. The way the points are placed by sina geometry requires a pseudo random process, so set.seed(10) makes it reproducible.

Next, step 2 initializes the ggplot with the car::Salaries data frame before requesting the sina geometry. This last is attached by ggforce's function, geom_sina(). Notice how we set the colors to represent sex and alpha to 0.5. This is not a perfect distribution representation though; if you try to plot a violin beneath it, you get that they are very similar for some bins and somehow a little bit different for others.

There are several new geometries, stats, and positions made available by ggforce; use them wisely--may the force be with you.

Using ggrepel to plot non-overlaying texts

Remember the times you wanted to plot texts or labels but feared that they would overlay? Fear no more, your troubles have met a sad end with ggrepel. This wonderful package shifts the text while adding a line segment to tell the audience from what place the text had come from.

This is wonderful for several reasons. When you want to plot pure text but over plotting is spoiling it or when text from your bubble plot is stealing the attention from some really small points, here is the solution. To understand it, we are back to our Armada bubble plot.

Getting Ready

Besides downloading `ggrepel`--as we are back to our armada plot--we need the `HistData` package again, so run the following:

```
> if(!require(ggrepel)){install.packages('ggrepel')}
> if(!require(HistData)){insertClassMethods('HistData')}
```

If everything went fine, you're are now locked and loaded.

How to do it...

For this recipe, we will be drawing a bubble plot and afterward making sure that the text is shown on the outside. Keep in mind that `ggrepel` is useful for a handful of other situations, for example, labeling several points and making sure that they do not overlay one another.

1. Design a base plot using `HistData::Armada` with `ggplot2`:

```
> library(ggplot2)
> library(HistData)
> bubble <- ggplot(Armada, aes(x = sailors, y = soldiers)) +
    geom_point(aes(colour = Armada, size = ships), alpha = .6) +
    scale_color_brewer(palette = 'Set3' ,guide = F) +
    scale_size_continuous(range = c(5,25)) +
    xlim(100,2000) + ggtitle('La Felicisima Armada')
```

2. Use one of the `geom_*_repel` functions carried by `ggrepel` to plot text or labels:

```
> library(ggrepel)
> bubble +
    geom_text_repel(aes(label = Armada),
                    point.padding = 3) +
    theme_classic()
```

Now the texts are plotted on the outer side of the points, so big texts do not overlay small bubbles:

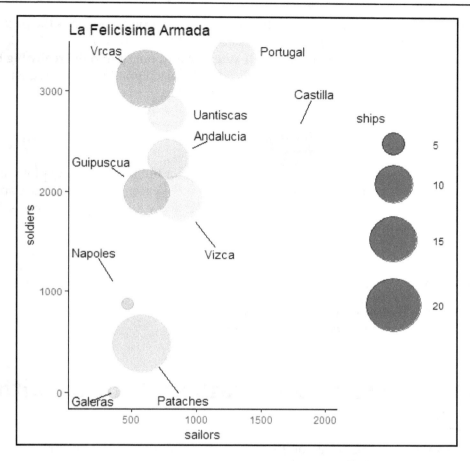

Figure 10.3 - working with ggrepel.

Now let's check how it worked.

How it works...

Step 1 draws a bubble plot. This is designed with `ggplot2` by working on the `Armada` data set coming from the `HistData` package. This plot is stored as an object called `bubble`. Simply adding `geom_text()` could cause some confusion as the big text would make difficult to visualize really small points.

The solution is to add texts (or labels) with `ggrepel`. The second step loads the package and adds non-overlaying texts. The function stacked with `bubble` was `geom_text_repel()`. To really make sure that text would not fit into the really big bubble, the recipe altered `point.padding` to 3; this is unnecessary if you have only regular sized points. At this step, the default theme was also changed to `theme_classic()`.

There's more...

Features coming from this package are not useful only for bubble plots. Any plot with overlaying text/labels crop great benefits from `ggrepel::geom_*_repel`. This is specially true for highly text-dependent plots. GitHub examples show this using the `mtcars` data set; check the *See also* section.

See also

- GitHub repository with `mtcars` example:
  `https://github.com/slowkow/ggrepel`

Visualizing relational data structures with ggraph

There are several ways of getting you free time to help other people. In his free time, Thomas L. Pedersen made this amazing R package called `ggraph`, which is built on top of `ggplot2`. This extension aims to handle relational data structures such as networks, trees, and graphs.

Most of the packages dealing with relational data focus only on one type of representation using different APIs; to handle many types would require you to learn several different packages. The advantage of using `ggraph` is that this package covers a wide variety of relational representations, all under the same `ggplot2` API.

`ggraph` covers lots of different types of data objects such as `hclust`, `network`, `dendogram`, and `igraph`. It can design plots in a very interactive way based on three basic concepts: layouts, nodes, and edges. I really hope you look for it the next time you need a relational data visualization.

This recipe will use Canadian migration data to demonstrate the `ggraph` network plot. Networks are frequently used to denote data complexity, get one's attention, confirm suspicions about data topology, and/or convey simple relations. This recipe starts by demonstrating how complex our data is right before narrowing down to simple relations.

Getting Ready

For this recipe, we need the `igraph` package to coerce our tabular data frame into a relational one. Data about Canadian migration is held by the `car` package, not to mention the star package here, `ggraph`:

```
>if(!require(car)){install.packages('car')}
 if(!require(igraph)){install.packages('igraph')}
 if(!require(devtools)){install.packages('devtools')}
 if(!require(ggraph)){
   devtools::install_github('thomasp85/ggraph')
 }
```

The last package can be downloaded from GitHub using `devtools`, which I recommend. Another alternative is to download it directly from CRAN using the `install.packages()` function.

How to do it...

In order to accomplish this recipe's goal, some data handling is required. It rolls a little bit different from the manipulations done on non-relational datasets.

1. Transform the `car::Migration` data frame into a `igraph` object using the `graph_from_data_frame()` function:

```
> library(car)
> library(igraph)
> graph <- graph_from_data_frame(Migration)
```

2. Create a node (vertices) attribute called `pops66` to hold population from source province on 1966:

```
> tmp_dt <- Migration[1:10,]
> V(graph)$pops66 <- tmp_dt$pops66[match(tmp_dt$source,V(graph)$name)]
```

3. Using `ggraph`, combine layouts from `ggraph()` with `geom_edge_*` and `geom_node_*` family functions to create a unique network:

```
> set.seed(10)
> library(ggraph)
> ggraph(graph, layout = 'lgl') +
    geom_edge_fan(aes(colour = migrants), alpha = .4) +
    geom_node_point(colour = 'darkgreen',size = 4) +
    theme_void()
```

As a result, we get ourselves the following image (Figure 10.4), which denotes data set complexity:

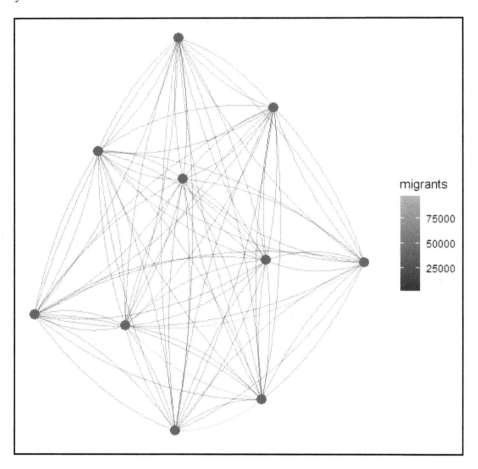

Figure 10.4 - Network denoting data complexity.

4. Simplify the visual by filtering the edges to be displayed using the `filter` argument:

```
> ggraph(graph, layout = 'star') +
  geom_edge_fan(aes(colour = migrants,
                    filter = migrants > 2*10^4),
                width = 1,
                arrow = arrow(length = unit(4, 'mm')),
                end_cap = circle(9, 'mm')) +
  geom_node_label(aes(label = name, size = pops66)) +
  theme_void()
```

Now the analysis get a little bit clearer, as following image (Figure 10.5) demonstrates:

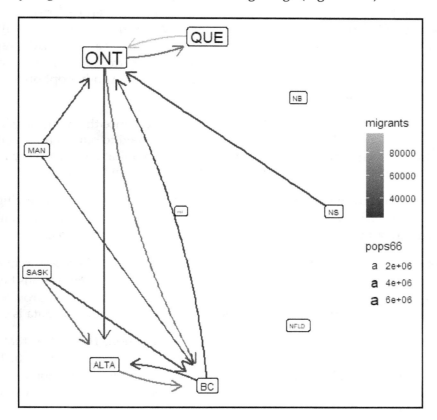

Figure 10.5 - simpler network.

Now let's see how we were able to get from there to here.

How it works...

Step 1 creates an `igraph` object from the `Migration` data frame, which came from the `car` package. To create this object, the `graph_from_data_frame()` function from the `igraph` package was called. The first two columns from data may work as "from" and "to" variables. At the end of this step, an object called `graph` is created.

What `ggraph` calls nodes, `igraph` calls vertices. If we want information from a data frame to be displayed as points, we first need to assign information as vertices into our `igraph` object. This can generally be done by calling the object in the `V()` function while adding a attribute with the `$` signal, like this: `V(<igraph object>)$<here attribute's name>`.

Step 2 makes the 1966 province population available as a graph vertices attribute, so we can display this kind of information by the nodes (points). After this step, `pops66` will be accessible by `geom_node_*` family functions. Although `ggraph` can deal with graphs from several packages, it's not made for graph manipulation. It's better to know the package from which relational data is coming so that you can manipulate it. Another option is to learn `tidygraph`, which is compatible with `ggraph`.

Step 3 is used to create a network graph to convince the audience that your data/problem is utterly complex. To create this visual, we begin by setting seed to our pseudo random generator. This is necessary as we will be relying on a layout that changes every time we run it (unless we set seed); the algorithm takes off from "random" positions.

The next lines tell us how generally `ggraph`'s viz is crafted. We start by initializing the graph with a layout, which is defined globally under the `ggraph()` function, similar to `ggplot()`. The layout picked was `'lgl'`; there are several more available.

Next, we define the nodes using a `geom_node_*` family function. These are connected using the `geom_edge_*` family functions. What the graph shows us is the migrations between Canadian provinces in 1971. We can't recall which points account for each province neither how much migration is carrying on, but we definitely put across that the data is complex.

 `ggraph` is built on top of `ggplot2` as an extension. This means that theme functions also work. Although the recipe used `geom_void()`, which looks fine for this kinds of viz, `ggraph` holds its own theme function called `theme_graph()`. Be aware that loading some fonts may be necessary.

Step 4 narrows down the problem. It also uses another layout, (`'star'`). `aes(filter)` is called inside `geom_edge_fan()` to show only the connections between nodes that had at least 20,000.00 migrations in 1971. This function also adds arrows to show migration direction.

Another change is that we now used `geom_node_label()` to display points. Labels are filled with Canadian province names' abbreviations while `size` represents its population in 1966. Now you know how generally layouts, nodes, and edges can be combined to brew unique networks using `ggraph`. This is not the only viz supported--it can display trees, dendrograms, and many more kinds.

Hope you liked this package and are instigated to learn more about it.

See also

- `ggraph` **package repository:** `https://github.com/thomasp85/ggraph`
- **Learn more about layouts:** `http://www.data-imaginist.com/2017/ggraph-introduction-layouts/`
- **Learn more about nodes:** `http://www.data-imaginist.com/2017/ggraph-introduction-nodes/`
- **Learn more about edges:** `http://www.data-imaginist.com/2017/ggraph-introduction-edges/`
- **Check out** `tidygraph`: `https://github.com/thomasp85/tidygraph`

Draw alternative lollipop and density plots with ggalt

This is another creation from the R master sorcerer, Bob Rudis. This package called `ggalt` displays lots of alternative geometries and statistical transformations addressed to `ggplot2`. For example, we could name `stat_bkde()` and `stat_bkde2d()`, which use alternative functions to create kernel density estimates (respectively for one and two dimensions).

This recipe demonstrates how to use `ggalt` to craft these two kinds of visuals with the help of the `car::Salaries` package. The recipe also demonstrates how to easily craft lollipop plots using `geom_lollipop()`. This last example uses the `car::Migration` dataset.

Getting Ready

Both `car` and `ggalt` packages can be obtained from CRAN:

```
if(!require(ggalt)){install.packages('ggalt')}
if(!require(car)){install.packages('car')}
```

With both packages installed we can go on.

How to do it...

While density estimates are drawn using the `Salaries` data frame, the lollipop plot uses `Migration`, both coming from the `car` package.

1. Store different data frames into different objects:

```
> library(car)
> dt1 <- Migration[1:10,]
> dt2 <- Salaries
```

2. After loading `ggalt`, stack `geom_lollipop()` with `ggplot()` to craft a lollipop plot:</li>

```
> library(ggalt)
> ggplot(data = dt1,
         aes(y=reorder(source, pops66),
             x=pops66)) +
    geom_lollipop(point.colour = 'navyblue',
                  point.size = 4,
                  horizontal = T) +
    theme_classic()
```

Following image (Figure 10.6) exhibits a lollipop plot showing Canadian provinces population in 1966:

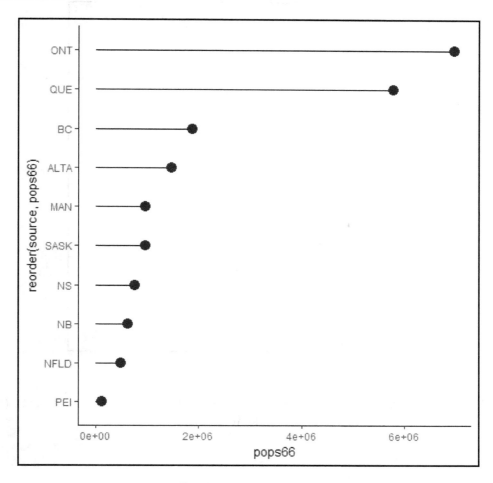

Figure 10.6 - Lollipop plot created by ggalt.

3. Call for geom_bkde() to draw kernel density estimates based on KernSmooth::bkde:

```
> ggplot(data = dt2,
        aes(x = salary,
            fill = discipline)) +
    geom_bkde(alpha = .2) + theme_classic()
```

The result is shown in the following image (Figure 10.7):

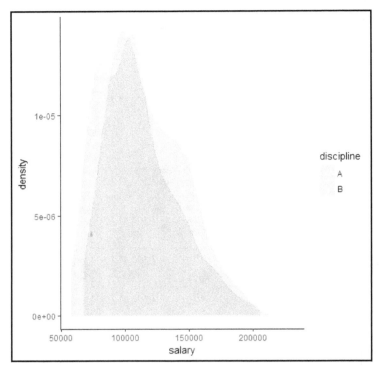

Figure 10.7 - ggalt kernel density estimates.

4. Alternatively, 2D kernel density estimates can be drawn by `stat_bkde2d()`, and `geom = 'plolygon'` can make it better:

```
> ggplot(data = dt2,
       aes(x = yrs.since.phd,
           y = yrs.service)) +
    stat_bkde2d(aes(fill = ..level..),
           geom = 'polygon')
```

The two-dimensional estimate is shown in Figure 10.8:

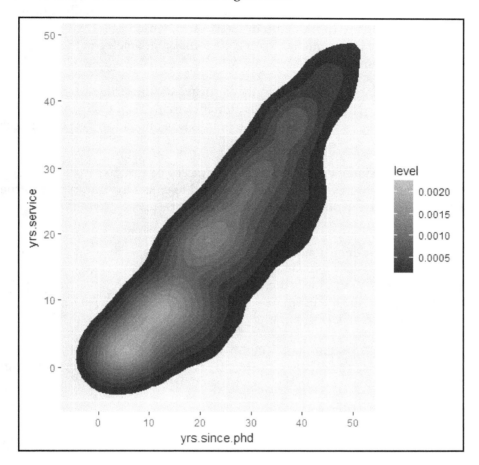

Figure 10.8 - ggalt 2D kernel density estimate.

The following section explains how each step rolled.

How it works...

Step 1 simply loads the `car` package and stores the data. The data frame to be used by the lollipop plot (`Migration`) is stored in the `dt1` object; only the first 10 rows are needed. The `Salaries` data frame will be used for both one and two density distribution drawings; this one is stored in the `dt2` object.

Step 2 draws the lollipop plot. It begins by loading `ggalt`, then drawing the `ggplot`. The first function designs the base aesthetics while reordering `source` (Canadian province name) with respect to `pops66` (population in 1966), our x variable.
Next, `geom_lollipop()` is summoned to give the lollipop geometry to the plot; `theme_classic()` is also stacked.

Once the categorical variable is assigned to the vertical axis, declaring `horizontal = T` is necessary inside `geom_lollipop()`. Other arguments are `point.size` and `point.colour`, which respectively change the point's size and color. You can check more arguments by typing `?geom_lollipop()`.

Step 3 draws one-dimensional density plots using `ggalt::geom_bkde()`. The main difference from `geom_density()` is the function used to create the underlying kernel density estimates. The `ggalt` one comes from `KernSmooth::bkde`, while `geom_density()` uses the base `density()` function.

Fourth step draws a two-dimensional density distribution. As we want polygon geometry on this plot, `stat_bkde2d()` was called instead of `geom_bkde2d()`; geometry was defined by the `geom = 'polygon'` argument then. While `stat_density_2d()` from `ggplot2` uses `MASS:kde2d()` to create the estimates, `ggalt::stat_bkde2d()` uses `KernSmooth::bkde2D()`.

There is a lot more to learn from `ggalt`. You can research the documentation. Another option is to seek the package's GitHub repository, which is filled with a lot of examples and descriptions. You can find the link in the See also section.

See also

- Lots of useful information plus a handful of examples can be found at `ggalt` GitHub repository:
  `https://github.com/hrbrmstr/ggalt`

11
Making Interactive Plots

This chapter covers the following recipes:

- Using `ggiraph` to create interactive plots
- Using `gganimate` to craft animated `ggplots`
- Crafting animated plots with `tweenr`

Introduction

Good visualizations intend to engage an audience's attention and hold it tight; they also aim to deliver good and precise information. There are a wide range of strategies to fit different situations. Whenever there is a place for it, making an interactive plot is advised; animations are welcome as well.

This chapter aims to introduce the use of three packages: `ggiraph`, `gganimate`, and `tweenr`. The first one can be used to make extra information available by hoovering the mouse; the two others animate a plot in a very *gify* way, usually culminating in very funny plots that attract too much attention.

 A little disclaimer before we go ahead: all the figures here are merely snapshots from the true outcomes. I do highly recommend you run each recipe so that you reach for what is really happening instead of getting only a glimpse.

Using ggiraph to create interactive plots

The `ggiraph` package is both an HTML widget and a `ggplot2` extension. There are a bunch of things you can do with it: design hover effects, set hover information, program JavaScript actions to trigger on click, and enable zoom. Changes such as these are mainly conducted under two families of functions: `*_*_interactive()` and `ggiraph()`. This recipe is about to introduce the usage of the last two, but once you get used to the stat/geom dynamic on `ggplot2`, the same logic is applied to `ggiraph`.

Getting ready

A recipe does not come without data, and this is coming from the DAAG package. We're using the `races2000` data set (Scottish Hill Races Data - 2000) to plot record time against distance. The race type will be displayed by colors, while record time in hours for females will be available by mouse hovering. Of course, all of that will be achieved using `ggiraph`:

```
> if(!require(DAAG)){install.packages('DAAG')}
>   if(!require(devtools)){install.packages('devtools')}
> if(!require(ggiraph))
    {devtools::install_github('davidgohel/ggiraph')}
```

To install the developer version of `ggiraph` we need `devtools` to be installed.

How to do it...

With only a few lines, it's possible to craft an interactive `ggplot` using `ggiraph` package.

1. Store the data set in a separated variable while creating other variable carrying a string that references JavaScript code:

   ```
   > library(DAAG)
   > dt <- races2000
   > dt$click <- 'window.open(\"http://www.hillrunning.co.uk\")'
   ```

2. Create and store a `ggplot` with the `ggiraph` package, using the `geom_point_interactive()` function:

   ```
   > library(ggiraph)
   > p <- ggplot(dt,
                 aes(x = dist,
                     y = time,
                     color = type)) +
   ```

```
geom_point_interactive( alpha = .8,
    aes(tooltip = timef,
        data_id = timef,
        onclick = click)) +
xlim(1.5,8) +
ylim(.2,.8)
```

3. Create a string for `css-style` and plot p using `ggiraph()`:

```
> css <- 'fill-opacity:.3;cursor:pointer;r:5pt;'
> ggiraph(code = print(p),
          hover_css = css,
          zoom_max = 2)
```

Following image (Figure 11.1) shows a snapshot of the real interactive output:

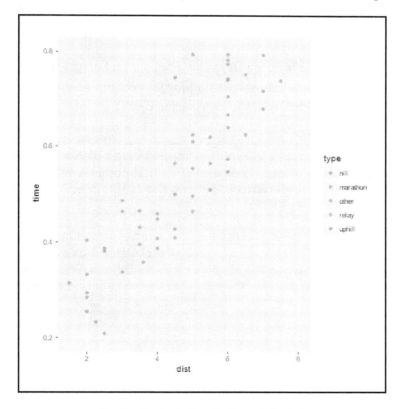

Figure 11.1 - Snapshot of an interactive plot created with ggiraph

This book can't display more than a simple static snapshot. I highly recommend you run this recipe in order to get the "real stuff" and understand it better. The following section describes what is going on and how.

How it works...

Whenever we click a point in the real graphic, a browser window might open a data set related page. Part of this is done in step 1—it loads the DAAG package, stores the races2000 data frame into an object called dt, while creates a new variable named click, a string that is carrying a JavaScript command.

The second step holds the ggplot creation. Notice that by loading ggiraph, ggplot2 was also loaded. Then, the recipe starts to build a ggplot object called p. The novelties come with geom_point_interactive(). ggiraph functions from the *_interactive family understands some new aesthetics:

- tooltip: Holds the information to be displayed when the mouse is over it
- onclick: Receives strings accounting for JavaScript codes to trigger on click
- data_id: Correspond to IDs to be associated with elements

All this aesthetics were properly set into the geom_point_interactive() function. At the end of this step, the xlim() and ylim() functions are being called to restrain data used to plot. Without this, plot limits would become so wide that points would cluster all together, not looking good at all. Even with the use of interactive family functions, calling p would not result in an interactive plot.

Interactivity is only achieved in step 3, by using ggiraph() function. The code argument is inputted with print(p). The hover_css parameter carries the css-style string ruling how elements should behave when the mouse hovers over them. For this recipe, those were stored in the object called css. Finally, the zoom_max argument is enabling the zoom.

This is generally how `ggiraph` can be used to craft very cool interactive plots under the same logic applied by `ggplot2`. If you'd like to learn more about this package, refer to the *See also* section.

See also

- `ggiraph` GitHub repository: https://github.com/davidgohel/ggiraph
- A vignette introducing the usage of `ggiraph`: https://cran.r-project.org/web/packages/ggiraph/vignettes/an_introduction.html

Using gganimate to craft animated ggplots

Animations are wonderful to attract attention to the information you want to display; they can make plots funnier, replace facets, and are very good matches to social media publications. Package `gganimate` makes it very simple to animate your `ggplot`. It takes you only to set a variable as `frame` aesthetic and then input your `ggplot` into `gganimate()` function create an animated version.

Animations created this way are very gif-like; in matter of fact, you can save you plot as `.gif` file. This recipe's goal is to show the general way plots made with `ggplot2` can be animated using `gganimate`. All this will be done under the `Titanic` data set framework. Let's create an animation that shows how many women and men survived across different classes. Requirements are very important here, get them from the next section.

Getting ready

First, make sure that ImageMagick (https://www.imagemagick.org) is downloaded in your system. For Mac users, Homebrew is recommended (https://brew.sh). Once ImageMagick is installed, we can proceed to package installation:

```
> if(!require(animation)){install.packages('animation')}
  if(!require(devtools)){install.packages('devtools')}
  if(!require(gganimate))
    {devtools::install_github('dgrtwo/gganimate')}
```

Make sure the `animation` package is also installed. Package `gganimate` package is being installed directly from its GitHub repository with the help of `devtools`.

How to do it...

Remember that the image in this book is a mere snapshot of the original figure. Run the recipe so you can get the original one:

1. Coerce `Titanic` data into a data frame object:

```
> dt <- data.frame(Titanic)
```

2. Draw a `ggplot2` bar plot as usual, but add a `frame` aesthetic to it:

```
> library(ggplot2)
> p <- ggplot(data = dt, aes(x = Class, fill = Survived,
                             weight = Freq, frame = Sex)) +
      geom_bar(position = 'identity')
```

3. Print it using the `gganimate()` function:

```
> library(gganimate)
> gganimate(p, interval = 2,
            filename = 'titanic.gif')
```

The original output shifts among `Male` and `Female` observations from time to time, it can be seen as an alternative to facets. Following image (Figure 11.2) shows a snapshot of the male data:

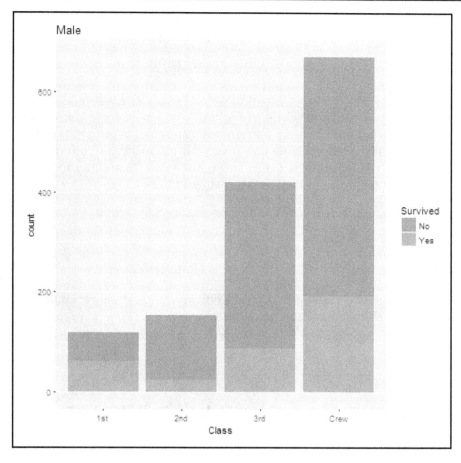

Figure 11.2 - A snapshot from an animated ggplot

The following section discusses what happened.

How it works...

Step 1 is a very simple one. It only takes the `Titanic` data set and turns it into a data frame so it can be inputted as data into `ggplot()`. The subsequent step is drawing the plot that later will fit the animation. It's very important to store this plot into an object; also make sure to declare the `frame` aesthetic, as this is the variable that later will command animations. Think of it as the variable that will group data into the different animation frames.

Be creative here—you can design absolutely any `ggplot` of your liking. Limits are given mostly by imagination, just do not forget the `frame` aesthetic.

The last step will give birth to the animated figure. It begins by loading `gganimate`, then calling the `gganimate()` function. The first argument has to be a `ggplot` with a `frame` aesthetic set. By declaring the `interval` argument, recipe is customizing the time between frames; `filename` can be used to create and save your animated plot into files. This recipe created a GIF file into the working directory itself, but a path to another folder can be coerced and yet other file formats are available, such as MP4.

For more information, you can follow the links in the *See also* section.

See also

- This package was created by David Robinson, a great data scientist. His Twitter is full of valuable information on data science: `https://twitter.com/drob`
- The GitHub repository holds a bunch of examples: `https://github.com/dgrtwo/gganimate`

Crafting animated plots with tweenr

Package `tweenr` package is another creation from Thomas Lin Pedersen. It works works well with `gganimate`, making it easier to interpolate your data between different states. With this package, a higher level of customization can be achieved with much less effort, and the possibilities are nothing but amazing.

There are mainly three functions used to create animations with `tweenr`, and this recipe introduces the most versatile of them all, `tween_elements`. It basically works with the data set by setting three roles to variables: time, id, and ease.

The following example does bear no meaning but the final result is very funny and shows what `tweenr` is capable of doing.

Getting ready

Package animation is sort of a requirement for both `gganimate` and `tweenr`. The last two packages work well together, so `gganimate` will also be requested:

```
> if(!requrie(animation)){install.packages('animation')}
> if(!require(devtools)){install.packages('devtools')}
> if(!require(tweenr))
    {devtools::install_github("thomasp85/tweenr")}
> if(!require(gganimate))
     {devtools::install_github('dgrtwo/gganimate')}
```

Do not forget ImageMagick (`https://www.imagemagick.org`). Now that we're locked and loaded, let's roll.

How to do it...

We are about to address a more customized animation by combining `tweenr` with `gganimate`. Again, this book shows only a snapshot of it; please run the recipe at your end to get the actual output:

1. Create a data frame with columns for `time`, `id`, and `ease`:

```
> dt <- data.frame(x = c(1:2,rep(3,5),4:5),
                   y = c(3,3,1:5,3,3), id = 1:9,
                   time = 1, col = 'red', alp = 0,
                   ease = as.character('linear'),
                   size = 1)
```

2. Create different data frames with different information for different times:

```
> dt1 <- dt
> dt1$time <- 2
> dt1$alp <- .4
> dt2 <- dt1
> dt2$x <- dt$y
> dt2$y <- dt$x
> dt2[,c('time','size')] <- 3
> dt2$ease <- 'bounce-out'
> dt2$col <- 'green'
> dt3 <- dt2
> dt3$x <- dt$x
> dt3$time <- 4
> dt3$col <- 'blue'
```

3. Bind all data frames together using `rbind()`:

```
> dt <- rbind(dt,dt1,dt2,dt3)
```

4. Load the `tweenr` package and manage the data using `tween_elements()`:

```
> library(tweenr)
> dt <- tween_elements(dt, time = 'time', group = 'id', ease =
'ease',
                        nframes = 300)
```

5. Create a `ggplot` using the `dt` data frame; do not forget to set `frame = .frame`:

```
> library(ggplot2)
  library(gganimate)
  p <- ggplot(data = dt, aes(x = x, y = y)) +
     geom_point(aes(size = size, color = col,
                    frame = .frame, alpha = alp)) +
     scale_size(range = c(1, 25), guide = 'none') +
     scale_alpha_identity(guide = 'none') +
     theme_void()
```

6. Plot `p` using `gganimate()`:

```
> animation::ani.options(interval = 1/20)
  gganimate(p, title_frame = F)
```

The following figure (figure 11.3) is only a snapshot of the real output:

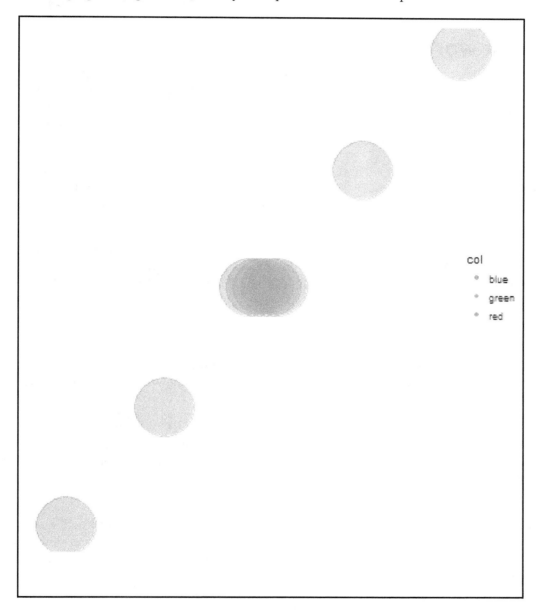

Figure 11.3 - Snapshot from an animated plot breed using tweenr and gganimate

The following section contains the explanation.

How it works...

The bottom line is that what `tweenr` does is to interpolate your data, requiring only little effort from you. This recipe demonstrated how to do that using `tween_elements()`. The primary step was creating a basic data frame (`dt`) to work as a departure point. We covered some variables that `ggplot` can put to good use: `x`, `y`, `col` (color), `alp` (alpha), and `size`. There are three additional ones: `time`, `id` and `ease`.

Having them named `time`, `id`, and `ease` is not a requirement; they only have to behave as follows. The `time` variable may rule the timeline of changes to occur during the animation, the `id` variable identifies different elements across different times, while `ease` commands the effects to happen between time shifts.

But until now, `dt` only held a single time point, which was not useful for our animation. Step 2 created a similar data sets while tweaking aesthetic variables and increasing `time`, sometimes changing the ease but not changing `id`s. Finally, step 3 bound them all using the `rbind()` function.

Step 4 used `tweenr` to interpolate data. The `tween_elements()` function was inputted with: the previous step data frame (`dt`); strings for `time`, `id`, and `ease` variables names; and a desired number of frames (`nframes`). The package then handled the data interpolation based on these three variables and outputted a new data frame with a new and useful variable called `.frame` -- `tweenr` created our frames.

The outputted data frame was selected to be our new `dt` object, overriding previous information. Step 5 used it to create a `ggplot` well suited for `gganimate`; notice how `aes(frame = .frame)` was set inside `geom_point()`. This particular plot was stored by an object named `p`. Step 6 animated it.

Last step began by tweaking the interval between frames using `animation::ani.options(interval = 1/20)`. In the sequence, the animation is created with `gganimate()`, and a good practice is to set `title_frame = F` whenever you are working with animations from `tweenr`, unless you want the frame number to be displayed as titles.

I hope you replicated this recipe on your end, and hope you found the resulting figure very funny, as I did. That is the thing about `tweenr`, once you combine it with `gganimate()` you reach for much higher levels of customization with so little extra effort. Other useful functions and more examples can be found at the GitHub repository; you can also find it in the *See also* section.

See also

- tweenr GitHub repository: `https://github.com/thomasp85/tweenr`

12
Building Shiny Dashboards

This chapter covers the following recipes:

- Installing and loading the `shiny` package
- Creating basic `shiny` interactive plots
- Developing intermediate `shiny` interactive plots
- Building a `shiny` dashboard

Introduction

Web applications and related interactive visuals are growing in importance nowadays and `shiny` certainly is the way to roll. It's not difficult to build web applications and interactive dashboards from your R console using `shiny`. Web applications can be enhanced with CSS themes, HTML widgets, and JavaScript actions.

This chapter aims to introduce the reader to the ways of crafting custom web applications and dashboards using `shiny` and `shinydashboard`. In this chapter, we reinforce a point: how the interactivity figures bred by `plotly` go well with `shiny` interactivity. Let's begin with the installation and loading.

Installing and loading a shiny package

This recipe is intended to show the reader how to download the `shiny` development package. It also teaches the reader how to load the package and craft an empty web application. Even an empty application is still useful to explain the very basics of working a web app with `shiny`.

How to do it...

Once we're looking for a package's development version, we must reach for GitHub, and that said, we need `devtools`.

1. Look for the `devtools` package. Once it's locked and loaded, we can proceed to make sure `shiny` will be installed:

```
> if(!require(devtools)){install.packages('devtools')}
> if(!require(shiny))
> {devtools::install_github('rstudio/shiny')}
```

2. Both `library()` and `require()` functions can be used to properly load the `shiny` package:

```
> library(shiny)
```

3. Design a simple user interface to get started with our web application:

```
> ui <- fluidPage(
    title = 'Hello World',
    titlePanel('hello_world'),
    sidebarLayout(
      sidebarPanel('togges usually are here',
                   br('more toggles')),
      mainPanel('this is the main panel',
                br('plots usually goes here'))
    )
  )
```

4. Create a function for receiving input and output as arguments, to work like a `server` for the application:

```
> server <- function(input,output){}
```

5. Input both the user interface (`ui`) and the `server` into `shinyApp()` to launch the application:

```
> shinyApp(ui = ui, server = server)
```

The application can be opened in your web browser window as the following image (Figure 12.1) demonstrates:

Figure 12.1 - Running a web app

As long you run the application, your R console will be unavailable. Click the **stop button** to put a hold on it and make the console available again.

How it works...

This recipe's first step begins by checking the devtools package. If it's not installed yet, it will look into the CRAN repository for it. Subsequently, the second if statement in this step will look for the shiny package. If it's missing, then it will use devtools::install_github() to get it directly from the GitHub depository; the later version is always there, which means new features and probably less issues.

Step 2 simply loads the shiny package. This is done under library() but can also be done by the require() function. The steps in this sequence teach us very important things about the package usage: (i) how to build a user interface; (ii) how to build a server; (iii) how to unite both to run a web application.

From the several layouts available, step 2 picks a very common one. The object to fit the user interface (ui, which is a preferable name by the way) is built with the fluidPage() function. The title argument sets the name to be displayed by the internet tab.

Following argument -- titlePanel() -- sets a title for the page while sidebarLayout() is picking a layout to fit the side and main panels. Functions sidebarPanel() and mainPanel() placed panels—order does matter here, and the first panel inputted is deployed at the left side when designed under sidebarLayout().

The third step shows how to define a server. It has to include a function handling at least two arguments: output and input. Sometimes it takes more arguments; another usual one is session. Instructions given to this functions rule how to build and rebuild objects displayed in the user interface.

Finally, step 5 runs the app. The shinyApp() function takes the the user interface (ui) and server to actually run the app. Remember, your R console will be unavailable while the application is running.

Creating basic shiny interactive plots

The previous recipe taught you how to install and load shiny, as well the basics of crafting and running a shiny app. This one introduces how to draw a basic interactive shiny plot (it's actually a shiny web app though). To do that, we shall demonstrate how to manipulate input and output while also taking advantage of plotly's interactivity.

Getting ready

Besides shiny, we also need three more packages, as follows:

```
> if(!require(plotly)){install.packages('plotly')}
> if(!require(Ecdat)){install.packages('Ecdat')}
> if(!require(dplyr)){install.packages('dplyr')}
```

The plotly package will be used to draw the plots, Ecdat will land the data, and dplyr will manipulate it. The data frame to be used is called USGDPpresidents and displays information about the **Real Gross Domestic Product (real GDP)** inflation index, presidents, wars, and more.

How to do it...

The main thing to pay attention to here is the general way that input is designated and used to construct the output:

1. Load all required packages before we start, as follows:

```
> library(shiny)
> library(plotly)
> library(Ecdat)
> library(dplyr)
```

2. The information on real GDP begins in 1970, so we filter the data based on the Year variable using dplyr::filter():

```
> data(USGDPpresidents)
> dt <- USGDPpresidents
> dt <- dt %>%
    filter(Year >= 1790)
```

3. Design a user interface (ui) while adding a sliderInput() by the side bar panel and asking for a plot (plotlyOutput()) at the main panel:

```
> ui <- fluidPage(
    title = 'shiny web app',
    titlePanel('U.S. Economy'),
    sidebarLayout(
      sidebarPanel(sliderInput(inputId = 'year', h3('Timeline'),
                               min = 1790, max = 2015,
                               value = c(1790, 2015))),
```

```
                 mainPanel(plotlyOutput(outputId = 'p'))
           )
        )
```

4. Take the information given by the slider (input$year) to craft the plot required at the main panel (output$p):

```
> server <- function(input,output){
  output$p <- renderPlotly({
    DT <- dt %>% filter(Year >= input$year[1] &
                        Year <= input$year[2])
    plot_ly(DT,x = ~Year, y = ~realGDPperCapita,
            type = 'scatter', mode = 'lines',
            text = paste('Excutive chief :', DT$executive))})

}
```

5. Run the app using shinyApp():

```
> shinyApp(ui = ui, server = server)
```

Our brand new web application shows a plotly line plot displaying the real US GPD. The timeline is held by the horizontal axis which can be controlled by a slider in the side bar panel. As a plotly plot, it can be zoomed in and out; hoover information tells us who was the executive at each time.

How it works...

Step 1 loads all the packages we need: shiny builds the application, plotly is used to draw the plot, Ecdat holds the data frame and dplyr manipulates it. The next step is attaching the USGDPpresidents data frame while drafting a filtered version of an object called dt. This filtering task is conducted by dplyr::filter() so that only existing information will be displayed—GDP is only available since 1790.

Step 3 is designing the user interface, and here we have two important novelties. The side bar panel includes a slider input made by sliderInput() function. First argument tells us the id attributed to the input -- once this recipe calls for 'year', information given by this slider bar (which the user can change any time) is reached by calling input$year.

The same function designates the bar range (min and max) and the starting value (value), and it can receive either a single value or two. Picking only one should result in a bar with a single slider. This recipe had two values picked, so there are two sliders which the current values can respectively reached by calling input$year[1] and input$year[2].

The other novelty is the output; the main panel is asking for a `plotly` output with `plotlyOutput()` function. The id chosen was `'p'` so the server function had to render an `plotly` object called `output$p`. This object will be displayed at the main panel. Notice that we called `plotlyOutput()`; if we wanted a `ggplot` to fit here we would call `plotOutput()` instead.

 There are two families of functions that can be used in the panels: `*Input()` and `*Output()`. While the first one creates and stores information in an object called `input`, the second one asks for some kinds of objects created as attributes from an object called `output`.

Fourth step is creating `server` function handle the inputs and draw the output; whenever an input is changed so is the output. This function creates the `output$p` object to be plotted at the main panel. To create it, `renderPlotly()` was called. It's important to outline the curly braces used to input the arguments—this is done so we can declare several lines of command inside it.

Functions from the `render*()` family are usually called by the server function; they render the output we need. Inside `renderPlotly()` we designated several lines of command to finally create a `plotly` plot. Input is called here and there when the `plotly` is being crafted so it can be manipulated by tweaking the toggles.

The last step ran the app by inputting both `ui` and `server` into the `shinyApp()` function. The `shiny` package cannot handle only plots, and it does not have only sliders to collect input. A useful guide is the *Shiny Cheatsheet* designed by Rstudio; the link can be found in the *See also* section.

See also

- The *Shiny Cheatsheet* made by RStudio: `http://shiny.rstudio.com/images/shiny-cheatsheet.pdf`

Developing intermediate shiny interactive plots

Applications can be enhanced by adding more toggles, more plots, and by exploring static HTML elements. More toggles and more elements can be added by simply calling more `*Input()` and `*Output()` functions separated by commas. The most popular static HTML elements have wrapper functions -- this recipe is using `h3()` a lot.

This recipe designs a `shiny` application with multiple toggles. Besides the `Timeline` toggle, this recipe will also create a toggle to pick Hoover information and two more toggles to choose the vertical axis variable displayed by each figure (yes, there will be two plots now).

Getting ready

The requirements are the same as in the previous recipe, and are as follows:

```
> if(!require(plotly)){install.packages('plotly')}
> if(!require(Ecdat)){install.packages('Ecdat')}
> if(!require(dplyr)){install.packages('dplyr')}
```

Now we can work with the application.

How to do it...

By calling functions from the `*Input()` family several times, several toggles are displayed, and the same idea is applied to the `*Output()` family, as follows:

1. Load all the packages that will be needed:

   ```
   > library(shiny)
   > library(plotly)
   > library(Ecdat)
   > library(dplyr)
   ```

2. Filter the data frame using `dplyr`:

   ```
   > data(USGDPpresidents)
   > dt <- USGDPpresidents
   > dt <- dt %>%
       filter(Year >= 1790)
   ```

3. Design a user interface with a bunch of `*Input()` and `*Output()` functions:

```
>  ui <- fluidPage(
    title = 'shiny web app',
    titlePanel('U.S. Economy'),
    sidebarLayout(
      sidebarPanel(sliderInput('year', h3('Year'),
                             min = 1790, max = 2015,
                             value = c(1790, 2015)),
                  selectInput('text', h3('Hoover text'),
                             choices = names(dt)[2:12],
                             selected = names(dt)[6]),
                  selectInput('var_y1', h3('Fig 1. Y-AXIS'),
                             choices = names(dt)[c(2:5,8,9,11)],
                             selected = names(dt)[5]),
                  selectInput('var_y2', h3('Fig. 2 Y-AXIS'),
                             choices = names(dt)[c(2:5,8,9,11)],
                             selected = names(dt)[8])),
      mainPanel(plotlyOutput(outputId = 'p1'),
               plotlyOutput(outputId = 'p2'))
    )
  )
```

4. Using the previously designed input, design a server function to create the `output$p1` and `output$p2` objects using `renderPlotly({})` functions:

```
> server <- function(input,output){
    output$p1 <- renderPlotly({
      DT <- dt %>% filter(Year >= input$year[1] &
                          Year <= input$year[2])
      plot_ly(DT, x = ~Year, y = DT[,input$var_y1],
             type = 'scatter', mode = 'lines', hoverinfo = 'text',
             text = paste(input$text, DT[,input$text])) %>%
        layout(yaxis = list(title = input$var_y1))})
    output$p2 <- renderPlotly({
      DT <- dt %>% filter(Year >= input$year[1] &
                          Year <= input$year[2])
      plot_ly(DT, x = ~Year, y = DT[,input$var_y2],
             type = 'scatter', mode = 'lines', hoverinfo = 'text',
             text = paste(input$text, DT[,input$text])) %>%
        layout(yaxis = list(title = input$var_y2))})
  }
```

5. Run the application with `shinyApp`:

```
> shinyApp(ui = ui, server = server)
```

The application programmed here has four toggles and two `plotly` figures. The discussion about how it worked follows.

How it works...

The first two steps are respectively loading the required packages and drafting the filtered data frame into an object named `dt`. Step 3 is handling some of the hard work. Here, four toggles are called by `*Input()` functions. The first one is the bar slider. The remaining returns variables from the data frame. Both the third and fourth ones we designed to return only continuous variables from the data frame, except for year. Some texts declared here fit inside `h3()` —this means HTML's level three headings.

These functions were all inserted into the side bar panel (`sidebarPanel()`). Two `*Output()` functions were called at the main panel (`mainPanel()`), asking for two `plotly` figures called `output$p1` and `output$p2`. Both were crafted by the next step within the `server()` function. Check how inputs are called to tweak the figures. One input is ruling x-axis range for both graphics at the same time, plus there is one input ruling the hoover information. Remaining two inputs are setting the variables to be displayed at the y-axis from each plot.

Finally, step 5 uses `shinyApp()` to run the application. As long as the application is running, the console will be unavailable; it's handling all the computation requited by the application.

There's more...

If you wish to share your application to the web you can always run it from a server. A very feasible (and free) option if you need to run only a few applications is to host them on `https://www.shinyapps.io/` by using the `rsconnect` package.

Building a shiny dashboard

Your `shiny` web application can be drawn as a dashboard. Translating a column `shiny` app to a dashboard version requires only small amounts of effort when you have the `shinydashboard` package installed. This recipe's goal is to introduce you to how to combine `shiny` and `shinydashboard` packages to design a web application within the dashboard format.

Getting ready

Besides `plotly`, `Ecdat`, and `dplyr` packages, we will also need the `shinydashboard` package:

```
if(!require(shinydashboard)){install.packages('shinydashboard')}
if(!require(plotly)){install.packages('plotly')}
if(!require(Ecdat)){install.packages('Ecdat')}
if(!require(dplyr)){install.packages('dplyr')}
```

The `shiny` package is still a requirement. Once all these are ready, we can go on and design a dashboard.

How to do it...

Instead of using `shiny` functions, the dashboards made by this recipe will greatly rely on functions designated by the `shinydashboard` package instead. The logic beneath the `shinydashboard` package is very similar to the one owned by `shiny`. Check it out:

1. Load all the packages that we need as follows:

   ```
   > library(shiny)
   > library(shinydashboard)
   > library(plotly)
   > library(Ecdat)
   > library(dplyr)
   ```

2. Draft a filtered version of the `Ecdat::USGDPpresidents` data frame into the `dt` object:

   ```
   > data(USGDPpresidents)
   > dt <- USGDPpresidents
   > dt <- dt %>%
       filter(Year >= 1790)
   ```

3. Design a user interface by combining `shinydashboard` package functions with `shiny` ones:

   ```
   > ui <- dashboardPage(
      title = 'shiny dashboard',
      dashboardHeader(title = 'Dashboard'),
      dashboardSidebar(
        menuItem('Figure', tabName = 'fig', icon = icon('line-
   chart'))
   ```

```
      ),
      dashboardBody(
        tabItem(tabName = 'fig',
                fluidRow(
                  box(
                    title = 'Plotly figure',
                    plotlyOutput(outputId = 'p1')),
                  box(
                    title = 'Control Panel',
                    sliderInput('year', 'Timeline',
                                min = 1790, max = 2015,
                                value = c(1790, 2015)),
                    selectInput('var_y1', 'y-axis variable',
                                choices = names(dt)[c(2:5,8,9,11)],
                                selected = names(dt)[5])))
                )
        )
      )
```

4. Create a server function to handle the `plotly` plot:

```
server <- function(input, output){
  output$p1 <- renderPlotly({
    DT <- dt %>% filter(Year >= input$year[1] &
                          Year <= input$year[2])
    plot_ly(DT, x = ~Year, y = DT[,input$var_y1],
            type = 'scatter', mode = 'lines',
            hoverinfo = 'text', text = DT[,'executive']) %>%
      layout(yaxis = list(title = input$var_y1))})
}
```

5. Reach for the dashboard by running the app with `shinyApp()`:

```
shinyApp(ui = ui, server = server)
```

When you run the app, a page very similar to the following screenshot (Figure 12.2) will appear:

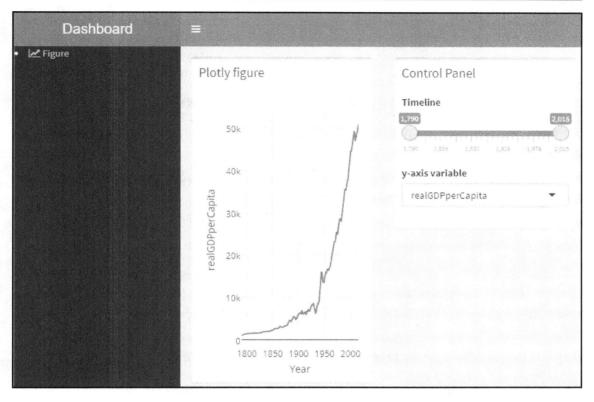

Figure 12.2 - Dashboard created with the shinydashboard package

The following section explains what was done by each step of this recipe in order to draw the dashboard.

How it works...

The recipe begins loading all the packages we need. `shiny` will work the web application, which works hand in hand with `shinydashboard` to deploy the dashboard design. `plotly` is used to draw a figure, `Ecdat` brings the data frame, and `dplyr` takes care of manipulating it. Step 2 is calling `dplyr` to filter data.

Step 3, is designing the user interface, and here we face some new ways of coding it. As we started with a main function used to describe it, this is now `dashboardPage()` and not `fluidPage()` anymore. To easily create a dashboard, refer to layout functions coming from `shinydashboard` and not `shiny` itself -- although the logic is pretty much the same.

Each major dashboard element is created by a function from the `dashboard*()` family. `dashboardHeader()` creates the dashboard header. Right after this one, there is `dashboardSidebar()`, which creates the side bar. Into this one we called `menuItem()` to create a single menu item.

 At the `menuItem()` function you can pick the icon tho be displayed by the menu item that you're creating. Name the `icon` argument under the `icon()` function to choose one. For icon references follow the link displayed at the *See also* section.

Next comes the creation of the dashboard body (`dashboardBody()`). Content to be described by the menu item is draw inside the `tabItem()` function; if there were more than one menu item it would be necessary to input each of them inside `tabItems()`. Two boxes are created (`box()`), one containing two toggles and the other one asking for a `plotly` output (`plotlyOutput()`).

Step 4 is creating the `server` function. This uses the input created at the user interface to craft the `plotly` output (`output$p1`) requested by `ui`. The last step simply takes both `ui` and `server` to run the `shiny` app which culminates in the dashboard.

See also

- Some of the icons referenced can be found here: `http://fontawesome.io/icons/`

Index

A

add_axis() function
  hacking, to operate as title function 36, 37, 38
alpha bending 49
animated ggplots
  crafting, gganimate used 317, 318, 319, 320
animated plots
  crafting, with tweenr 320, 321, 323, 324
area plots
  coloring, geom_area() used 127, 128, 129, 130
  crafting, geom_area() used 127, 128, 129, 130

B

bar graphic
  plotting, with aggregated data 165, 166, 167
basic scatterplot
  plotting 32, 33, 34
basic shiny interactive plots 330, 331, 333
bivariate dot plots
  drawing, ggplot2 used 84, 85, 86, 87
box plots
  combining, with dot plots 91, 93
  jitters, adding to 81, 82, 83
  notches, adding to 81, 82, 83
bubble plot
  drawing 266, 268

C

car package
  installing 76, 77
choropleth maps
  crafting, ggplot2 used 190, 191, 193
color reference palette
  reference 115
colors
  scatterplot, plotting with 38

contour plots
drawing, ggplot2 used 242, 243, 244, 246
contours
  labeling, directlabels package used 249, 250, 251
custom number of contour lines
  picking 246, 247, 248, 249
custom theme function
  wrapping 284, 285, 286

D

density plots
  drawing, geom_density() used 130, 131, 132, 133
  drawing, with ggalt 307, 308, 309, 310, 311, 312
directlabels package
  used, for labeling contours 249, 250, 251
dot plots
  box plots, combining with 91, 92, 93

E

ellipsis 17
extrafont package
  new fonts, importing 277, 278, 280

F

facet box plot
  creating 220, 221, 222
faceted bar graph
  creating 214, 215, 216, 217
faceted histograms
  crafting 218, 219, 220
faceted line plot
  crafting 222, 225
faceted maps
  creating 228, 229, 230, 231, 233

reference 233
faceted scatterplots
   making 226, 227, 228
facets
   drawing, plotly used 233, 234, 235, 236
fonts
   importing, with extrafont package 277, 278, 280

G

geom_area()
   area plots, coloring 127, 129, 130
   area plots, crafting 129, 130
geom_col()
   bar graphic, plotting with aggregated data 165,
     166, 167
geom_density()
   density plots, drawing 130, 131, 132, 133
geom_dotplot()
   suitable colors 87, 88, 89, 90
   univariate colored dot plots, drawing 133, 134,
     135, 136, 137
geom_errorbar()
   variability estimates, adding to plots 167, 168,
     169, 170
geom_histogram()
   histogram, creating 118, 119, 120, 121, 122
geom_rug()
   used, for rugging margins 52, 53, 54
geometry
   picking 259
ggalt
   density plots, drawing 307, 308, 309, 311, 312
   lollipop, drawing 307, 308, 309, 310, 312
   reference 312
gganimate
   used, for crafting animated ggplots 317, 318,
     319, 320
ggExtra
   used, for adding marginal histograms 56, 57
ggforce package
   reference 296
   sina plots, drawing 297, 299
   wonderful zoom facets, drawing 294
ggiraph
   used, for creating interactive plots 314, 316

ggplot2
   point geometry, using to work as dots 94, 95, 96,
     97
   raster plots, creating 255, 256, 258
   reference 12
   tile plot, crafting 251, 253
   used, for crafting choropleth maps 190, 191,
     193
   used, for drawing bivariate dot plots 85, 86, 87
   used, for drawing contour plot 242, 243, 244,
     246
   used, for plotting twitter words frequencies 142,
     143, 144, 145, 146
   using 13, 14, 15, 16, 17, 18
ggraph
   relational data structures, visualizing 302, 303,
     305, 306
ggrepel
   non-overlaying texts, plotting 299, 300, 302
ggsci
   reference 277
   sci themes, applying 274, 276, 277
ggtech
   used, for mimicking tech companies themes 280,
     281, 283
ggthemes
   reference 274
   themes, setting 269, 270, 272, 273
ggvis CRAN-R documentation
   reference 12
ggvis
   point geometry, using to work as dots 96, 97
   references 21
   using 13, 14, 16, 17, 18, 19
graphics packages
   installing 8, 9, 10, 11
   loading 8, 9, 10, 11
gridExtra
   used, for drawing marginal histograms 57, 59,
     60

H

hexagon plot
   adjusting 176, 177, 178
high quality faceted bar graph

plotting 236, 238, 239
histogram
  creating, geom_histogram() used 118, 119, 120,
    121, 122
  number of bins widths 122, 123, 124, 125, 126
  with custom colors 122, 123, 124, 125, 126
Homebrew
  reference 317
hrbrthemes
  misspells, checking 287, 289, 290
  reference 291

I

ImageMagick
  reference 317
interactive cholera map
  creating, plotly used 187, 188, 189, 190
interactive globe
  crafting, plotly used 205, 206, 207, 208
interactive hexagon plots
  making 174, 175, 176
interactive plots
  creating, ggiraph used 314, 316
intermediate shiny interactive plots 334, 336

J

jittering points 46, 48
jitters
  adding, to box plots 81, 82, 83
joy package
  used, for replacing violins 109, 110, 111

L

line plots
  making 170, 171, 172, 173
lollipop
  drawing, with ggalt 307, 308, 309, 310, 312

M

maps
  creating, based on map projection types 197,
    198, 199, 200
  high quality maps, creating 209, 210, 211, 212
  simple maps, making 184, 185, 187

zooming in on 194, 195, 196
margin plots
  making, with plotly 60, 61
marginal histograms
  adding, ggExtra used 55, 56, 57
  drawing, gridExtra used 57, 59, 60
margins
  rugging, with geom_rug() 52, 53, 54
Middle Earth
  mapping 201, 203

N

non-overlaying texts
  plotting, ggrepl used 299, 300, 302
notches
  adding, to box plots 81, 82, 83

O

over-plotting
  dealing with 43, 44, 45, 46, 48, 51

P

pirate plots
  reference 111
plotly
  point geometry, using to work as dots 96, 97
  reference 12
  three-dimensional plot, designing 259, 261
  used, for crafting interactive globe 205, 206,
    207, 208
  used, for creating interactive cholera map 187,
    188, 189, 190
  used, for drawing facets 233, 234, 235, 236
  used, for making margin plots 60, 61
  using 13, 14, 15, 16, 17, 18
plots
  making, primitives used 21, 22, 23, 24, 25, 27,
    28
  variability estimates, adding to 167, 169
primitives
  used, for making plots 21, 23, 24, 25, 27, 28
proportional stacked bar
  crafting 157, 158, 159, 160
publication quality contour plot
  crafting 261, 263, 264

publication quality violin plots
  creating 111, 112, 114, 115
publish quality density plot
  drawing 147, 148, 149
publish quality proportional stacked bar graph
  developing 179, 181
publish-quality scatterplots
  drawing 68, 69, 70, 71, 73

Q

quantile regression lines
  adding 65, 66, 67, 68

R

raster plots
  creating, with ggplot2 255, 256, 258
reducing points 43, 44, 45
regression lines
  adding 62, 63, 64
relational data structures
  visualizing, with ggraph 302, 303, 305, 306
rtweet
  used, for plotting twitter words frequencies 142,
    143, 144, 145, 146

S

scatterplot
  plotting, with colors 38, 40
  plotting, with shapes 38, 40
sci themes
  applying, with ggsci 274, 276, 277
shape reference palette
  plotting, for ggplot2 42
shapefiles
  handling 201, 203, 204
shapes
  scatterplot, plotting with 38, 40
Shiny Cheatsheet
  reference 333
shiny dashboard
  building 336, 337, 340
shiny package
  installing 327, 328, 329, 330
  loading 327, 328, 329, 330
side-by-side bar graph

  plotting 161, 163, 164
simple box plots
  drawing 78, 79, 80, 81
sina plots
  drawing, with ggforce 297, 299
stacked bar graphs
  creating 152, 154, 155
stat_summary
  used, for customizing violin plots 101, 102, 103,
    104
static hexagon plots
  making 174, 175
suitable colors
  for geom_dotplot 87, 89, 90

T

themes
  applying 287, 289, 290
three-dimensional plot
  designing, with plotly 259, 261
tile plot
  crafting, with ggplot2 251, 253
tweenr
  animated plots, crafting 320, 321, 323, 324
  reference 325
twitter words frequencies
  plotting, ggplot2 used 142, 143, 144, 145, 146
  plotting, rtweet used 142, 143, 144, 145, 146

U

univariate bar charts
  crafting 138, 140, 142
univariate colored dot plots
  drawing, geom_dotplot() used 133, 134, 135,
    136, 137
utils package 10

V

variability estimates
  adding, to plots 167, 168, 169
violin plots
  crafting 98, 99, 100, 101
  customizing, stat_summary used 101, 102, 103
violins
  coloring 105, 106, 107, 108

replacing, joy package used 109, 110, 111
sorting, manually 105, 106, 107, 108

Z

zoom facets
    drawing, ggforce package used 294, 296

www.ingramcontent.com/pod-product-compliance
Lightning Source LLC
Chambersburg PA
CBHW080615060326
40690CB00021B/4699